ARTHAVIRA

THE JOURNEY OF NIKHIL

LAKSHMI NARSIMHAN

Dedication

To the Honourable Mr. P. S. Sreedharan Pillai, Governor of Goa, whose wisdom, and encouragement have been a guiding light throughout this journey—thank you for your inspiring leadership and unwavering support.

Your guidance has been instrumental in shaping my path, and your belief in my potential has been a constant source of motivation. Your unwavering commitment to excellence and your visionary approach has inspired me to strive for greatness. I am deeply grateful for your mentorship and the invaluable lessons you have imparted. Your support has been a cornerstone of my success, and I am honored to have had your guidance.

To my parents, whose love, sacrifice, and belief in my dreams provided the foundation upon which everything was built—I owe everything to your strength and guidance. Your unwavering support and endless sacrifices have been the bedrock of my success. From the countless sleepless nights to the endless words of encouragement, you have been my pillars of strength. I am forever grateful for your love and for instilling in me the values that have guided me through every challenge. Your constant belief in my potential and your relentless efforts to ensure my success have been truly inspiring. Your love has been a source of comfort and motivation, pushing me to strive for excellence. I am deeply thankful for the lessons you have taught me and the unwavering support you have provided. Your sacrifices have not gone unnoticed, and I am honored to be your child.

Thank you for everything.

To Miss Savita Sharma, whose words motivated me to take the leap and author this book—thank you for your unwavering belief in my story. Your encouragement gave me the courage to pursue my passion and transform my dreams into reality. Your insightful feedback and constant support have been invaluable throughout this journey. I am deeply grateful for your mentorship and for believing in the power of my words. Your belief in my potential was the spark that ignited this entire project. You saw something in my story that I hadn't fully recognized myself, and your confidence in my abilities gave me the strength to push forward. Your guidance has been a beacon of light, helping me navigate through the complexities of writing and publishing. Without your encouragement, this book might have remained just an idea. Thank you for being a steadfast supporter and a true inspiration.

Your constant inputs and inspiration have been the backbone of this project. From the initial drafts to the final manuscript, your suggestions and insights have shaped the narrative in profound ways. You were always there to provide constructive criticism,celebrate the small victories and offer words of wisdom when I faced challenges. Your dedication to my success has been truly remarkable, and I am honored to have had you by my side throughout this journey. Your unwavering support and belief in my story have made all the difference. Thank you for everything.

To my dear friends, Renjith Nair, and Pooja Nair, who stood by me through every triumph and failure, offering advice, laughter, and perspective when I needed it most—your friendship means the world to me. Your unwavering support and companionship have been a source of immense strength. Through every high and low, your presence has been a constant reminder that I am never alone. Thank you for your endless patience, for listening to my rants, and for celebrating every milestone with me. Your friendship is a treasure that I hold close to my heart.

Your belief in me has been a driving force, pushing me to strive for greatness even when the path seemed uncertain. Your encouragement has been a beacon of light, guiding me through the darkest moments and celebrating the brightest ones. The laughter we've shared has been a balm to my soul, and your advice has been a compass, steering me in the right direction. Your perspective has helped me see challenges as opportunities and failures as stepping stones to success.

I am deeply grateful for your unwavering support, which has been a pillar of strength throughout this journey. Your friendship has been a source of inspiration, reminding me that with the right people by my side, anything is possible. Thank you for being my confidants, my cheerleaders, and my rock. Your presence in my life has made all the difference, and I am honored to call you, my friends. Here's to many more adventures, shared dreams, and countless memories together. Your friendship is a gift I cherish every day.

And finally, to all those who dream big but start small, this book is for you. Never stop believing in the power of perseverance and the possibility of greatness. Your dreams are valid, and your journey is unique. Embrace every challenge, cherish every victory, and never lose sight of your goals. This book is a testament to the power of determination and the beauty of chasing your dreams. Keep pushing forward and remember that greatness is within your reach.

Contents

Contents

Contents

Epigraph

” Success is not final; failure is not fatal: It is the courage to continue that counts."- Winston Churchill

xiii

First Page By Mr. P. S. Sreedharan Pillai, Honourable Governor Of Goa

P S Sreedharan Pillai
Governor of Goa

First Page

Raj Bhavan
Goa-403004

19/11/2024

Readers generally prefer to read imaginative stories.The reason why they like such stories is that many things are feasible in imaginative world that are not easily practicable in our day to day life.It paints our dreams about the world around us.besides it release us from the harsh realities for a while.

Although fiction is the favourite to read, motivational books inspires readers the most.But fiction and motivation combined in one book can do wonders for readers.We saw that miracle in Paulo Coelho 's Alchemist.Like Alchemist,Arthavira is a novel that combines fiction and motivation.The novelist paints a dreamlike growth story of a hardworking and dedicated ordinary entrepreneur.The life of Nikhil,the hero of the novel,is like that of a phoenix bird rising from the ashes.Reading this book will help you to realise the inner potential of each person.

All the best to Arthavira and its author Lakshmi Narsimhan.

P S Sreedharan Pillai
Governor of Goa

Foreword By Mr. Shripad Naik

श्रीपाद नाईक
राज्य मंत्री
नवीन और नवीकरणीय ऊर्जा एवं विद्युत
भारत सरकार

SHRIPAD NAIK
Minister of State for
New and Renewable Energy & Power
Government of India

FOREWORD

6th November, 2024

Arthavira: The Journey of Nikhil is more than a story—it's a call to action for dreamers, doers, and those who dare to break the mold. In these pages, you will not only read about triumphs and challenges, but you will also witness the raw, relentless spirit of a young man who refused to let circumstances define his destiny. Lakshmi Narsimhan masterfully weaves a narrative that grips your heart and fuels your ambition. Nikhil's journey reminds us all that the greatest achievements are born from perseverance, and that every setback is merely a stepping stone to a greater victory.

This book is a powerful reminder that the path to success is not for the faint of heart, but for those who are ready to rise, again and again. I am honored to be part of this momentous launch, and I am confident that Nikhil's story will light a fire in the hearts of all who read it.

(Shripad Naik)

New & Renewable Energy : 7th Floor, Atal Akshay Urja Bhawan, Lodhi Road, New Delhi-110003
Tel. : 011-20849074-75, 20849141, E-mail : mos-mnre@gov.in; shripad.naik@sansad.nic.in
Power : Room No. 200, Shram Shakti Bhawan, Rafi Marg, New Delhi-110001, Tel.: 011-23720450-51
Res. (Delhi) : 1, Lodhi Estate, New Delhi-110003, Tel.: 011-24635396, Fax : 011-24656910
Res. (Goa) : "Vijayshree" House No. 111, St. Pedro, Old Goa, Goa-403402, Tel.: 0832-2444510, 2444088

Preface

The idea of authoring this book took shape during a casual chat with Miss Savita Sharma, who always had a knack for offering insightful observations. We were deep in conversation when she suddenly remarked, "You know, your writing feels almost mechanical at times—like talking to ChatGPT." I chuckled at the comparison but knew she had a point. I often found myself laying out ideas systematically, breaking down complex thoughts into simple, clear narratives, much like an AI model would.

Intrigued, I jokingly responded, "Maybe I should be training ChatGPT if my writing feels that way!" Without missing a beat, she said, "Why not write a book instead? If you can communicate so well and with such clarity, why not share your journey with others?"

Her comment stayed with me. It was one of those moments where something so casual sparked a much deeper idea. I realized that while my writing might have seemed structured or methodical, it was a strength that could be channeled into something far more impactful. Miss Sharma had pointed out something I hadn't seen in myself—that my experiences, challenges, and lessons could be crafted into a story that could inspire others.

That simple conversation gave me the push I needed. If I could train a machine, why couldn't I shape my life's journey into a narrative that might help others? With Miss Sharma's encouragement, the decision was made that I would author this book. Not just as a reflection of my journey, but as a testament to the fact that, no matter how structured or mechanical our thinking may sometimes seem, the heart behind our stories can always connect with others.

And so, this book was born—written for anyone who has ever felt unsure of their path but willing to keep pushing forward.

Author's Note

This book is inspired by real events, and while many parts of the story are deeply personal, I have taken creative liberties to enrich the narrative. The essence of this journey remains true: the determination to rise after each fall, to face challenges head-on, and to continue moving forward despite the odds.

My hope is that readers find not only inspiration in these pages but also a reminder that success is built on resilience, failure, and constant learning. This story is a celebration of those who dare to dream and work tirelessly to achieve those dreams.

In sharing this journey, I aim to highlight the power of perseverance and the importance of embracing every setback as a steppingstone towards success. Life is filled with unexpected twists and turns, and it is our response to these challenges that defines our path. Through the highs and lows, the victories, and defeats, it is the unwavering spirit to keep pushing forward that truly matters.

Every chapter of this book is a testament to the human spirit's resilience and the relentless pursuit of one's goals. It is a reminder that no dream is too big and no obstacle too insurmountable when you have the courage to keep going. The stories within these pages are not just mine; they are a reflection of the countless individuals who have faced adversity and emerged stronger.

As you read through these pages, I hope you find a piece of your own journey mirrored in these words. May this book serve as a beacon of hope and a source of motivation, encouraging you to chase your dreams with unyielding determination. Remember, success is not a destination but a journey, one that is paved with hard work, resilience, and the willingness to learn from every experience.

This book is a tribute to all the dreamers, the fighters, and the believers. It is a celebration of the human spirit's capacity to overcome, to adapt, and to thrive. Let these stories inspire you to rise after every fall, to face your challenges head-on, and to continue moving forward, no matter the odds. Your dreams are within reach—keep striving, keep believing, and never give up.

Acknowledgements

Authoring a book is never a solo endeavor, and there are countless people I thank for their unwavering support and encouragement throughout this process.

First and foremost, to the Honorable Governor of Goa, Mr. P. S. Sreedharan Pillai, your guidance has been a beacon of light, illuminating the path and inspiring me to strive for excellence. Your wisdom and encouragement have been instrumental in shaping this journey, and I am deeply grateful for your support.

To my parents, whose love, sacrifices, and unwavering belief in my dreams have made everything possible—I am forever indebted to you. Your endless patience, sleepless nights, and constant encouragement have been the bedrock of my success. Thank you for instilling in me the values that have guided me through every challenge.

Miss Savita Sharma, your unwavering belief in my story and your constant encouragement gave me the courage to pursue my passion. Your insightful feedback and steadfast support have been invaluable. Thank you for pushing me to tell my story and for believing in its value.

To my dear friends, Renjith Nair and Pooja Nair, your friendship has carried me through the darkest moments. Your advice, laughter, and perspective have been a source of immense strength. I am so fortunate to have you both in my life, and your unwavering support has been a constant reminder that I am never alone.

ACKNOWLEDGEMENTS

To the countless colleagues, mentors, and friends who have supported me through every venture, your insight and encouragement have been a guiding force. Thank you for your invaluable contributions and for believing in my vision.

Finally, to the readers—thank you for taking the time to read this story. I hope it inspires you as much as it has inspired me to write it. This book is a celebration of resilience, determination, and the power of dreams. May it serve as a beacon of hope and motivation, encouraging you to chase your dreams with unyielding determination. Thank you for being a part of this journey.

Introduction

Nikhil's journey from the small town of Ernakulam to the heights of entrepreneurial success is a compelling narrative of resilience, personal growth, and unwavering determination. This book delves into the various facets of his life, illustrating how each experience, whether a triumph or a setback, contributed to his ultimate success.

Starting from his humble beginnings in Ernakulam, Nikhil faced numerous challenges that tested his resolve. The book chronicles his early struggles, highlighting the obstacles he encountered and the lessons he learned along the way. It paints a vivid picture of his relentless pursuit of knowledge and his unyielding desire to improve himself, both personally and professionally.

As Nikhil ventured into the world of business, he encountered failures and setbacks that could have easily derailed his ambitions. However, it was his ability to rise above these challenges that set him apart. The book explores how he turned each failure into a learning opportunity, using these experiences to build a stronger foundation for his future endeavors. His journey is a testament to the power of resilience and the importance of maintaining a positive mindset, even in the face of adversity.

Throughout the narrative, readers will find themselves inspired by Nikhil's unwavering determination and his ability to adapt to changing circumstances. His story serves as a powerful reminder that success is not defined by where we start, but by our willingness to keep moving forward, regardless of the obstacles in our path.

Whether you are an aspiring entrepreneur, someone facing challenges in your own career, or simply a lover of stories about perseverance, this book offers valuable insights and inspiration. It underscores the importance of resilience, continuous learning, and the courage to pursue one's dreams. Nikhil's journey is a celebration of the human spirit's capacity to overcome adversity and achieve greatness.

In summary, this book is not just about business success; it is about the personal growth and determination that drive us to rise above every challenge. It is a story that will resonate with anyone who believes in the power of perseverance and the relentless pursuit of one's dreams.

CHAPTER 1
SMALL TOWN BEGINNINGS

Nikhil's journey began in the heart of Ernakulam, a small town nestled on the western coast of Kerala. The town, with its rich cultural tapestry and lush green landscapes, provided a picturesque backdrop to his early years. Ernakulam was a place where tradition met modernity, where ancient temples stood alongside bustling markets, and where the whispers of the past mingled with the aspirations of the future.

Nikhil was born into a close-knit, joint family that upheld the traditional values of Kerala. His home was a sprawling ancestral house, a typical Kerala tharavadu, with red-tiled roofs, wooden pillars, and a central courtyard where the family gathered for meals and celebrations. The house was always alive with the chatter of relatives, the aroma of spices from the kitchen, and the sound of the monsoon rains drumming on the rooftops.

Nikhil's father was a respected government employee, known for his integrity and dedication to his work. His mother, a homemaker, managed the household with grace and efficiency, ensuring that the family's needs were always met. She was a woman of few words but possessed a quiet strength that Nikhil admired deeply. Growing up, Nikhil was surrounded by love and warmth, but also by the elevated expectations that came with being part of such a traditional family.

His grandmother played a significant role in shaping his early years. An expert storyteller, she would often gather Nikhil and his cousins in the evenings to narrate tales from Indian epics like the Mahabharata and Ramayana. Her stories were not just about heroes and gods; they were lessons in morality, courage, and the importance of perseverance. These stories ignited Nikhil's imagination and planted the seeds of ambition in his young mind.

Ernakulam itself was a town of contrasts. On one hand, it was steeped in tradition, with its vibrant festivals, Kathakali performances, and age-old customs. On the other hand, it was a town on the cusp of change, with new industries emerging, and a growing emphasis on education and technology. The town's unique blend of the old and the new had a profound impact on Nikhil. He learned early on that while it was important to honor tradition, it was equally important to embrace change and innovation.

As a child, Nikhil was curious and introspective. He would often spend hours exploring the town, observing the daily lives of the people around him. He was fascinated by the local craftsmen who created intricate wooden sculptures and brass lamps, and by the way technology was slowly making its way into the lives of the townspeople. These early observations fueled his interest in how things worked and how they could be improved.

At school, Nikhil was a bright student, though he was often shy and reserved. He excelled in his studies, particularly in science and mathematics, subjects that allowed him to delve deeper into his curiosity about the world. His teachers recognized his potential and encouraged him to participate in various competitions and science fairs. While Nikhil enjoyed the challenges, he often found himself more comfortable with books and experiments than with people.

Nikhil's introverted nature meant that he struggled to make friends easily. He preferred the company over the books or the solitude over a small workshop he had set up at home. Here, he would spend hours dismantling and reassembling gadgets, trying to understand how they worked. His parents, while proud of his academic achievements, worried about his lack of social interaction. They encouraged him to participate in more extracurricular activities, but Nikhil remained focused on his studies and his experiments.

Despite his reserved nature, Nikhil was deeply connected to his family. He admired his father's work ethic and his mother's quiet strength. His grandmother's stories continued to inspire him, teaching him the values of resilience, courage, and the importance of staying true to one's principles. These values would become the foundation upon which Nikhil would build his future.

As Nikhil grew older, the pressure to excel academically increased. In a family where education was highly valued, there was an unspoken expectation that Nikhil would follow in the footsteps of his father and pursue a respectable career. However, Nikhil's interests were not limited to academics. He had a growing fascination with technology and innovation, and he began to dream of creating something that could make a difference in the world.

The town of Ernakulam, with its blend of tradition and modernity, had a noteworthy influence on Nikhil's aspirations. He saw how the town was evolving, how new opportunities were emerging, and he wanted to be a part of that change. He wanted to create something that would not only honor the values he had been taught but also embrace the future.

In the evenings, as the sun set over the lush green fields and the aroma of jasmine filled the air, Nikhil would sit in the courtyard of his home, contemplating his future. He knew that the path ahead would not be easy, but he was determined to make a mark, to create something that would be remembered. The stories of the heroes and gods his grandmother had told him echoed in his mind, reminding him that every great journey begins with a single step.

And so, with a heart full of dreams and a mind brimming with ideas, Nikhil took his first steps on the path that would eventually lead him to become an entrepreneur, a leader, and a visionary. But as he would soon learn, the journey to success is rarely straightforward. It is a path filled with challenges, setbacks, and moments of doubt. Yet, it is also a journey of discovery, growth, and ultimately, triumph.

CHAPTER 2

CHILDHOOD DREAMS

Nikhil's childhood was a mixture of curiosity, solitude, and a deep desire to understand the world around him. From an early age, he was drawn to the mysteries of how things worked—whether it was the old radio in his father's study or the way the monsoon rains brought life to the fields in his hometown of Ernakulam. His mind was constantly filled with questions, ideas, and dreams.

After completing his early education in a local school, Nikhil's parents decided to enroll him in Triveni, a prestigious boarding school near Chennai. Their decision was driven by a desire to provide him with the best education possible, but it also meant that Nikhil would have to leave behind the comfort of his family and the familiarity of Ernakulam. At just six years old, he found himself in a unique environment, surrounded by unfamiliar faces and a sprawling campus that felt both exciting and overwhelming.

The transition was difficult. The first few weeks at Triveni were marked by intense homesickness. Nikhil missed the warmth of his home, the sound of his grandmother's voice telling stories, and the simple pleasures of life in Ernakulam. The boarding school, with its rigid schedules and strict discipline, felt cold and impersonal. The large dormitories, echoing with the sounds of other children, only deepened his sense of isolation.

Despite the initial struggles, Nikhil soon found solace in his studies. The structured environment of Triveni, while challenging, provided him with the intellectual stimulation he craved. He quickly emerged as one of the top students in his class, excelling particularly in science and mathematics. His teachers recognized his potential and encouraged him to participate in science fairs and competitions. However, Nikhil's introverted nature led him to spend most of his time buried in books and experiments, rather than engaging in social activities.

One of the most significant aspects of Nikhil's time at Triveni was the small workshop he set up in his hostel room. With permission from his teachers, he collected old clocks, radios, and other discarded gadgets, which he would dismantle and attempt to repair. The process of taking things apart and understanding how they worked fascinated him. While other boys played sports or socialized in the common room, Nikhil could often be found hunched over his workbench, tinkering with wires, gears, and circuits.

Nikhil's passion for science and technology wasn't just limited to the confines of his workshop. He was equally fascinated by the natural world. He closely observed the monsoons, which were a constant presence during his early years in Kerala. At Triveni, he began to study the patterns of rainfall, the impact it had on agriculture, and the science behind weather systems. These early explorations laid the groundwork for his later interest in environmental technology.

However, Nikhil's school life was not without its challenges. Being introverted made it difficult for him to make friends, and he often found himself on the outskirts of social circles. His reserved nature and academic focus made him a target for bullies. Some of the more aggressive boys in his dorm would mock his solitary habits and his obsession with gadgets. They would hide his tools, sabotage his projects, and tease him mercilessly for preferring books over sports.

These experiences were painful for Nikhil. The bullying made him feel even more isolated, and he often wondered why he couldn't just fit in like everyone else. The teasing was particularly harsh during the school holidays when most of the students went home to be with their families. Nikhil, however, often had to stay back at the hostel due to his parents' busy schedules. During these times, the dormitories would empty out, leaving Nikhil alone in the vast, echoing halls.

The loneliness during these vacations was overwhelming. With no one to talk to and nothing to distract him, Nikhil spent most of his time in the workshop, pouring himself into his projects. The silence of the empty school was both a comfort and a reminder of his isolation. It was during these solitary hours that Nikhil's resolve began to harden. He decided that if he couldn't fit in with the other boys, he would focus on what he was good at—his studies and his inventions.

Despite the bullying and the loneliness, Nikhil found a friend in Arjun, another quiet student who shared his love for science. The two boys bonded over their mutual interests, spending countless hours discussing their latest experiments and challenging each other's ideas. Arjun's friendship provided Nikhil with the companionship he had been missing. Together, they entered several science competitions, often winning top prizes for their innovative projects.

As Nikhil grew older, his dreams began to take shape. He was no longer content with just understanding how things worked—he wanted to create something new, something that could make a real difference in the world. His mind was constantly buzzing with ideas for inventions, from a machine that could harness renewable energy to a device that could improve agricultural productivity. These ideas were the first sparks of what would later become his entrepreneurial journey.

However, Nikhil's ambitions were not without challenges. The pressure to succeed, both academically and socially, weighed heavily on him. The expectations from his family, combined with the competitive environment of Triveni, often left him feeling overwhelmed. There were times when the loneliness and the constant striving for excellence took a toll on his mental health. But every time he felt like giving up, he would remember the stories his grandmother told him—stories of heroes who faced insurmountable odds but never gave up. These stories, coupled with his own determination, kept him going.

One of the defining moments of Nikhil's childhood came during a national science competition in the eighth grade. He had spent months working on a project that combined his love for technology and his concern for the environment—a solar-powered irrigation system that could help farmers in rural areas. The project was ambitious, and there were times when Nikhil doubted whether he could pull it off. But with the encouragement of his teachers and the support of Arjun, he persevered.

The competition was fierce, with students from all over the country highlighting their best work. Nikhil's project was met with skepticism by some of the judges, who doubted whether a boy of his age could develop something so complex. But when he presented his working model, explaining the science behind it and its potential impact, the skepticism turned into admiration. Nikhil won the first prize, and the recognition gave him a newfound confidence in his abilities.

The success of his project was a turning point for Nikhil. It was the first time he genuinely believed that his ideas could make a difference. The win also brought him the attention of several prominent educators and scientists, who encouraged him to continue pursuing his interests in science and technology. For Nikhil, the competition was not just about winning a prize—it was about realizing that his dreams were within reach.

As he progressed through the remaining years of school, Nikhil continued to excel academically, but his focus was increasingly on his own projects and ideas. He spent less time worrying about fitting in and more time developing the skills and knowledge that would eventually lead him to his entrepreneurial journey. The dream of creating something meaningful, something that could change the world, had taken root in his heart, and there was no turning back.

By the time Nikhil graduated from Triveni, he was not just a top student—he was a young man with an unclouded vision of what he wanted to achieve. The seeds of entrepreneurship had been sown, and his childhood dreams.

CHAPTER 3

SCHOOL YEARS

The years Nikhil spent at Triveni marked a critical period of growth and self-discovery. While his early years at the school had been marked by loneliness and homesickness, as he progressed, Nikhil found ways to channel these feelings into his studies and projects. Triveni, with its sprawling campus and rigorous academic environment, became the crucible where Nikhil's academic and personal identity began to form.

From the outside, Nikhil appeared to be thriving. He was consistently at the top of his class, excelling in subjects like science and mathematics. Teachers regularly praised him for his discipline and curiosity, encouraging him to explore his ideas further. But while he earned respect for his academic prowess, Nikhil's social life remained a struggle. His introversion and awkwardness in social situations made it difficult for him to connect with his peers. He often felt like an outsider, observing the world from a distance rather than participating in it.

As he grew older, the gap between Nikhil and his classmates only widened. Many of the boys at Triveni were drawn to sports, pranks, and the kinds of activities that were far from Nikhil's interests. He preferred spending his free time in the library or the small workshop he had set up in his hostel room. His love for taking things apart and understanding how they worked continued to grow, and the workshop became his sanctuary. It was the one place where he felt in control, where the chaos of the outside world could not intrude.

Yet, this isolation did not go unnoticed by his classmates. Nikhil's quiet demeanor and singular focus on his studies and gadgets made him a target for ridicule. The bullying, which had started in his early years, intensified as he moved through the middle grades. The boys would tease him for spending his time with machines rather than with people, calling him names like "robot" and "machine man." They would hide his tools, make fun of his inventions, and exclude him from group activities. The worst moments came during holidays, when most of the boys would leave for home and Nikhil would be left alone in the empty dormitories.

Those vacations were particularly tough. With the entire school almost deserted, the silence in the dorms felt deafening. While his classmates spent time with their families, Nikhil was often left to his own devices. The loneliness during these times became almost unbearable. The vast, empty corridors of the school, which were normally filled with the sounds of laughter and activity, now echoed with nothing but Nikhil's footsteps.

Despite this, Nikhil learned to cope by focusing even more intensely on his projects. He convinced himself that if he could not fit into the social fabric of the school, he would excel in the one area where he felt comfortable—his inventions. Each holiday, he would use the solitude to dive deeper into his work, often losing himself in his experiments until the early hours of the morning. His isolation turned into a strange kind of strength, pushing him to excel even when it felt like the world had turned its back on him.

One of his major turning points came during his ninth year at Triveni. Nikhil had been working on a project to create a low-cost water purification system, inspired by the issues of water scarcity in rural areas of India. The system was designed to be simple enough for any household to use, relying on basic filtration techniques that could remove harmful impurities from contaminated water. He had spent months perfecting the design, sourcing materials, and testing prototypes in his workshop.

The school science fair was approaching, and Nikhil knew this project could be his breakthrough. However, the bullying reached a new level just before the fair. Some of the boys, jealous of Nikhil's dedication and frustrated by their own lack of achievement, sabotaged his project. They damaged the prototype he had been working on for months, leaving Nikhil devastated just days before the competition.

For a moment, Nikhil considered quitting. The emotional toll of the bullying, combined with the failure of his project, felt like too much to bear. But something inside him refused to give up. It was in these moments of despair that he remembered the stories his grandmother used to tell him—tales of heroes who overcame impossible odds to achieve greatness. He knew that quitting now would mean letting his tormentors win, and that was something he could not accept.

With a renewed sense of determination, Nikhil locked himself in his workshop and worked tirelessly to rebuild his project. He barely slept in the days leading up to the fair, using every spare moment to fix the damage and improve the design. When the day of the science fair arrived, Nikhil stood nervously by his booth, unsure of how his hastily rebuilt project would be received.

To his surprise, the judges were impressed. Not only did the water purification system work, but it also addressed a critical issue facing many communities across India. Nikhil's project was awarded first prize, and he received special recognition for his innovation and perseverance in the face of adversity. This victory was more than just a win at a science fair—it was a personal triumph, a validation that his hard work and dedication could overcome even the most difficult obstacles.

The success of the project earned Nikhil the respect of his teachers and, surprisingly, some of his classmates. While the bullying did not stop entirely, it lessened as his peers began to see him not just as the "weird, quiet boy," but as someone who could achieve remarkable things. The incident also marked a shift in Nikhil's own self-perception. He realized that while he might never fit in with the crowd, his unique talents and perspective could set him apart in ways that mattered.

As Nikhil progressed through his final years at Triveni, he continued to excel academically. His reputation as a brilliant student and innovator grew, and he began to take on more ambitious projects. The school, recognizing his potential, provided him with additional resources and mentorship from teachers who saw in him the makings of a future leader.

One of those teachers was Mr. Iyer, the head of the science department, who took Nikhil under his wing.

Mr. Iyer had a keen eye for talent and was impressed by Nikhil's work ethic and intellectual curiosity. Under Mr. Iyer's guidance, Nikhil was exposed to advanced scientific concepts and encouraged to think beyond the textbook. It was Mr. Iyer who first planted the idea in Nikhil's mind that his innovations could have a real-world impact, far beyond the walls of the school.

By the time Nikhil graduated from Triveni, he had transformed from a quiet, introverted boy into a confident young man with a clear sense of purpose. The years of isolation, bullying, and struggle had not broken him—they had shaped him into someone who understood the value of perseverance, resilience, and self-belief. While his school years had been far from easy, they had forged in him the qualities that would become essential in his later life as an entrepreneur.

Nikhil left Triveni with not only academic accolades but also a deeper understanding of who he was and what he was capable of. The lessons he had learned—both inside and outside the classroom—would guide him as he embarked on the next phase of his journey. The road ahead was still uncertain, but for the first time in his life, Nikhil felt ready to face whatever challenges awaited him.

CHAPTER 4

TEENAGE TRIALS

As Nikhil entered his teenage years, life at Triveni continued to challenge him in new and unexpected ways. The pressure to perform academically had intensified. With each passing year, the stakes grew higher, and the expectations from his family, teachers, and even himself weighed heavily on him. The competitiveness of the academic environment made it clear that only the best would secure places at top universities or land scholarships. The stress of maintaining his position at the top of the class was unrelenting.

Though Nikhil had become more confident in his abilities, the isolation that had characterized his earlier years remained. While he had gained the respect of some of his classmates after his victory in the science fair, he never truly found a place within their social circles. His time at school remained a solitary experience, defined by long hours in the library or workshop, and the constant grind of academic work.

But something new was beginning to stir inside Nikhil. The teenage years brought with them a heightened sense of ambition. What had once been a vague interest in technology and invention was now crystallizing into something much more focused. Nikhil wasn't just interested in excelling in his studies anymore—he wanted to build something unique, something that would set him apart. He was drawn to problem-solving, especially when it required out-of-the- box thinking. His mind buzzed with unconventional ideas that challenged the traditional ways of doing things.

More than anything, Nikhil began to realize that his real passion lay in business and strategy. While many of his peers were preparing for careers in engineering or medicine, Nikhil was increasingly fascinated by the idea of building a consulting firm—one that could provide innovative solutions to the problems businesses faced. He wanted to create a company that helped businesses think differently, solving their challenges in ways they hadn't imagined.

The consulting industry was a world that Nikhil found captivating. He was drawn to how consultants could come into a company, analyze its weaknesses, and then provide strategic solutions to drive growth. This appealed to his problem-solving nature, and he spent hours reading about successful business consultants, studying their methods, and dissecting case studies of companies that had turned around because of outside advice. He believed that his ability to think creatively, to approach problems from unique angles, could be his competitive edge in this field.

However, Nikhil's interest in consulting and business strategy wasn't easily understood by those around him. His teachers, while supportive, had always seen him as a top student destined for a career in engineering. His family, particularly his father, had similar expectations. His father envisioned Nikhil following a safe, stable path—one that involved a respected profession with steady income and job security. Entrepreneurship, in his father's eyes, was risky and unpredictable.

The tension between Nikhil's ambitions and his family's expectations came to a head during a family visit in his final year at Triveni. His father, proud of his son's academic achievements, expected Nikhil to speak about his plans to pursue engineering at one of the top institutes. But when Nikhil revealed that he wanted to build a consulting firm, his father's response was less than enthusiastic.

"A consulting firm?" his father asked, his voice tinged with disbelief. "Nikhil, do you know how difficult it is to succeed in that world? It's not as simple as starting a business. You need connections, capital, experience. Why take such a risk when you could have a stable career as an engineer? You've always been good at academics, why not stick to something more certain?"

Nikhil had anticipated his father's skepticism, but it still stung to hear the doubt in his voice. He understood his father's concerns, but Nikhil couldn't shake the feeling that he was meant for something more than just following the traditional path. His mind was filled with ideas for helping businesses solve their problems, and he was determined to prove that his approach—thinking creatively—was the way forward. "I know it's risky," Nikhil replied, trying to keep his voice steady. "But I believe that with the right approach, I can offer businesses something unique. It's not just about following the conventional path. I want to create solutions that no one else has thought of."

His father sighed but didn't push the issue further. Though the conversation ended, the unspoken tension between Nikhil's dreams and his father's expectations lingered. Nikhil knew that to pursue his entrepreneurial ambitions, he would need to prove himself—first to his family, and then to the world.

At school, Nikhil found solace in his projects. He threw himself into studying business strategies and innovative problem-solving techniques, often staying up late to pore over case studies of companies that had been transformed through consulting. His mind was alive with ideas, and he began to draft business plans, mapping out how he could create a consulting firm that would offer services beyond the standard approaches.

But as his final year at Triveni progressed, Nikhil was faced with the ultimate test—the entrance exams for top engineering institutes like the Indian Institutes of Technology (IIT). His family expected him to secure a place, and the pressure to perform was immense. While his heart was increasingly drawn toward business and consulting, his mind knew that failing the exam would bring disappointment to those who had always believed in his academic potential. Despite his focus on out-of-the-box thinking, Nikhil couldn't ignore the importance of the IIT exams. He spent long hours preparing for them, balancing his studies with his passion for business. But the more he prepared, the more he felt a growing disconnect between the path his family envisioned for him and the path he wanted to carve for himself. The night before the exam, Nikhil lay awake, torn between meeting his family's expectations and following his own dream of entrepreneurship.

When the results came out, Nikhil's worst fears were realized—he hadn't made the cut for IIT. The failure felt like a heavy blow, not just to his academic record, but to his sense of identity. He had always been the top student, the one who excelled, and now he had to face the reality of disappointing his family. For weeks, Nikhil struggled with the shame of falling short.

But as the initial sting of failure began to fade, Nikhil found clarity. He realized that while he had failed to secure a spot at IIT, the setback gave him the freedom to pursue what he genuinely wanted. The dream of becoming an entrepreneur, of building a consulting firm that offered innovative, unconventional solutions, had always been in the back of his mind. Now, with the IIT door closed, Nikhil saw a new opportunity in front of him—the chance to fully commit to his vision.

Instead of wallowing in disappointment, Nikhil applied to Presidency College, one of the best institutions for commerce studies. While it wasn't the path his family had expected, it was the one that would provide him with the business acumen he needed to navigate the consulting world. For Nikhil, this was a pivotal moment—one where he chose to follow his passion for problem-solving and strategy, rather than conform to expectations.

In his final days at Triveni, Nikhil reflected on the lessons he had learned. The years of isolation, the struggles with his identity, and the pressures of academic achievement had all shaped him into someone who could think independently. He realized that his talent for thinking creatively, for coming up with unique solutions to problems, would be the key to his success.

As Nikhil left Triveni behind, he knew that his journey was just beginning. The road ahead would be full of challenges, but for the first time, he felt confident that he was on the right path—a path that was his alone.

CHAPTER 5

FIRST VENTURES

Entering Presidency College marked a pivotal moment in Nikhil's life. Unlike his time at Triveni, where he had often felt out of place, college offered a fresh start. Surrounded by young minds eager to carve out their own paths, Nikhil finally found an environment where his entrepreneurial spirit could take root and grow.

From the moment he set foot on campus, Nikhil was clear about one thing—he wasn't there just to get a degree. He was there to build something, to begin the process of turning his dreams into reality. While his peers focused on lectures and exams, Nikhil was already thinking about his first venture. Inspired by the idea of consulting, he began sketching out plans for a small business that could provide strategic advice to local enterprises. He didn't have the experience of seasoned consultants, but what he lacked in experience, he made up for in determination and out-of-the-box thinking.

Presidency College had a vibrant startup culture, and Nikhil quickly became involved in the college's entrepreneurship club. Here, he found like-minded students who shared his passion for business and innovation. Together, they would spend hours brainstorming ideas, discussing market trends, and attending workshops on everything from marketing to economic management. Nikhil thrived in this environment, constantly pushing himself and those around him to think creatively about the challenges they wanted to solve.

His first significant project was a consulting service called Strategic Edge. The idea behind it was simple—Nikhil would offer business strategies and problem-solving solutions to small, local companies that couldn't afford larger consulting firms. He believed that his unique ability to think creatively would allow him to offer fresh perspectives to businesses that were struggling to grow or adapt to changing market conditions.

Setting up Strategic Edge wasn't easy. Nikhil had to juggle his coursework with the demands of running a fledgling business. His days were long, and his nights even longer, filled with meetings, research, and project deadlines. With no real capital to speak of, Nikhil relied on his network of friends and classmates, who helped him with everything from market research to designing the company's branding. Most of the work was done in the college library or in makeshift meeting rooms they set up in dormitories.

One of the biggest challenges Nikhil faced early on was convincing local businesses to take him seriously. At just 19 years old, he lacked the credentials and track record that most companies looked for in a consultant. His first few pitches were met with skepticism, and there were several moments when Nikhil wondered if he had taken on more than he could handle But Nikhil wasn't one to give up easily. He understood that if he was going to make Strategic Edge successful, he needed to prove his value. So, instead of waiting for businesses to come to him, he started offering free consultations to small companies in exchange for testimonials and case studies. His first clients were small family-owned businesses—a local café struggling with its pricing strategy and a boutique store that needed help improving customer retention. Nikhil worked tirelessly on these projects, pouring all his energy into finding innovative solutions to their problems.

The café, for example, was losing customers to larger, more established chains in the area. After studying the market, Nikhil suggested a unique loyalty program that offered personalized rewards for regular customers. He also proposed a revamp of their menu to include locally sourced ingredients, capitalizing on the growing trend of sustainable and organic eating. Within a few months, the café's customer base had grown significantly, and the owner was thrilled with the results.

Similarly, for the boutique store, Nikhil implemented a digital marketing strategy, helping the store develop an online presence and engage with customers through social media. His fresh perspective on their operations breathed new life into the business, and the owner, impressed by his insights, referred him to other small business owners. Word began to spread, and soon, Strategic Edge was gaining momentum. The testimonials from his early clients gave Nikhil the credibility he needed to approach bigger businesses. As his reputation grew, so did his confidence. He began taking on more challenging projects, including helping a mid-sized manufacturing firm streamline its supply chain and advising a local tech startup on scaling its operations.

Despite the early successes, running Strategic Edge wasn't without its challenges. Nikhil often found himself stretched thin, juggling his college work with client demands. There were times when he barely slept, staying up late to meet deadlines or prepare for client meetings. He also faced financial constraints—while the consulting firm was gaining traction, it wasn't yet profitable, and Nikhil was still relying on the goodwill of his friends to keep the business running.

Moreover, there were failures along the way. Not every project went smoothly, and Nikhil had his share of missteps. One particularly painful experience was a consulting project for a local IT company. Nikhil had proposed an ambitious digital transformation strategy, but the execution fell short due to poor communication and lack of resources. The project was a failure, and the client was dissatisfied, leading Nikhil to reflect deeply on what had gone wrong.

But failure didn't discourage him. If anything, it made Nikhil more determined to improve. He used the experience to refine his approach, learning from his mistakes and adjusting his strategies to better fit the needs of his clients. Each setback was a lesson, and each success was a step closer to realizing his dream of building a successful consulting firm.

Outside of his work on Strategic Edge, Nikhil's time at Presidency College was filled with other entrepreneurial pursuits. He became deeply involved in the college's startup incubator program, where he mentored younger students who were launching their own ventures. This experience not only helped him sharpen his business skills but also gave him a sense of purpose. He enjoyed helping others realize their entrepreneurial dreams, and it further fueled his passion for innovation.

By the time Nikhil graduated from Presidency College, Strategic Edge had grown from a small side project into a reputable consulting firm with a solid client base. He had developed a reputation for delivering creative, out-of-the-box solutions, and his business was beginning to show signs of profitability. More importantly, Nikhil had proven to himself and to those around him that his unconventional path—one driven by innovation and risk-taking—was the right one.

Nikhil's first venture, while far from perfect, had given him a taste of what was possible. It had taught him the importance of resilience, adaptability, and, most of all, the value of thinking differently. He knew that his journey was just beginning, and that there were bigger challenges and opportunities waiting for him in the world beyond college. As he packed his bags and prepared to leave the halls of Presidency College, Nikhil felt a sense of accomplishment. But more than that, he felt excitement. The world of business consulting was vast and full of possibilities, and Nikhil was ready to take it on.

CHAPTER 6

HIGHER EDUCATION AND NEW HORIZONS

After graduating from Presidency College, Nikhil found himself at a crossroads. His first venture, Strategic Edge, had taught him valuable lessons about business, consulting, and, most importantly, himself. He knew he had the drive to succeed, but he also realized that the world beyond college would present much bigger challenges. With this in mind, Nikhil decided to pursue higher education to sharpen his skills and broaden his understanding of business strategy and management.

Nikhil had always been a high achiever, and after careful consideration, he set his sights on joining one of the premier business schools in the country—Indian Institute of Management Ahmedabad (IIM A). It was a place where the brightest minds converged, and where Nikhil knew he could further refine his consulting ideas while gaining exposure to new fields of study. The competitive nature of getting into IIM A was daunting, but Nikhil's persistence and determination paid off. After months of preparation and the rigors of the Common Admission Test (CAT), Nikhil earned his place at IIM A, a moment of pride for both him and his family.

From the outset, Nikhil found IIM A to be a completely different world compared to Presidency College. Here, the competition was fiercer, the workload more intense, and the expectations even higher. But

Nikhil thrived in this environment. He saw IIM not just as a place to earn a degree, but as a training ground for bigger ventures. He immersed himself in courses on business strategy, operations management, and entrepreneurship, learning from some of the most accomplished professors in the country.

One of the most transformative experiences at IIM A was the exposure to real-world case studies. These weren't just hypothetical exercises—many of the cases involved analyzing the challenges faced by some of the world's biggest companies. Nikhil loved dissecting these problems, often coming up with unconventional solutions that caught the attention of his professors and classmates. It was during these sessions that Nikhil's confidence in his ability to think differently truly flourished. But beyond academics, IIM A also gave Nikhil the opportunity to work on two entrepreneurial ventures that would shape his approach to business forever.

The first venture was FoR (Furniture on Rent). Nikhil had noticed a growing trend among students and young professionals: many of them moved frequently, and investing in expensive furniture wasn't practical. Nikhil saw a gap in the market and realized there was potential in offering furniture on rent as a more flexible and affordable alternative. Together with a group of classmates, Nikhil worked on launching for, a service that provided stylish and affordable furniture rentals to students and young professionals in cities where relocation was frequent.

The project was both a success and a learning experience. Nikhil handled operations and logistics, coordinating with suppliers and customers while ensuring that the company could scale. While FoR gained traction in urban areas and the idea was well- received, the challenges of managing inventory and customer service proved daunting. Nevertheless, the experience gave Nikhil a taste of managing a bona fide business on a larger scale, with moving parts that required coordination and precision.

The second venture was more personal to Nikhil and reflected his desire to make a social impact. It was called Talking to Silence, an NGO venture focused on addressing the growing issue of elder loneliness. Nikhil had observed that many elderly individuals were left behind by their children who had moved to other cities or countries for work. The project aimed to create safe spaces where elderly people could share their life stories, find companionship, and connect with younger generations through organized events and community programs.

Nikhil's role in Talking to Silence was largely strategic, as he used his consulting mindset to streamline operations and secure funding from local businesses and philanthropists. Though it was an emotionally challenging project—listening to the stories of elderly individuals who had been left alone—Nikhil felt a deep sense of purpose. It wasn't just about making profits anymore; he was now using his skills to make a positive social impact.

Both ventures provided Nikhil with the practical knowledge he needed to navigate the complex world of business. He learned how to manage teams, allocate resources, and handle the ups and downs of entrepreneurship. Importantly, he began to see the value of building a network. Whether it was securing suppliers for or finding sponsors for Talking to Silence, Nikhil realized that his success would depend heavily on the relationships he built and the trust he earned.

But as Nikhil's time at IIM An ended, he knew that his next move would need to be even bigger. He had proven to himself that he could launch ventures and take on the challenges of entrepreneurship, but now he wanted to apply these skills in the real world—on a global scale. He had always dreamed of working for a large, multinational company where he could learn from the best and push himself even further. With his heart set on this goal, Nikhil began exploring job opportunities after graduation.

It wasn't long before an opportunity presented itself. Nikhil was offered a position at GE Aircraft, a division of the global conglomerate General Electric. The role, as a Six Sigma Black Belt, involved working on process improvement and operational efficiency, applying Six Sigma methodologies to streamline operations within the company. For Nikhil, this was a dream job. Not only was GE one of the world's largest companies, but it also offered him the chance to work on a global scale, solving complex problems and learning from the brightest minds in the industry.

Nikhil's initial stint with GE was in India, where he worked on optimizing supply chain processes and reducing inefficiencies in manufacturing operations. But within a year, his talents were recognized, and he was given the opportunity to move to the United States to work at GE's headquarters. This was a significant moment for Nikhil. Moving to the U.S. not only expanded his professional horizons, but it also exposed him to innovative ideas, new ways of doing business, and a new level of competition.

During his time at GE in the U.S., Nikhil had the chance to meet and learn from some of the biggest names in the business world. Two figures, in particular, stood out: Jack Welch and Jeff Immelt, both legendary CEOs of GE. Their leadership philosophies, especially Welch's focus on performance and innovation, deeply influenced Nikhil's approach to business. He absorbed their lessons, learning how to lead teams, drive change, and maintain a relentless focus on excellence.

While Nikhil enjoyed his work at GE and the global exposure it provided, he never lost sight of his entrepreneurial ambitions. He knew that at some point, he would return to building his own business—something that would allow him to combine his passion for consulting, strategy, and innovation. But for now, GE was the perfect platform for Nikhil to continue growing, learning, and refining his skills.

As his time at GE continued, Nikhil began to feel more confident in his abilities. He had mastered the art of process improvement, worked with some of the best minds in the world, and gained invaluable experience in a global company. But the entrepreneur inside him was stirring once again. He knew that it wouldn't be long before he would return to the world of startups and consulting, this time with a wealth of knowledge and experience that would make him even more formidable.

Nikhil's time at IIM A and GE had expanded his horizons in ways he could never have imagined. He had learned the value of both structure and creativity, of following processes and breaking the mold when necessary. Most importantly, he had discovered that the key to success wasn't just about thinking outside the box—it was about building the right team, forging the right connections, and having the courage to take risks.

As Nikhil prepared for the next phase of his journey, he knew one thing for certain: the road ahead was going to be challenging, but he was ready for it.

CHAPTER 7

ENTERING THE REAL WORLD

After his transformative experience at IIM Ahmedabad and his initial success at GE Aircraft, Nikhil felt ready to tackle even bigger challenges. Working at a global conglomerate had given him exposure to the complexities of large-scale operations, and his interactions with visionary leaders like Jack Welch and Jeff Immelt had only deepened his understanding of leadership and innovation. However, despite his achievements in the corporate world, Nikhil's entrepreneurial spirit continued to drive him toward building something of his own.

By 2001, Nikhil's reputation at GE had grown, and his role as a Six Sigma Black Belt saw him leading key process improvement projects across multiple divisions. This experience, while invaluable, began to feel limiting. Nikhil found himself increasingly drawn toward the idea of returning to India to explore new opportunities. He had a vision of applying the strategic and operational lessons he had learned at GE to businesses back home, particularly in emerging sectors where innovation and efficiency were desperately needed.

Nikhil knew that this decision would not come without risk. Leaving a stable and well-paying job at GE to return to the uncertainties of entrepreneurship in India was a gamble, but one that Nikhil was willing to take. He was confident that his unique blend of consulting expertise and out-of-the-box thinking could help businesses in India thrive. Armed with this conviction, he resigned from his position at GE and made the move back to India.

Upon his return, Nikhil took up a position at HSBC, one of the world's largest banking and financial services organizations. The role allowed him to continue building on his experience while also exploring how financial institutions operated. This move, however, was more than just a job—it was part of a bigger plan. Nikhil saw his time at HSBC as an opportunity to learn about financial markets, corporate banking, and the challenges businesses faced in securing capital. These lessons would prove crucial for his own ventures later on.

At HSBC, Nikhil's primary focus was on improving operational efficiency within the organization. He led several key initiatives aimed at reducing costs, optimizing workflows, and enhancing the overall customer experience. His background in Six Sigma made him well-suited to this role, and his ability to think creatively about solving complex problems earned him recognition from senior leadership. Over time, Nikhil took on more responsibility, leading projects that spanned across various divisions, including retail banking, corporate finance, and asset management.

While his corporate career at HSBC flourished, Nikhil couldn't ignore the entrepreneurial itch that continued to tug at him. Even as he worked on improving processes within HSBC, his mind was always buzzing with innovative ideas for how businesses could be run more effectively. He frequently attended startup events, business conferences, and networking meetups, where he found himself surrounded by India's emerging entrepreneurs. The energy and innovation in these circles excited him and reminded him of the consulting firm he had built during his college days.

It was during this period that Nikhil began laying the groundwork for his next big entrepreneurial leap. Drawing from his experiences at GE and HSBC, Nikhil decided to venture into the world of strategic consulting—this time, on a much larger scale. He saw a growing need for businesses in India to adopt more efficient management practices and innovative business models, especially as the economy was rapidly globalizing. This led to the conceptualization of his next major venture: NHD Consulting.

NHD Consulting was designed to offer a full suite of services aimed at helping businesses optimize their operations, improve profitability, and implement sustainable growth strategies. Unlike his college venture, which had been focused on smaller, local businesses, Nikhil's vision for NHD was much broader. He wanted to work with mid-sized and large enterprises, helping them navigate the complexities of growth, scale, and innovation in an increasingly competitive market. Launching NHD Consulting wasn't easy. The market was crowded with established players, and Nikhil knew that he would need to offer something unique to stand out. Drawing from his deep understanding of process improvement and strategy, Nikhil positioned NHD as a firm that specialized in driving efficiency and innovation, two areas that many businesses in India struggled with. His ability to blend traditional management practices with cutting- edge innovation made NHD an attractive option for companies looking to transform.

However, like most entrepreneurial journeys, Nikhil's venture into the consulting world came with its fair share of challenges. Early on, he faced difficulty securing large clients. Many businesses were hesitant to trust a new firm, and the competition from well- established consulting giants made it tough to break into the market. Nikhil's initial pitches were often met with skepticism, and he faced numerous rejections. But he wasn't discouraged. If there was one thing Nikhil had learned throughout his career, it was the importance of persistence.

Undeterred, Nikhil tapped into his personal and professional networks, reaching out to former colleagues from GE and HSBC, as well as the connections he had made during his time at IIM A. Slowly but surely, he began landing small consulting gigs—process optimization projects for mid-sized manufacturing firms, advisory roles for tech startups, and efficiency improvement initiatives for retail chains. These early projects, while modest, helped Nikhil build a portfolio and establish a reputation for delivering tangible results.

One of the most significant breakthroughs for NHD Consulting came when Nikhil secured a contract with a large retail conglomerate that was struggling to improve its operational efficiency across multiple locations. The company had been losing market share to more agile competitors, and its leadership team was eager for a turnaround. Nikhil's consulting team worked closely with the company's executives to identify bottlenecks in the supply chain, streamline inventory management, and enhance customer service protocols.

The project was a resounding success. Not only did the company see a dramatic improvement in its operational performance, but it also regained its competitive edge in the market. The success of this project helped cement NHD Consulting's reputation as a firm that could deliver transformative results. Word of Nikhil's expertise spread, and soon, NHD was securing larger and more lucrative contracts.

However, despite the growing success of NHD, Nikhil faced personal and professional challenges that would test his resilience. Running a consulting firm required long hours, and the pressure to continually deliver results took a toll on Nikhil's mental and physical health. There were moments when the stress felt overwhelming, and Nikhil wondered whether he had made the right decision in leaving the relative stability of his corporate career for the uncertainties of entrepreneurship. But Nikhil had never been one to shy away from adversity. He had built NHD from the ground up, and he wasn't about to let the pressures of leadership derail his vision. He knew that the road ahead would be difficult, but he was committed to seeing it through. Over time, Nikhil learned to manage the demands of running a business, delegating more responsibility to his growing team, and focusing on strategic decision- making rather than getting caught up in day-to-day operations.

As NHD Consulting continued to grow, Nikhil found himself at the center of India's rapidly evolving business landscape. He was frequently invited to speak at industry conferences and seminars, where he shared his insights on innovation, efficiency, and the future of consulting. His ability to combine global best practices with a deep understanding of the Indian market made him a sought-after speaker and advisor.

But despite the accolades and success, Nikhil never lost sight of the bigger picture. He had always believed that business was about more than just profits—it was about creating value, driving change, and making a positive impact on society. This belief guided his leadership at NHD and shaped the company's mission to help businesses not only succeed but thrive in a way that was sustainable and ethical.

As Nikhil looked back on his journey—from his early days at Presidency College to his time at GE, HSBC, and finally as the founder of NHD Consulting—he felt a deep sense of fulfillment. The road had been long and difficult, filled with setbacks, challenges, and moments of doubt. But through it all, Nikhil had stayed true to his vision and his belief in the power of innovative thinking.

The real world, as Nikhil had learned, was full of uncertainty. But for those willing to take risks, think differently, and persevere through the toughest challenges, it was also a place of endless opportunity.

CHAPTER 8

FIRST MAJOR FAILURE

Success, as Nikhil had learned, was never linear. For every victory, there were setbacks—sometimes minor, sometimes devastating. His growing success with NHD Consulting had given him the confidence to think even bigger. But it also set the stage for what would become his first major failure—one that would test his resolve in ways he had never experienced before.

With NHD Consulting steadily gaining traction, Nikhil began exploring other business ventures. He had always been drawn to the idea of innovating within multiple industries, and one area that particularly piqued his interest was retail. The retail sector in India was undergoing significant changes, driven by globalization and the rise of e-commerce. Nikhil believed that there was room for a new player—one that could combine innovative technology with traditional retail practices to create a unique shopping experience.

With this vision in mind, Nikhil launched Retail InnovateX, a venture that aimed to revolutionize the shopping experience for middle-class consumers. The concept was ambitious: a hybrid model that integrated physical retail stores with an innovative digital platform. Customers could walk into a store, browse products, and receive personalized recommendations based on data-driven insights, while also having the option to purchase products online for home delivery. The idea was to create a seamless, omnichannel experience that blurred the lines between physical and digital shopping.

Nikhil was confident that Retail InnovateX would be a significant change. He had conducted extensive market research, assembled a talented team, and secured funding from investors who were excited about the potential of the project. On paper, everything seemed perfect. But as the saying goes, "The best-laid plans often go awry," and Nikhil was about to learn that even the most well-conceived ideas can fail.

From the very beginning, Retail InnovateX faced a series of challenges. The retail landscape was far more competitive than Nikhil had anticipated. Established players with deep pockets were already dominating the market, and customers were slow to adopt the hybrid model. Many preferred to stick with either traditional shopping or the convenience of online platforms, leaving Retail InnovateX struggling to find its niche.

Operational issues further compounded the problem. The seamless integration of physical stores and a digital platform proved to be far more complex than anticipated. Technical glitches plagued the online platform, causing delays in orders and frustrating customers. In the physical stores, inventory management became a logistical nightmare, with frequent stock shortages and delays in restocking. As the operational headaches piled up, Nikhil found himself grappling with problems that seemed to multiply by the day.

Despite these issues, Nikhil remained optimistic. He was used to solving problems, and he believed that with enough time and effort, he could turn things around. But time was not on his side. The financial pressures of running a retail business were immense, and the company was bleeding money. Overhead costs for the physical stores were far higher than expected, and the revenue from online sales was not enough to offset the losses.

Nikhil tried everything to keep Retail InnovateX afloat. He poured more money into improving the technology, hired additional staff to address the operational issues, and launched aggressive marketing campaigns to attract customers. But no matter what he did, the problems persisted. The stores were losing money, the online platform was struggling to gain traction, and investors were growing increasingly impatient.

As the months went by, it became clear that Retail InnovateX was on the verge of collapse. Nikhil faced a harsh reality: his ambitious vision had not only failed to take off, but it had also drained his resources and strained his reputation. The decision to shut down the venture was one of the hardest Nikhil had ever made. He had invested so much—financially, emotionally, and mentally—into Retail InnovateX, and admitting defeat felt like a personal failure But Retail InnovateX wasn't the only venture pulling Nikhil down. Around the same time, Nikhil had ventured into the café business, launching a quirky, music-themed café called Kaafo. The idea behind Kaafo was to create a vibrant space for young people—a place where music and culture could come together in a café setting. With live performances, themed interiors, and a cozy atmosphere, Kaafo quickly became a popular hangout spot for college students and young professionals. The café was buzzing with energy, and for a while, it seemed like Nikhil had hit on a winning formula.

But the success of Kaafo came with its own set of problems. As the café gained popularity, it began attracting the wrong crowd—youngsters who used the space not just for coffee and music, but for more illicit activities. Nikhil soon discovered that some patrons were peddling and consuming prohibited substances within the café. The situation escalated quickly, and before long, the local authorities had caught wind of it.

Dealing with the police was a nightmare. While Nikhil had no involvement in the illegal activities, the fact that they had occurred in his café put him squarely in the spotlight. The cops demanded answers, and Nikhil found himself embroiled in a legal and public relations battle that he hadn't anticipated. The once-thriving café was now under constant scrutiny, and Nikhil's reputation began to take a hit.

Adding to the chaos was the growing tension with the residents of a nearby colony. The music, which had once been a key attraction for Kaafo, was now the source of numerous noise complaints. Residents from the adjacent colony began lodging formal complaints, accusing the café of disturbing the peace. The situation became even more volatile when local goons, claiming to represent the neighborhood, began showing up at Kaafo demanding money in exchange for "protection."

Nikhil found himself caught between the police, the agitated residents, and the criminal elements that were trying to extort money from him. His dream of running a successful café was turning into a nightmare. The pressure mounted, and Nikhil struggled to keep the business afloat. The financial strain of Kaafo, combined with the collapse of Retail InnovateX, pushed Nikhil to his breaking point. His personal savings were rapidly depleting, and he found himself sinking into debt.

The once-inviting atmosphere of Kaafo turned sour. With police visits becoming a regular occurrence, patrons began to stay away, and business plummeted. The café that had started with so much promise was now a shadow of its former self. Nikhil, who had always prided himself on his ability to solve problems, found himself facing challenges on all fronts—legal, financial, and personal.

As Kaafo struggled, Nikhil was forced to make yet another painful decision. Shutting down the café felt like another failure, and it weighed heavily on him. His once-thriving ventures were now crumbling around him, and the toll it took on his morale was immense. For the first time in his career, Nikhil questioned whether he had what it took to continue as an entrepreneur. The strain on his finances was crushing, and the constant battles with law enforcement and local goons had worn him down.

The failure of Retail InnovateX and Kaafo marked a dark period in Nikhil's life. He had always believed that hard work and perseverance could solve any problem, but these ventures had shown him the harsh realities of entrepreneurship. Despite his best efforts, despite his creativity and determination, he had been unable to save the businesses. It was a humbling experience, one that left him feeling lost and uncertain about his future.

But as time passed, Nikhil began to reflect on the lessons he had learned. The failure of these ventures had been a humbling experience, but it had also taught him valuable lessons about the realities of entrepreneurship. He realized that even the most innovative ideas could fail if the execution wasn't right. He had been so focused on the vision that he had overlooked critical operational details, and the market had been less receptive than he had anticipated.

More importantly, Nikhil realized that failure was not the end—it was a stepping stone. He had always believed in the power of resilience, and now he had the opportunity to put that belief into practice. Instead of dwelling on what had gone wrong, Nikhil chose to focus on what he could learn from the experience. He spent months analyzing the mistakes he had made, studying the market and reflecting on how he could approach future ventures differently.

The failure of Retail InnovateX and Kaafo had been painful, but they had also given Nikhil the perspective he needed to move forward. With newfound clarity, he prepared to rebuild—this time with a more pragmatic approach and a deeper understanding of the risks involved. Nikhil knew that his entrepreneurial journey was far from over. The lessons he had learned would shape his future, and he was ready to rise from the ashes.

Here's a revised version that amplifies Nikhil's emotional struggle and the deep sense of pain and failure he felt while re-entering corporate life:

CHAPTER 9

RISING FROM THE ASHES

The failures of Retail InnovateX and Kaafo had left Nikhil devastated—his finances were in ruins, and his confidence shattered. The man who had once believed in the power of persistence, of innovation, now found himself standing at the edge of a precipice. The optimism and ambition that had defined his career now seemed like distant echoes. The weight of failure hung heavy on his shoulders, and for the first time in his life, Nikhil felt completely lost.

In the months following the collapse of his ventures, Nikhil's reality became harsher with each passing day. His savings were gone, drained by his attempts to keep Retail InnovateX and Kaafo alive. The mounting debt was overwhelming, and every bill he received felt like a punch to the gut. He had sunk everything into those ventures—his time, his money, his belief—and now, he had nothing to show for it.

The pressure from his family and friends was relentless. His father, who had always been a pillar of pragmatism, no longer minced his words. "Nikhil enough is enough," he would say, his voice laced with concern but also a sharpness that Nikhil wasn't used to. "You've tried. You've given it your best shot, but it's time to face reality. Go back to the corporate world. Secure yourself. You can't keep living like this." His friends, too, echoed the same sentiments. They watched as he spiraled deeper into debt, unable to understand why he still clung to his entrepreneurial dreams. "You're burning yourself out," they told him. "Why keep chasing this? It's time to get a job, get stable again."

Their words were well-intentioned, but they stung. The belief Nikhil had in his vision was crumbling under the weight of his failures. He had once been so sure of himself, so certain that he could create something remarkable. But now, the doubts began creeping in. His mind was a battlefield, and every day felt like he was losing another piece of himself.

The BizBoost framework, the innovative consulting model he had poured his heart into, remained unfinished sitting like an unfulfilled promise on his desk. Nikhil believed in it, but the more he worked on it, the more unreachable it seemed. He tried pitching the idea to potential clients, but each attempt felt like a slap in the face. Rejection after rejection came, with polite dismissals and cold skepticism. His past failures followed him like a shadow—no one wanted to take a risk on the man whose last ventures had publicly collapsed.

Financially, things were getting worse by the day. Nikhil's debts were piling up faster than he could manage, and with no income, the future looked bleak. He had fought as hard as he could, but it felt like life was boxing him into a corner. His stomach turned every time he thought about how close he was to losing everything.

In the darkest moments, Nikhil had no choice but to face a painful reality: his family and friends were right. He couldn't survive like this anymore. He couldn't keep chasing a dream that wasn't paying the bills, which wasn't giving him the lifeline he so desperately needed. And so, with a heavy heart and a growing sense of dread, Nikhil made the decision that haunted him the most—he would return to the corporate world.

But even that, as it turned out, was not going to be easy. The corporate doors he had once walked through with confidence now seemed firmly closed. Nikhil's career had taken a long break, and prospective employers viewed him with suspicion. His stellar resume was marred by the very thing he had been proud of—his entrepreneurial ventures. His failures overshadowed everything else, and the corporate world was unforgiving. They didn't want to hear about innovation or ambition—they wanted results, and Nikhil didn't have them.

Rejection after rejection followed. Every job interview felt like an interrogation, where his career break was scrutinized, his choices questioned, and his failures laid bare. Nikhil's nerves were frayed as he sat through each of these interviews, trying to explain himself to people who only saw him as a risk. "Why did you leave corporate?" they asked, skepticism in their eyes. "Why should we hire someone who hasn't been in the corporate world for years?"

Every rejection was another blow to his already fragile self-esteem. The sting of humiliation burned deeper with each passing day. The man who had once been at the top of his game, advising businesses, and driving innovation, was now being turned away from jobs he knew he was overqualified for. He felt like a beggar, pleading for a chance in a world that had no place for him anymore. And every rejection was a reminder of how far he had fallen.

Finally, after months of being worn down by rejections and dwindling hope, Nikhil managed to secure a position—very different from the roles he had once held. It wasn't the job he wanted; it was the job he needed. The salary wasn't impressive, the title was underwhelming, and the work felt hollow. But at least it offered a steady paycheck, a lifeline out of the debt that was suffocating him. But every day felt like a compromise—like he had traded in his dreams for survival. The flame that had once burned so brightly inside him was now little more than a flicker, kept alive by the hope that somehow, some way, he could claw his way back to the world of entrepreneurship.

Despite the corporate job, BizBoost never left his mind. It was the last vestige of his ambition, the one idea he couldn't let go of. In the stolen moments between meetings, during the long commute home, or late at night when the world was asleep, Nikhil worked on refining it. But the weight of his corporate life made it harder to hold on to. His spirit was fractured, and with each passing day, it felt like the dream was slipping further away.

It wasn't until a chance encounter at a networking event that the tides began to shift. A former client from his NHD Consulting days recognized him and struck up a conversation. They talked about business challenges, and without thinking, Nikhil mentioned BizBoost—not with the enthusiasm he once had, but with a cautious tone, wary of another rejection.

To Nikhil's surprise, his associate was intrigued. "That's actually a solid concept," he said. "Why don't you try pitching this to a few of my contacts? I think they'd be interested."

Nikhil felt a flicker of hope for the first time in what felt like an eternity. He cautiously began arranging meetings, refining his pitch, but the emotional scars of his failures were still fresh. He was terrified of another rejection, terrified that his fragile hope would be shattered once more. But this time, something was different. Slowly, bit by bit, the pieces began to fall into place. His contacts saw the potential in BizBoost, and Nikhil secured his first client for the revamped framework—a manufacturing company that was struggling to stay afloat.

The project reignited something in Nikhil that had long been dormant. He threw himself into the work, using every lesson he had learned from his failures to make sure this project didn't go off the rails. And, against all odds, it worked. The company turned around. Profits soared, operations streamlined, and Nikhil's success with BizBoost became the talk of the industry.

For the first time in years, Nikhil felt alive again. His belief in his vision had been restored, not by blind optimism, but by hard-won success. The breakthrough with BizBoost marked a turning point in his life—professionally and personally. And the man who had once been on the verge of losing everything had risen from the ashes, stronger and more determined than ever.

But this time, Nikhil understood something deeper. His journey wasn't about one success or one failure. It was about resilience, about getting back up every time life knocked him down. The pain he had endured, the humiliation he had felt while clawing his way back into corporate life, had forged him into something new. He had learned that the world would keep throwing challenges his way, but it was up to him to decide how to respond.

As NHD Consulting grew, Nikhil finally realized that the scars of his failures were not signs of defeat—they were proof of his ability to persevere. He had risen, repeatedly, and he knew that no matter what came next, he would rise again.

CHAPTER 10

BizBoost Takes Flight

Before BizBoost could take off, survival became Nikhil's immediate priority. He was desperate to keep his dreams alive, but his financial situation had left him with few options. To make ends meet, Nikhil turned to what he knew best: process optimization. He began offering Green Belt and Black Belt Six Sigma training courses to small corporates across the globe. From late- night online workshops to in-person seminars, Nikhil became a traveling instructor, toggling between continents just to stay afloat. His reputation as a sharp mind in the field of operational efficiency allowed him to secure clients, but the work was grueling and relentless.

What set Nikhil apart was his unique certification in Lean Lego, a rare distinction that made him one of the few trainers certified by the prestigious Lego Serious Play Organization. Nikhil used the Lego methodology to teach corporations how to visualize and design efficient systems using the playful yet powerful tool. It was innovative, hands-on, and effective. For many businesses, learning Lean through Lego was eye- opening, and Nikhil's approach earned him praise in niche circles. Yet, despite the recognition, he still felt like he was running on a treadmill, unsure if he was actually moving forward or just keeping himself from collapsing. The workshops helped pay the bills, but they didn't quench Nikhil's thirst for more. His real passion, the BizBoost framework, was still a concept he couldn't let go of. Each night, after exhausting days of facilitating training sessions and traveling between cities, Nikhil would retreat to his desk and work on refining BizBoost. With deadlines pressing on both sides, Nikhil toggled between his corporate job and the endless revisions of his proposals. The hours seemed to blur together—one pitch deck after another, one email at a time.

Sleep became a distant memory. Coffee was his constant companion. He worked through the nights, fueled by nothing but caffeine and sheer determination. The clock would strike 2 a.m., then 3 a.m., and still, Nikhil would be sitting at his desk, eyes bloodshot, mind racing. He couldn't afford to slow down. If he wasn't teaching corporate workshops, he was refining business proposals. And if he wasn't drafting proposals, he was chasing clients. His life had become an endless loop of meetings, flights, workshops, and restless nights.

As much as he threw himself into his work, Nikhil couldn't shake the loneliness that clung to him. Success was within reach, but so was exhaustion. The pressure was unbearable, and the endless toggling between his corporate job and the nascent BizBoost framework left him feeling stretched thin—physically, emotionally, and mentally. He craved stability, not just professionally but personally. He felt as if he was on autopilot, functioning without truly living. He had alienated himself from friends, family, and any semblance of emotional stability.

His relationships had suffered under the strain of constant work. Conversations with his family had dwindled, replaced by hurried updates over the phone. His social life was non-existent, his friendships neglected as the weight of his ambitions grew heavier. Though outwardly he presented the image of someone driven and relentless, internally, he was fragile teetering on the edge of burnout, unsure how much longer he could keep juggling everything.

It was during this tumultuous period that Nikhil realized something had to give. He couldn't keep toggling between his job, his clients, and his personal ambitions without breaking. But giving up wasn't an option. BizBoost was the one idea that still gave him a reason to keep pushing forward. It was his lifeline—his last chance to build something that truly mattered. And so, Nikhil doubled down on his efforts, even as the world around him felt increasingly unstable.

The breakthrough came when he managed to secure a high-profile contract with a small, struggling manufacturing company. It wasn't the scale of the contract that mattered—it was the opportunity to test BizBoost in a real-world setting. This was his chance to prove the framework's value and turn his sleepless nights into something tangible. Nikhil poured everything he had into the project. The company was hemorrhaging money due to inefficient processes and an outdated supply chain. Using BizBoost, Nikhil's team overhauled their operations from the ground up—streamlining production, cutting waste, and implementing new strategies for growth. It was a complete transformation, and when the results began to show, Nikhil felt the weight of months of doubt and frustration lift off his shoulders. Profits rose, inefficiencies disappeared, and the company's leadership marveled at the results.

Word about BizBoost began to spread, slowly at first, but then like wildfire. Nikhil's success with the manufacturing company was the validation he had been searching for. He had proven that the BizBoost framework wasn't just an idea scribbled on paper—it was a working model that could save businesses. Offers from larger corporations started to trickle in, and Nikhil soon found himself facing a new challenge: scaling BizBoost to meet the growing demand.

But scaling was easier said than done. Nikhil needed a team to handle the workload, but hiring the right people was an uphill battle. His reputation was still scarred from his previous failures, and many professionals were hesitant to take a chance on someone who had been on the brink of financial collapse just months before. Interviews were grueling, and Nikhil often found himself defending his vision, trying to convince potential hires that BizBoost was more than just another consulting trend. Still, Nikhil pressed forward. Slowly, he began to build a team—people who, like him, were willing to take a risk on something new. They weren't industry veterans, but they were hungry for success and shared his belief in BizBoost. With the right people in place, Nikhil's consulting firm began to gain traction.

The next major breakthrough came when BizBoost was applied to a large retail chain struggling to compete with the rise of e-commerce. The retail industry had changed dramatically, and traditional brick-and-mortar stores were finding it increasingly difficult to keep up with the efficiency and scale of online giants. The chain's CEO, desperate to turn things around, decided to take a chance on Nikhil's approach.

This was the opportunity Nikhil had been waiting for—a project large enough to establish BizBoost as a transformative force. But the stakes were enormous. The retail chain's future was on the line, and Nikhil knew that any failure here could undo all the progress he had made. His team spent months analyzing the business, identifying inefficiencies, and crafting a comprehensive strategy to streamline operations and improve customer retention.

The work was intense, and the pressure to deliver was overwhelming. Nikhil often found himself lying awake at night, unable to sleep, his mind racing with thoughts of the project. He had pushed his body to the limit, surviving on coffee and adrenaline, but he knew that this was his make-or-break moment. He couldn't afford to fail—not again. In the end, Nikhil's persistence paid off. The retail chain underwent a complete transformation. By implementing BizBoost, they streamlined their supply chain, improved customer engagement, and saw a dramatic increase in profits. The success of the project catapulted BizBoost into the spotlight, and suddenly, Nikhil was no longer the man scraping by on corporate workshops—he was a leader in the consulting world.

With the retail project as a case study, more companies began reaching out to BizBoost, eager to replicate the success. It was a surreal moment for Nikhil—after years of struggle, rejection, and failure, he had finally built something that people believed in. But even as BizBoost began to soar, Nikhil couldn't help but reflect on the emotional toll the journey had taken. He had fought tooth and nail to get here, sacrificing sleep, relationships, and his own emotional well-being along the way.

But in the end, it had been worth it. He had risen from the ashes of his failures, stronger and more resilient than ever before. The road ahead was still uncertain, but for the first time in a long while, Nikhil felt ready for whatever came next.

CHAPTER 11

THE PINNACLE AND NEW CHALLENGES

Nikhil sat at his desk, staring at the screen in front of him, the numbers, and graphs swimming before his eyes. Another late night in the corporate world, another set of reports that needed his attention. But his mind wasn't here—hadn't been here for a long time. He glanced at his phone, where his personal emails were stacking up, all relating to BizBoost. His consulting firm was growing faster than he had ever dreamed, but his corporate job was pulling him deeper into responsibilities that had long lost their appeal.

The constant juggling act had left him exhausted. Days bled into nights, and nights bled into the next day, with little to no rest in between. The success of BizBoost had come at a cost—his energy, his health, his peace of mind. But as much as the consulting world excited him, Nikhil was chained to his corporate role by a financial reality he couldn't ignore. Every time he thought about quitting, the cold facts slapped him back to reality: the five-year cooling-off period.

The five-year wait was unavoidable. Transitioning BizBoost from a sole proprietorship to a private limited company had been the smartest move he could make. The old tax structure had suffocated his business, swallowing up his profits as quickly as he made them. Incorporating had given him the protection and tax advantages he needed, but with it came this burdensome period where he had to continue working his corporate job for stability.

The pressure was mounting. While BizBoost was gaining traction, larger companies refused to take a chance on a small, boutique firm like NHD Consulting. It didn't matter that his framework was transformative—it wasn't "big enough." The doors of opportunity were still slammed shut. The consulting industry was dominated by big players, and the big players weren't interested in working with what they considered a risky, small operation. It was demoralizing.

In his corporate job, Nikhil's role kept expanding, pushing him into more leadership positions, drowning him in more responsibilities. Every promotion felt like a tighter leash around his neck. His workload was ballooning, and there were days when sleep became a luxury he could only dream of. He was suffocating. He'd work until late in the night on corporate projects, only to switch gears at 2 a.m. and dive headfirst into BizBoost, responding to client emails, drafting new proposals, and chasing deals. It wasn't just about growing a business anymore—it was about surviving, about holding on to what he had started.

There were moments when he wondered if it was all worth it. How much longer could he keep up this charade, pretending to care about corporate strategies that didn't matter to him anymore? How much longer could he maintain the façade of a high-performing corporate executive when all he wanted was to immerse himself fully in the world of entrepreneurship?

The tension was palpable. He would sit through high-stakes corporate meetings, discussing strategies for clients he barely cared about, while in the back of his mind, BizBoost was always there, tugging at him, calling him. His phone would vibrate in his pocket—another message from a client, another opportunity slipping away because he didn't have the time to nurture it. It felt like drowning. But every time he considered walking away, the looming financial obligations kept him tied down.

The five-year cooling-off period was dragging him through the mud. Nikhil's health began to suffer. He felt the weight of the endless nights, the caffeine-fueled days, and the emotional toll of splitting his life in two. His relationships strained. His friends stopped calling because they knew he'd cancel last minute. His family saw less and less of him. He was there, but he wasn't present—mentally, he was always elsewhere, thinking about the next step for BizBoost.

And yet, there was no way out—at least, not yet. The clock was ticking, but the finish line felt further and further away.

But deep down, Nikhil knew giving up wasn't an option. The alternative—returning fully to the corporate world—was a nightmare he couldn't accept. He had come too far. He had sacrificed too much. And so, with every ounce of strength he could muster, he began to fight back. If the world wasn't going to give him a break, he would create one.

That's when the idea hit him: diversification.

If BizBoost was going to survive the cooling-off period and break into the larger market, he needed to offer more than just a singular framework. He needed to make his firm indispensable. So, Nikhil dove into creating new service lines—consulting packages specifically tailored to industries that were desperate for innovation but didn't know where to find it. Retail, healthcare, manufacturing—these sectors were bleeding for efficiency, for transformation. He knew that if he could crack open these markets, the big players would have no choice but to pay attention.

The late nights became even later as he worked on diversifying BizBoost's offerings. Leadership training programs, business process optimization modules, and innovative operational strategies were developed—one after the other. These weren't just add- ons; they were game-changers. Nikhil was building a suite of services that would make BizBoost stand out in a crowded marketplace. He wasn't just fighting to survive anymore—he was fighting to dominate.

Every small victory felt like a lifeline. A new client here, a successful project there—it all added up. Slowly, the doors that had been slammed in his face began to creak open. Companies that had once written him off as "too small" were now interested. His persistence was paying off. But the pressure was relentless. The corporate world still demanded everything from him, and he had no choice but to deliver. His responsibilities grew, and there were times when he felt like he was running on fumes. But quitting was never an option. He had tasted what it meant to build something of his own, and nothing could compare to that feeling. Not even the promotions, the accolades, or the six-figure salary his corporate job offered.

As the final year of the cooling-off period approached, Nikhil began to prepare for his exit from the corporate world. He started delegating more within BizBoost, relying on his senior consultants to handle day-to-day operations. He built out a structured plan for the company's growth, ensuring that when the time came, he could scale it without losing momentum.

And finally, the day arrived. Five years of sacrifice, sleepless nights, and pushing himself to the brink—Nikhil submitted his resignation. His colleagues were shocked. To them, he was a rising star, someone destined for the top echelons of corporate leadership. They didn't know that every step he had taken in the corporate world was a step closer to freedom.

As he walked out of the office for the last time, Nikhil felt the weight of the last five years lift off his shoulders. He was free—free to build BizBoost into the company he had always envisioned, free to dedicate himself fully to the clients who believed in him, free to chase his dreams without the burden of a double life. The road had been long, and the sacrifices had been immense. But Nikhil knew, as he took those steps into the unknown, that it had all been worth it. He had built something extraordinary, something that would outlast the challenges he had faced. And as he looked ahead to the future, he knew this was only the beginning.

With the world finally at his feet, Nikhil was ready to conquer it. BizBoost wasn't just a business anymore—it was a movement. A testament to what could be achieved when you refuse to give up, no matter how heavy the burden or how long the journey.

62

CHAPTER 12

STEPPING INTO THE UNKNOWN

When Nikhil resigned from his corporate job, the rush of freedom was intoxicating. The weight of five years of split focus, sleepless nights, and constant juggling had finally lifted from his shoulders. BizBoost was now his world—his sole focus, his only job, his future. But as the days turned into weeks, the reality of what lay ahead slowly began to sink in. This wasn't the victory lap he had imagined. The stakes were higher than ever before.

Gone were the safety nets of a steady corporate salary and the security of a large organization. Now, every decision, every deal, every mistake was on his shoulders alone. There was no fallback, no cushioned corporate job to lean on. He was all in, and if he failed, there would be no one to catch him.

The first few months were a blur of optimism and adrenaline, but soon enough, the cracks began to show. While BizBoost had secured a handful of clients, landing the bigger fish—the contracts with multinational corporations that would push his firm into the big leagues—was proving impossible. No matter how many proposals he pitched, the response was always the same: "We like your approach, but you're too small." Every rejection was a blow. Nikhil found himself at meetings with top executives, pitching his heart out, only to walk away empty-handed. He would sit in his car afterward, the weight of failure pressing down on his chest like a vice. No matter how much he refined his strategies, no matter how innovative his solutions were, BizBoost was always deemed too "boutique" to handle the demands of large-scale

"Boutique." That word echoed in Nikhil's mind long after those meetings ended. It wasn't just a rejection of his business; it felt like a rejection of him. He had built BizBoost from the ground up, driven by passion, innovation, and a relentless work ethic. But none of that seemed to matter in a world that favored the big, established players. No matter how much value he could bring to the table, they couldn't see past his firm's size.

Every rejection took a little more wind out of his sails. He would return to the office, force a smile for his team, and dive into the next project, hoping the next pitch would be different. But behind closed doors, the pressure was suffocating. At night, Nikhil lay awake, staring at the ceiling, his mind racing with doubts. What if this wasn't enough? What if all these years of sacrifice led to failure?

It wasn't just the client rejections that gnawed at him. The financial strain was becoming unbearable. BizBoost was growing, but so were the expenses. Hiring new talent, expanding operations, maintaining an office space—it all cost money, and the payments from clients were staggered, often delayed for months. The cash flow problems were mounting, and Nikhil found himself constantly shuffling funds, dipping into his personal savings just to keep the company afloat.

The reserves were dwindling. Every time he checked the bank balance, a knot of anxiety tightened in his stomach. He would run his fingers through his hair, staring at the numbers on the screen, wondering how much longer they could hold on. His personal finances were stretched thin, and with each day that passed without a major client win, the sense of impending doom grew heavier.

And yet, Nikhil refused to give up. Failure was not an option—it couldn't be. He had worked too hard, sacrificed too much, to walk away now. But the toll was becoming undeniable. There were nights when Nikhil would sit alone in his office, the faint hum of the city outside, feeling the crushing weight of responsibility. His health was deteriorating—he was running on fumes, barely sleeping, living off caffeine and adrenaline. His personal life had all but disappeared. Friends stopped inviting him out; family gatherings became rare, and when they did happen, Nikhil was always mentally absent, too consumed by work to engage.

The emotional toll was immense. BizBoost had been his dream, but now it felt like a trap—one he couldn't escape. He couldn't shut off the constant stream of worries about unpaid invoices, high overheads, and the never-ending chase for new clients. The business world was unforgiving, and he was feeling its full force. He was the founder, the CEO, the strategist, and the firefighter—putting out one problem after another, barely able to catch his breath before the next crisis hit.

One afternoon, Nikhil found himself on a call with a prospective client. It was a major deal, the kind that could turn things around for BizBoost—the kind of contract that could stabilize the business for months. He had prepared for this pitch meticulously, knowing it could be his shot at breaking into the big leagues. But halfway through the call, his voice faltered. He could feel it—he was losing them. The client's tone shifted from interest to hesitation. And then it came, the polite brush-off: "We're not sure if you're the right fit for us at this scale."

Nikhil felt the familiar sting of disappointment wash over him. As the call ended, he sat there in silence, staring at the blank screen. The rejection wasn't new, but this one felt different. It felt final. He had given everything he had in that pitch, and it still wasn't enough. For a moment, he felt the crushing urge to walk away, to leave it all behind, to admit defeat.

But something inside him rebelled against that thought. This wasn't the end. It couldn't be.

Nikhil took a deep breath, leaned back in his chair, and closed his eyes. He reminded himself of why he had started this journey in the first place. It wasn't just about building a successful company; it was about proving that he could. It was about the dream he had nurtured for years, the sacrifices he had made, and the countless times he had pushed forward when everything seemed impossible.

"Not yet," he whispered to himself. "Not like this."

The next day, Nikhil called a meeting with his core team. He looked around the room at the faces of the people who had stood by him, who had believed in his vision even when the world didn't. His voice was firm but filled with resolve. "We're going to make this work. No matter what it takes. I know things look tough right now, but we've survived tougher times. We've built this company with our own hands, and I refuse to let it go down without a fight. This is not the end—it's just the beginning."

The room was silent for a moment, but then the energy shifted. His team nodded, their determination mirroring his own. They weren't giving up either. They were in this together.

In the weeks that followed, Nikhil doubled down on his efforts. He reached out to past clients, asking for referrals, testimonials—anything that could help boost BizBoost's credibility in the eyes of bigger companies. He spent hours reworking proposals, refining his pitch, and making sure no stone was left unturned. Every rejection fueled his fire. Every "no" was another reason to push harder, to prove that he and BizBoost could stand alongside the giants of the consulting world. But it wasn't easy. The financial strain continued to weigh heavily on him. There were days when payroll seemed like a distant dream, and Nikhil was faced with the reality of having to let people go to keep the company afloat. It was one of the hardest decisions he ever made, knowing that his choices affected not just the business, but the livelihoods of the people who had put their trust in him.

Despite the emotional and financial turmoil, something inside Nikhil remained unshaken. He had come too far to quit now. The setbacks were painful, the obstacles seemingly insurmountable, but deep down, he knew he had the strength to keep going. He wasn't just fighting for BizBoost; he was fighting for himself—for the belief that no matter how hard the journey got, he wouldn't back down.

BizBoost wasn't just a company anymore—it was a symbol of his resilience, his refusal to quit even when everything seemed stacked against him. And with each passing day, with each small victory, Nikhil felt the momentum starting to shift. The struggle wasn't over, but neither was the fight. He wasn't done yet.

CHAPTER 13

CLIMBING THE NEXT MOUNTAIN

The next few months were a whirlwind for Nikhil and his team. After the heart-to-heart conversation where he reignited their collective fire, everyone threw themselves into their work with renewed energy. There was no room for hesitation—no space for doubt. Every project, every client interaction was now a crucial step in proving that BizBoost could break into the upper echelons of consulting.

But it wasn't just the external pressure from clients and finances that weighed on Nikhil; it was the growing responsibility within his own company. BizBoost was expanding, but the challenges were expanding too. The more work they took on, the more cracks began to show in their internal processes. Projects were getting delayed, communications between team members were becoming strained, and the pace of growth was outpacing their ability to manage it.

Nikhil knew something had to change. The relentless pursuit of perfection had led to burnout within his team, and he could feel it—the once- unstoppable drive was starting to falter. Meetings that used to buzz with excitement and collaboration now felt tense, as everyone struggled to keep up with the relentless demands. There was friction, and Nikhil could sense that the pressure he had been putting on himself was spilling over onto his team.

One evening, after another long day, Nikhil sat in his office, staring at the whiteboard where the week's priorities were scrawled in red marker. He knew that his team was giving everything they had, but it wasn't enough. They were stretched too thin. The weight of leadership had never felt heavier. It was his job to keep this ship afloat, to steer them through the storm. But how could he inspire them when he himself was starting to feel defeated?

Nikhil's phone buzzed. A message from his operations manager, Priya, popped up: "Can we talk? I think we need to regroup."

Nikhil leaned back, exhausted but determined. He replied with a simple "Yes," and a few moments later, Priya knocked on his office door.

Priya had been with him from the start. She was the calm in the chaos, always ready to bring clarity when things seemed overwhelming. But tonight, even Priya looked worn down. Her eyes, usually sharp with focus, were tired.

"We're at a breaking point, Nikhil," she said, sitting down across from him. "Everyone's feeling the pressure, and morale is dipping. The team is working around the clock, but we're not seeing the results we need. It's not sustainable. We can't keep going like this." Nikhil sighed. He knew she was right. He had seen it in their faces, heard it in their voices. The enthusiasm that once fueled their long nights and weekend marathons was fading, replaced by frustration and exhaustion. They were running on empty, and it was starting to show.

"We've taken on too much," Priya continued. "We need to focus. We can't be everything for everyone."

Her words hit him hard. Focus. It was something he preached constantly, but somehow, in his desperation to grow, to succeed, he had lost sight of it himself. He had spread his team too thin, chasing every opportunity that came their way, hoping that the next client would be the one that changed everything. But instead, it had led them here—overworked, overwhelmed, and underperforming.

Nikhil nodded slowly. "You're right," he said, his voice heavy with the weight of realization. "We need to regroup. Reprioritize. If we keep pushing like this, we'll break."

The next morning, Nikhil called an all-hands meeting. His team, still reeling from the pressure, looked apprehensive as they gathered in the conference room. Nikhil stood at the front, ready to address them, but this time, it wasn't just about motivating them to push harder. It was about admitting that they needed to change the way they were working. "We've been trying to do too much," he began, his voice calm but filled with conviction. "We've been chasing every client, every project, thinking that growth means taking on more. But what I've realized—what we all need to realize—is that real growth doesn't come from doing more. It comes from doing better. We need to focus on the clients that matter, the projects that can take us to the next level. We need to stop spreading ourselves so thin and start being strategic."

The room was silent, but Nikhil could see the shift in his team's posture. There was relief in their faces. They had been feeling the same pressure, the same sense of drowning, but now they had permission to slow down, to be more intentional with their work.

"We're going to take a step back," Nikhil continued. "We'll refocus our energy on our key clients, the ones that align with our vision. And I want each of you to take a breath. We've been sprinting for so long, but this isn't a sprint—it's a marathon. Let's run at a pace that will get us to the finish line in one piece."

As the meeting ended, there was a palpable sense of relief. The tension that had been building over the past few months started to ease, and for the first time in weeks, Nikhil saw a glimmer of the team's old spark returning. They weren't giving up; they were resetting.

But while the team began to regroup, Nikhil's challenges were far from over. The financial strain was still looming over him like a dark cloud. BizBoost was burning through cash at an alarming rate, and the delays in client payments were becoming more than just an inconvenience—they were a threat to the company's survival, Nikhil found himself sitting down with the finance team late into the night, reviewing spreadsheets, cash flow statements, and invoices. The numbers didn't lie. They had just a few months of runway left before things became dire. It was a sobering reality, one that kept Nikhil awake at night, staring at the ceiling, wondering if he had made the right choices.

Every day felt like a race against time. He pushed himself harder, chasing down clients, following up on unpaid invoices, doing everything in his power to keep the cash flowing. But the payments were slow, and the bills were piling up faster than the money was coming in.

One evening, as Nikhil sat at his desk, staring at a growing list of overdue payments, he felt the familiar weight of defeat creeping in. What if it wasn't enough? What if all the sacrifices, all the long hours, all the sleepless nights led to nothing?

The doubts circled in his mind like vultures, waiting to devour whatever hope was left. But just as he felt himself slipping into despair, a thought sparked deep inside him—this wasn't the first time he'd faced impossible odds.

Nikhil leaned back in his chair, closing his eyes, trying to block out the noise of his thoughts. He had been here before, staring down failure, wondering if he would make it through. But every time, he had found a way. Every time, when the pressure was at its highest, he had pulled through.

This was no different. He couldn't allow the doubt to win. He couldn't let this moment define him or his company. BizBoost was too important, not just to him but to the people who believed in it, the clients who depended on it, and the team that had given everything to help build it.

With a deep breath, Nikhil opened his eyes, the familiar fire returning to his chest. No more distractions. No more chasing. Focus. It was the lesson he had learned repeatedly, and now, more than ever, he needed to apply it.

The next morning, Nikhil walked into the office with renewed purpose. The team could sense the shift in his energy, and it spread through them like wildfire. The focus was clear now—no more trying to do everything at once. They were going to build BizBoost the right way—slow, steady, and unbreakable.

And though the financial challenges still loomed, Nikhil knew one thing for certain: they weren't done yet.

CHAPTER 14

BUILDING BRIDGES AND FACING STORMS

The meeting room buzzed with quiet tension as Nikhil stood at the head of the table, reviewing the agenda for the day. It had been a week since their regrouping meeting, where they'd refocused on fewer, high-priority clients. The energy within the team had shifted since then—they were more focused, more intentional. But there was still an underlying current of stress. The financial strain hadn't disappeared, and Nikhil knew they were walking a tightrope.

Today's meeting was different, though. They were preparing for a crucial client call with one of the biggest potential deals they had ever landed. If they managed to win this client, it could be the turning point BizBoost desperately needed.

Nikhil cleared his throat, gathering his thoughts. Priya, his operations manager, was sitting to his right, her usual calm demeanor masking the tension that hung in the room. Anuj, their lead strategist, flipped through his notes, clearly nervous. The rest of the team, though smaller now after some difficult layoffs, looked eager to prove themselves.

"Alright," Nikhil began, looking around the table. "This is it. We've been through worse, but we've never faced an opportunity like this before. This client could take us to the next level. They've seen our work, they know what we can do, but today, we need to show them why they need us and only us."

Anuj nodded, but his fidgeting betrayed his anxiety. Priya leaned forward, her eyes meeting Nikhil's, offering silent support. She knew as well as he did that this deal was a make-or-break moment for BizBoost.

"Anuj," Nikhil said, turning his focus to the strategist, "we need to be sharp. No second-guessing yourself. You've got this."

Anuj gave a tight smile. "I know," he said, but his voice wavered. "It's just... this is big. And I know they've been talking to the bigger firms. What if they see us as too small again? I mean... we've heard it before, right?"

Nikhil paused for a moment, choosing his words carefully. He knew the team's confidence had taken a hit with all the rejections they had faced, and Anuj's fear was valid. But there was no room for doubt now.

"They may think we're small," Nikhil said, his voice steady, "but that's where our strength lies. We're nimble, we're adaptable, and we're not bogged down by bureaucracy like those big firms. That's what we need to show them. They need a partner who can move quickly, who can innovate without getting stuck in red tape. That's us. We've been through too much to let this slip. We deserve this deal." The room was quiet for a moment as Nikhil's words hung in the air. Then, slowly, Anuj nodded, his shoulders straightening.

"You're right," Anuj said, more to himself than anyone else. "We've got this."

Nikhil gave him a small nod, then turned to the rest of the team. "Priya, I'll lead with the overview of our framework, but I'll need you to back me up when we get into the implementation. You know the operational side better than anyone."

"Absolutely," Priya said, her voice calm and steady. "I've got it covered."

"And everyone else," Nikhil continued, his eyes moving across the room, "I need you all to stay sharp. Be ready to answer any questions they throw at us. This is a team effort. We don't win this alone."

The team nodded, more resolute now, and Nikhil felt the familiar weight of leadership settle on his shoulders. They weren't just pitching a project today—they were pitching their future. The success of BizBoost depended on this deal. But beyond the financials, Nikhil felt something deeper—he was fighting for his team. They had been through so much together, and he couldn't let them down.

The call began promptly at 3 p.m. The client's team joined the video conference, their faces stoic and professional, betraying no emotion. The CEO, a sharp-looking man named Mr. Verma, led the conversation. "Alright, Nikhil," Mr. Verma began, his voice smooth but commanding, "we've reviewed your

proposal. There's a lot we like, but before we proceed, I need to understand how your team is positioned to handle a project of this scale. We've been working with bigger firms up until now, and frankly, we need assurances that your firm has the bandwidth and expertise to deliver."

Here it was. The same question that had sunk so many of their pitches before.

Nikhil leaned forward, his heart pounding but his voice steady. "I understand your concerns, Mr. Verma," he said. "I know we're not the size of the bigger firms you've worked with, but that's exactly why we're the right choice for you. With a smaller team, we can give you more focus and personalized attention. Every single member of my team will be fully dedicated to your project. We won't treat you like just another client—we'll treat you like our only client."

He paused for a moment, letting his words sink in before continuing. "We've structured our team to be agile. We can pivot quickly, solve problems on the spot, and tailor our approach to your specific needs in a way that larger firms simply can't. With us, you're not just getting a service—you're getting a partnership. And I think that's what sets us apart." Mr. Verma raised an eyebrow, intrigued but not yet convinced. "That's all well and good, but at the end of the day, results are what matter. Can you guarantee that your team can deliver what we need, on time and at the level we expect?"

Nikhil didn't hesitate. "We can, and we will. Our track record speaks for itself. We've consistently delivered on complex projects, even when faced with limited resources. We're used to punching above our weight, and we thrive in high-pressure situations. This project is exactly the kind of challenge we're built for."

Priya chimed in then, her voice clear and confident. "Mr. Verma, I handle the operational side of things, and I can assure you that we have the processes in place to meet your timeline and quality standards. We don't just throw resources at a problem—we approach every project with strategy, precision, and focus. You won't get lost in the shuffle with us."

There was a moment of silence as Mr. Verma considered their words. Nikhil could feel the tension in his shoulders, but he kept his expression calm, waiting for the client to respond.

Finally, Mr. Verma leaned back in his chair. "Alright," he said slowly. "You've made your case. I'll need to review a few things with my team, but... I like what I'm hearing. Let's keep the conversation going."

The call ended soon after, and Nikhil let out a breath he hadn't realized he was holding. It wasn't a "yes" yet, but it wasn't a "no" either. It was progress.

As the team debriefed after the call, the mood was lighter, more optimistic. They hadn't won the deal yet, but they were in the game, and that was something.

"Good work, everyone," Nikhil said, his voice filled with cautious optimism. "We're not there yet, but we've moved the needle. Now, we just need to keep pushing."

The team nodded, a sense of relief washing over them. The stakes were high, but they were still in the fight.

As the day ended and the office emptied out, Nikhil sat at his desk, reflecting on the day's events. The journey wasn't over. There were still obstacles to overcome, challenges to face, and battles to fight. But for the first time in a long time, Nikhil felt hope.

They weren't just surviving anymore. They were climbing. And no matter how steep the climb got, he knew one thing for sure—BizBoost was here to stay.

CHAPTER 15

STRUGGLING TO STAY AFLOAT

The initial relief from the client meeting lasted only a few days. Despite Mr. Verma's positive response, the deal wasn't sealed. There were follow-up questions, more details requested, and endless back-and-forth that dragged the process longer than Nikhil expected. With every passing day, the pressure grew, and the financial strain on BizBoost became more acute.

Nikhil sat in his office late one night, staring at the cash flow projections. The numbers were grim. They were running out of runway fast. If they didn't close this deal soon or find another source of revenue, BizBoost could hit a wall. Payroll was coming up, and Nikhil knew they wouldn't have enough to cover everyone if things didn't turn around quickly.

His phone buzzed. It was Priya. "Can you talk?" her text read.

Nikhil sighed and dialed her number. She answered on the second ring.

"We've got a problem," she said, not wasting any time. "Anuj just called. He's been in touch with the client, and they're asking for a significant reduction in fees if we want to move forward. They're using our size against us—again."

Nikhil closed his eyes, frustration bubbling up. "How much of a reduction?"

"Twenty percent," Priya said flatly. "Which means we'll be working on razor-thin margins. Honestly, Nikhil, I don't think we can afford to take it."

A long silence followed. Nikhil knew she was right, but what choice did they have? They needed the revenue, even if it was far from ideal. But taking on a project that wouldn't be profitable could lead to more trouble down the line.

"Tell Anuj to set up another call with them tomorrow," Nikhil said finally. "We can't just roll over on this."

"You think they'll budge?" Priya asked, doubt clear in her voice.

"They have to," Nikhil said, though he wasn't entirely convinced. "We'll figure something out."

After hanging up, Nikhil felt the familiar weight of uncertainty press down on him. Every decision he made felt like walking a tightrope—one wrong step, and everything could collapse. The next morning's call with the client would be crucial, but the truth was, they were at a disadvantage. BizBoost was small, and they couldn't offer the kinds of discounts the bigger firms could afford. The next day, Nikhil gathered his team for a strategy session before the client call. Priya, Anuj, and the rest of the core team sat around the conference table, their expressions a mixture of exhaustion and determination.

"Alright," Nikhil began, "here's the situation. The client wants a fee reduction—twenty percent. Obviously, that's not something we can easily accommodate. But we need this deal. So, we're going to push back. We'll offer a smaller discount, but in exchange, we need to lock them into a longer-term contract. If we can guarantee repeat business, the lower margins on this deal won't kill us."

Anuj raised an eyebrow. "You think they'll go for that?"

"They might," Nikhil said. "It's our best shot. We need to show them that we're willing to be flexible, but we can't afford to cut our own legs out from under us."

Priya spoke up. "I'm worried about the team, Nikhil. Everyone's feeling the strain. We've been running lean for too long, and the constant pressure is starting to wear people down. If we keep pushing like this without some kind of win, we might lose more than just this client."

Nikhil knew she was right. The team had been giving their all, but morale was sinking. The endless cycle of near-misses, financial strain, and constant uncertainty was wearing them thin. They needed a win—something to remind them why they were fighting so hard.

"I know," Nikhil said softly. "We're on the edge. But we've been on the edge before, and we pulled through. We'll pull through this time, too."

Priya gave him a tight smile, but Nikhil could see the fatigue in her eyes. She had been his rock through all of this, but even rocks crack under enough pressure.

"I'll take the lead on the call," Nikhil continued. "I'll push them hard, but I'll need you all ready to jump in if they start asking for specifics."

The call that afternoon felt like walking into a lion's den. Mr. Verma and his team were sharp and direct, questioning every line of the proposal, pressing hard for the fee reduction. Nikhil fought back, his voice steady even though his insides were in knots.

"I understand where you're coming from," Nikhil said, his tone measured, "but I need you to understand that we're not a giant firm that can throw resources at a problem and charge you for the extras. What we offer is lean, effective, and focused. We don't just bring a solution—we bring a relationship. A partnership. And that's something the larger firms can't match."

There was a pause on the other end of the line.

Nikhil held his breath.

"I hear you, Nikhil," Mr. Verma finally said. "But the reality is, we're running a business too, and cost is a major factor. We're willing to negotiate, but we need some flexibility on your end."

Nikhil felt the tension spike, but he pressed on. "We can offer a ten percent reduction in fees, but only if we're looking at a two-year partnership. We're not interested in being a one-and-done vendor. If we're going to commit to this, we need to know there's a long-term plan in place."

Another silence. Nikhil could hear the murmurs of Mr. Verma's team on the other end, discussing the offer.

He glanced at Priya, who was watching him closely, her fingers crossed under the table.

Finally, Mr. Verma spoke. "Alright. We'll need to review this internally, but I think we can work with that. Let's circle back tomorrow."

As the call ended, Nikhil leaned back in his chair, his heart still racing. It wasn't a win—not yet—but it was progress. And right now, progress was all they could ask for.

After the meeting, the team gathered around the table, everyone visibly drained but cautiously optimistic.

"Good job," Priya said, offering Nikhil a small smile. "That's the best we could've hoped for."

"Yeah," Nikhil said, rubbing his temples. "But it's not over yet. We need to be ready for anything tomorrow." The next morning, Nikhil arrived early to the office, the tension weighing heavily on his shoulders. The call with Mr. Verma would either seal the deal or push them back to square one, and there wasn't much room left for failure. He sipped his coffee, staring at his computer screen but unable to focus.

Just then, Priya walked in, holding her tablet. "You ready for this?" she asked, her voice soft but steady.

Nikhil looked up, meeting her eyes. "Ready as I'll ever be," he said.

Priya sat down across from him, her expression serious. "You know, Nikhil, no matter what happens with this deal, you've done everything you could. You've fought harder than anyone else would have. And even if it doesn't go our way... we'll figure it out."

Nikhil smiled, grateful for her words. "Thanks, Priya. I just... I don't want to let anyone down."

"You won't," she said firmly. "We're in this together."

A few hours later, the team gathered in the conference room, nerves buzzing as they waited for the call. The air was thick with anticipation, every moment feeling like an eternity.

The call finally came through, and Mr. Verma's voice echoed through the room. "Nikhil, after reviewing everything with my team... we're ready to move forward. Let's make this happen."

For a split second, the room was silent. And then, an explosion of relief and celebration filled the air. Nikhil felt the weight lift off his shoulders as his team erupted in cheers.

They had done it. Against all odds, they had won.

As the celebration died down and the team dispersed, Nikhil sat alone in the conference room, staring out the window. This wasn't just a win—it was survival. But he knew that the road ahead was still long. The battles weren't over, and the challenges would keep coming.

But for the first time in a long time, Nikhil felt something he hadn't felt in months: hope.

CHAPTER 16
THE PRESSURE OF SUCCESS

Winning the Verma deal should have felt like the end of one journey and the start of a more stable future. But for Nikhil, the victory came with its own set of challenges. While the immediate financial strain was temporarily lifted, BizBoost now had to prove that it could deliver—on a bigger scale and in less time than they had ever managed before.

The team, still riding the high from securing the deal, quickly realized they were stepping into uncharted territory. The size of the project was massive, and there was little room for error. Every mistake would be magnified, and Nikhil knew that one misstep could cost them everything they had just won.

It was only a week into the project when the cracks began to show.

Nikhil stood in the middle of the office, the sound of furious typing and whispered conversations filling the space around him. His team was scattered, working on different parts of the project, but the energy that had fueled their success was starting to wane. They had pushed themselves so hard to win the deal, and now they were struggling to keep up with the relentless pace.

Priya walked over, her expression troubled. "We need to talk," she said quietly.

Nikhil nodded, following her into the small conference room they had claimed as their war room for the project.

"What's going on?" he asked as soon as the door closed.

Priya leaned against the table, arms crossed. "We're stretched too thin. I've been talking to the team, and they're burning out fast. We've got so many deliverables due in the next week, and I don't know how we're going to meet all of them."

Nikhil exhaled, rubbing the back of his neck. He had sensed it, too—the exhaustion creeping in, the late nights turning into even later ones. The team had been running at full speed for months, and there was no sign of it letting up.

"We can't fail on this one," Nikhil said, more to himself than to Priya. "We just can't."

"I know that," Priya replied, her voice soft but firm. "But we're going to hit a wall if we don't slow down. We need more resources, more hands on deck. Otherwise, we're going to burn out, and the quality of our work is going to suffer."

Nikhil paced the room, his mind racing. She was right. BizBoost was still operating with a lean team, and while that had been a strength before, it was quickly becoming a liability. He had pushed them hard to secure this deal, but now he was asking too much. They couldn't keep up this pace without help.

"Okay," he said finally, stopping to face her. "We need to bring in more people—freelancers, contractors, whoever we can find. I'll reach out to my network, and you do the same. We'll bring in fresh hands to handle the lower-level work so our core team can focus on the big picture."

Priya nodded, relief washing over her face. "That's a good plan. But we need to move fast."

"I know," Nikhil said. "We'll make it work. We have to."

The rest of the day was a blur of phone calls, emails, and frantic coordination. Nikhil reached out to every contact he had, pulling in favors, scrambling to bring in temporary help. By the end of the day, they had secured a small group of freelancers to assist with the heavy lifting, but Nikhil knew it was only a temporary fix.

As he walked back to his office, Priya caught up with him. "We've got some good freelancers coming in," she said. "But we need to think long-term. If we're going to keep growing like this, we need to start hiring more full-time staff. We can't keep relying on short- term solutions."

Nikhil sighed, leaning against his desk. "I know. But we don't have the budget for it right now. This project is supposed to stabilize us financially, but we're still running thin."

Priya frowned, clearly frustrated. "Then we need to figure out how to make it work, Nikhil. We're going to keep getting projects like this, and we can't just scramble for help every time. We need stability."

Nikhil nodded, the weight of the situation pressing down on him. The success of the Verma deal was supposed to be a turning point for BizBoost, but instead, it had only brought more pressure, more demands, and more uncertainty.

Later that evening, Nikhil sat alone in the office, staring at the endless list of tasks that needed to be done. The lights in the office were dim, the hum of the air conditioner the only sound as his team had finally left for the night. He had tried to send them home earlier, knowing they needed rest, but he couldn't bring himself to leave just yet.

The truth was, Nikhil felt more alone now than ever. The success he had dreamed of had come, but it felt hollow, overshadowed by the fear of losing everything he had worked for. The constant need to prove himself—to clients, to his team, to himself—was eating away at him.

He pulled out his phone and scrolled through his contacts, stopping at a familiar name: Raghav, an old friend from his corporate days who had gone on to become a successful entrepreneur himself. Raghav had always been a source of wisdom, someone who had weathered the storms of building a business and come out the other side stronger.

Nikhil hesitated for a moment before hitting the call button. The phone rang twice before Raghav picked up.

"Hey, man," Raghav's voice was warm, instantly cutting through the isolation Nikhil felt. "It's been a while. What's going on?"

Nikhil exhaled, leaning back in his chair. "I don't even know where to start. We landed this big deal—our biggest yet—and it's supposed to be the thing that turns everything around. But I feel like I'm drowning, man. We're stretched so thin, and I don't know if we can pull this off without burning out. Every day feels like I'm fighting to stay above water."

There was a brief pause on the other end of the line before Raghav responded. "I know that feeling," he said quietly. "I've been there. Success isn't always what it seems. You work so hard to get it, and then when it comes, it brings a whole new set of problems."

Nikhil closed his eyes, grateful for the understanding in Raghav's voice. "I thought winning this deal would solve everything," he admitted. "But it's only made things harder."

"That's the trap," Raghav said. "You think that once you reach a certain point, it'll get easier. But it doesn't. The stakes just get higher. The pressure gets more intense. But you have to remember why you started this in the first place. It's not about the deal or the money. It's about building something that lasts. And that takes time, Nikhil. You can't rush it."

Nikhil nodded, feeling the tension in his chest ease slightly. Raghav was right. He had spent so much time chasing success, thinking that once he reached a certain level, everything would fall into place. But building a business—building a legacy—wasn't about shortcuts. It was about persistence, about weathering the storm and coming out stronger on the other side.

"You've come too far to let this break you," Raghav continued. "It's going to be hard, but you're tougher than you think. You've built something incredible, and you've got people who believe in you. Lean on them. You don't have to do this alone."

Nikhil felt a wave of gratitude wash over him. "Thanks, Raghav. I needed that."

"Anytime, man," Raghav said. "And remember, if you need anything, just call. We've all been through this. You're not alone in this fight."

As Nikhil hung up the phone, he felt a sense of clarity return. The road ahead was still long and difficult, but he wasn't alone. He had a team, friends, and allies who believed in him, and most importantly, he believed in himself.

He glanced at the whiteboard on the wall, where the project milestones for the Verma deal were written in bold. There was still so much work to be done, so many challenges ahead. But for the first time in days, Nikhil felt a glimmer of hope. They weren't just surviving—they were building.

And no matter how hard it got, Nikhil knew one thing: he wouldn't quit.

CHAPTER 17

THE WEIGHT OF GROWTH

The Verma deal was moving forward, but the pace at which things were unfolding was starting to wear on everyone. Nikhil had hoped that winning this contract would relieve some of the pressure, but instead, it had only amplified it. The project deadlines were tighter than anticipated, and the client's demands were growing more complicated by the day.

One Friday morning, the office felt unusually tense. The team had been working late nights and weekends to stay on top of the deliverables, but it was clear that exhaustion was creeping in. Even Priya, who had always maintained her calm exterior, was starting to show signs of wear.

Nikhil looked around at his team, noting the dark circles under their eyes, the slow pace at which they moved. They were burnt out, and he was running out of ways to keep their morale up. He needed to find a way to keep them pushing forward without pushing them over the edge.

Later that day, Nikhil gathered his core team for a meeting. Priya, Anuj, and a few key consultants sat around the conference table, their faces a mixture of exhaustion and frustration. The room was silent, the usual buzz of conversation muted by the weight of the workload.

Nikhil cleared his throat, breaking the silence. "I know things have been intense lately," he began, his voice steady but serious. "We've been pushing hard, and I can see that it's taking a toll. I want to hear from you—how are we doing? Where are we struggling?"

There was a long pause before Anuj finally spoke up. "Honestly, Nikhil, we're drowning," he said bluntly, rubbing his temples. "The client's requests are getting more and more specific, and they're asking for things that weren't even in the original scope. We're already stretched thin, and now we're being pulled in a hundred different directions. It's... overwhelming."

Priya nodded in agreement, her tone softer but just as concerned. "It's not just the workload, Nikhil. It's the pace. We're working nonstop, and it's unsustainable. If we keep going like this, we're going to make mistakes. Big ones. And that's the last thing we need right now."

Nikhil took a deep breath, running his hand through his hair. He had seen this coming, but hearing it from his team made it real. He had been so focused on delivering for the client that he hadn't taken the time to step back and evaluate how it was affecting his people.

"You're right," Nikhil admitted. "We've been in crisis mode for too long, and it's not fair to you. I know you're all giving everything you have, and I appreciate it more than I can say. But we can't keep pushing like this."

Priya leaned forward, her expression serious. "We need to push back, Nikhil. The client is overstepping the boundaries of the contract. We agreed on a specific scope of work, and they keep expanding it without adjusting the deadlines or the budget. We can't keep saying yes to everything."

Nikhil nodded slowly. She was right. The client was taking advantage of them, and in his desperation to keep the project moving, he had allowed it to happen. But that needed to change—they needed to set boundaries.

"Okay," Nikhil said, his voice more resolute. "Here's what we're going to do. I'll set up a call with Mr. Verma and his team, and we'll address this head-on. We'll renegotiate the scope, the timeline, and the fees. I'll make it clear that we can't keep absorbing the extra work without compensation. It's not fair to us, and it's not sustainable."

The team looked relieved, but there was still an undercurrent of doubt in the room. They had pushed back before, but clients like Mr. Verma often had the upper hand. And while Nikhil knew the conversation would be difficult, it was one that had to happen.

"Do you think they'll agree to that?" Anuj asked, his tone uncertain.

Nikhil met his eyes. "They'll have to. We can't deliver the quality they expect if we're being overworked and underpaid. I'll make them see that."

The next day, Nikhil prepared for what he knew would be a difficult conversation. He had dealt with demanding clients before, but this was different—the stakes were higher, the pressure more intense. The Verma deal had kept BizBoost afloat, but if they couldn't renegotiate, it could end up sinking them.

The call began, and as expected, Mr. Verma wasn't happy. He listened to Nikhil's concerns, his expression growing more impatient as the conversation continued.

"Nikhil, I hear what you're saying," Mr. Verma said finally, his tone clipped. "But the reality is, we need these deliverables on time. We're running on a tight schedule ourselves, and if you can't keep up, we'll need to find someone who can."

Nikhil felt the familiar surge of frustration. This was the threat they always used—the idea that they could be replaced, that there was always someone else who could do the job faster, cheaper, better. But this time, Nikhil wasn't going to back down.

"With all due respect, Mr. Verma," Nikhil began, his voice firm, "we agreed on a specific scope of work, and we've done everything in our power to meet your needs. But your team has consistently added new tasks and expanded the scope without adjusting the timeline or the budget. My team is working around the clock to keep up, but it's simply not sustainable. We need to revisit the terms of our agreement, or we won't be able to deliver the quality you're expecting."

There was a long silence on the other end of the line, and Nikhil could feel the tension building.

Finally, Mr. Verma spoke, his tone more measured. "I understand where you're coming from, Nikhil. Let's review the contract and see where we can make adjustments. But I need you to understand—we're counting on you to deliver. This project is critical to our business."

Nikhil nodded, feeling the weight of Mr. Verma's words. They weren't out of the woods yet, but it was progress. The client had agreed to revisit the contract, and that was a win in itself.

After the call ended, Nikhil leaned back in his chair, exhaustion washing over him. He had been so focused on keeping the client happy that he had lost sight of what was fair for his own team. But now, they had a chance to level the playing field. They just needed to hold their ground.

As he walked back to the conference room to debrief with his team, Nikhil felt a sense of determination settle over him. The road ahead was still uncertain, and there were no guarantees that the renegotiation would go entirely in their favor. But they had made their stand, and that was a step in the right direction. When Nikhil entered the room, his team looked up at him, their expressions a mix of curiosity and hope.

"How did it go?" Priya asked.

Nikhil smiled, though he felt the exhaustion pulling at him. "They're willing to renegotiate. It's not a done deal yet, but it's a start."

The tension in the room eased, and Nikhil could see the relief on his team's faces. They weren't out of the woods, but they had bought themselves some time.

"We're going to make this work," Nikhil said, his voice filled with quiet conviction. "But we need to stick together. We need to keep pushing, but we also need to protect ourselves. We can't let the client or the pressure break us."

The team nodded, and Nikhil could feel their resolve strengthening. They weren't just fighting for the Verma deal anymore—they were fighting for their company, for each other. And that was a fight Nikhil knew they couldn't afford to lose.

As the day wound down and the office began to empty, Nikhil found himself sitting alone in the quiet conference room, his mind racing with thoughts of the future. The pressure was immense, the stakes higher than ever, but for the first time in a long time, he felt a sense of clarity.

They had faced bigger challenges before, and they had survived. They would survive this, too. BizBoost wasn't just a company—it was their legacy. And no matter how hard things got, Nikhil knew one thing for sure: they would keep fighting.

CHAPTER 18

HOLDING THE LINE

A week had passed since Nikhil's call with Mr. Verma. The renegotiation process was underway, and while it was a step in the right direction, the project was still draining the team's energy. The tighter deadlines and expanded scope had taken a toll, but for now, they were holding steady.

One morning, Nikhil arrived at the office early. The quiet of the morning hours had become his sanctuary—a brief respite before the demands of the day consumed him. As he sat at his desk, sipping his coffee, he felt the weight of the past few months settle on him. BizBoost was growing, but with growth came problems he hadn't fully anticipated.

The door to his office creaked open, and Priya stepped in, looking unusually tense.

"We need to talk," she said, her voice low.

Nikhil set his coffee down, gesturing for her to sit. "What's going on?"

Priya sat down across from him, her hands clasped together tightly. "I've been talking to the team," she began, her eyes meeting his. "And I'm worried. Really worried. The burnout is worse than I thought. Anuj mentioned to me yesterday that he's considering taking a break—he's not sure he can keep going like this."

Nikhil's heart sank. Anuj was one of their key strategists, someone he had leaned on heavily to navigate the Verma deal. The thought of losing him, even temporarily, was a blow Nikhil wasn't prepared for.

"He said that?" Nikhil asked, his voice tight.

Priya nodded, her expression grim. "He's not the only one feeling it. We've all been running on fumes for too long, Nikhil. We need to do something before more people start considering walking away."

Nikhil leaned back in his chair, his mind racing. He had known the team was feeling the strain, but hearing it so bluntly from Priya hit him harder than he expected. The pressure was breaking them, and if he didn't act soon, it could fracture the entire company.

"What do you think we should do?" Nikhil asked, his voice quieter now, laced with concern.

Priya sighed, brushing a strand of hair from her face. "We need to lighten the load. I know we're in the middle of the Verma project, but we can't keep working like this. The deadlines are killing us. We need to push back harder on the client—extend the timelines, reduce the scope. If we don't, we're going to lose more than just Anuj."

Nikhil nodded, absorbing her words. She was right, but renegotiating the project was already a delicate balance. Mr. Verma had agreed to revisit the terms, but pushing too hard could backfire. They needed the revenue, but they also needed a team that could function.

"I'll talk to Mr. Verma again," Nikhil said finally. "I'll make it clear that we need to ease up on the deadlines, or we won't be able to deliver at the level they're expecting."

Priya gave him a small, relieved smile. "Thank you. I know this isn't easy, but it's necessary. We can't afford to lose people, Nikhil."

After Priya left, Nikhil sat alone in his office, the reality of the situation weighing heavily on him. Leadership was a lonely place, and moments like this made it even lonelier. His team was depending on him, but the balancing act was growing harder by the day.

He knew he needed to act quickly. BizBoost had come too far to falter now, but the emotional and physical toll on everyone—including himself—was mounting.

Later that day, Nikhil called Anuj into his office. The young strategist walked in looking exhausted, his usual energy drained. He sank into the chair across from Nikhil, his eyes downcast.

"Priya mentioned you've been thinking about taking a break," Nikhil said gently, not wanting to overwhelm him.

Anuj nodded, rubbing the back of his neck. "Yeah, I have. I just... I don't know if I can keep up with this pace. It's like we're constantly sprinting, and I'm out of breath, Nikhil. I need a break before I burn out completely."

Nikhil studied him for a moment, understanding the toll it had taken. Anuj was one of his brightest stars, and the idea of losing him—temporarily or otherwise—was a gut punch. But he couldn't ignore what Anuj was saying. He had to take care of his people.

"I get it," Nikhil said quietly. "I know we've been pushing hard, and it's not sustainable. But I want you to know that we're not expecting you to carry this on your own. I've been pushing back on the client, trying to give us more breathing room. I don't want you to burn out."

Anuj looked up, his expression softening slightly. "I appreciate that, Nikhil. But it's not just about this one project. It's everything. The pressure, the constant deadlines... it's just a lot."

"I know," Nikhil said. "And I'm working on making things more manageable. But I need you here, Anuj. BizBoost needs you. You're a huge part of what we're building, and I don't want to lose that. But if you need a break, I'll support it. We'll figure out a way to make it work."

Anuj nodded, clearly conflicted. "I'm not saying I'm leaving, Nikhil. I just need to find some balance, you know?"

"I understand," Nikhil said, offering him a small smile. "Let's get through this project, and then we'll figure out how to take some of the load off you. You're not alone in this. We're all in it together."

Anuj gave a tired smile in return. "Thanks, Nikhil.

I needed to hear that."

As Anuj left the office, Nikhil leaned back in his chair, his mind racing. The conversation with Anuj had been a reminder of just how fragile the situation was. BizBoost had come so far, but they were teetering on the edge of burnout. It was up to him to keep things balanced, to protect his team while still delivering for their clients.

The next day, Nikhil sat down for another call with Mr. Verma. The renegotiation had been going smoothly enough, but Nikhil knew they needed to push even harder on the deadlines if they were going to survive this project.

"Mr. Verma, we've made a lot of progress, but I need to be upfront with you," Nikhil began, his tone firm but respectful. "We need more time to complete the project at the level you're expecting. My team is doing everything they can, but the current deadlines aren't realistic with the expanded scope. If we don't adjust, I'm worried the quality will suffer."

Mr. Verma was silent for a moment, and Nikhil braced himself for resistance. But instead, Mr. Verma sighed. "I understand, Nikhil. We've been feeling the pressure on our end, too. I don't want to compromise on quality, so if we need to extend the timelines, let's make it happen."

Nikhil exhaled in relief. "Thank you. That'll make a huge difference."

After the call, Nikhil gathered his team to share the good news. The relief in the room was palpable. For the first time in weeks, they weren't running headlong into a wall. There was breathing room, a chance to slow down and regroup.

"We're not out of the woods yet," Nikhil said, his voice calm but encouraging. "But we've got some space now. Let's take advantage of it. Let's refocus and get this done the right way."

The team nodded, their spirits visibly lifted. They weren't giving up, but they were finally getting a chance to catch their breath. BizBoost was still in the fight, and Nikhil knew they could make it through.

As the day wound down, Nikhil stood at the window of his office, watching the city lights flicker on as the sun set. The weight of leadership was heavy, but tonight, it felt a little lighter. They had taken a step in the right direction, and for now, that was enough.

Nikhil knew the road ahead was still full of challenges. The pressure wouldn't disappear overnight, and there would always be new hurdles to face. But in this moment, as he watched the world outside his window, he felt a quiet sense of resolve.

They were going to make it. BizBoost wasn't just a business—it was a testament to everything they had built together. And no matter how hard the fight, Nikhil was ready to lead them through it.

CHAPTER 19

THE BREAKING POINT

The team was beginning to catch its breath, but Nikhil knew the reprieve was temporary. The extended deadlines bought them time, but the Verma project was still a beast that loomed over them. With the new schedule in place, Nikhil had hoped the pressure would ease, but what came next was far from what he expected.

It was just past 6 p.m. when Priya rushed into Nikhil's office, her face pale and her phone clutched tightly in her hand.

"Nikhil, you need to see this," she said, her voice barely above a whisper.

Nikhil's heart sank as he watched her approach. He had seen that look before—the kind that only meant bad news.

Priya handed him her phone, and Nikhil quickly skimmed through an email from Mr. Verma's assistant. It wasn't the usual status update or project inquiry. It was a notice of reevaluation.

"They're reconsidering the contract," Priya said, her voice wavering. "They're not satisfied with our progress and are reviewing their options."

Nikhil froze, his mind racing. This couldn't be happening. They had just renegotiated, just secured more time. How could the client be backtracking now? He felt a cold sweat break across his forehead.

"This... this doesn't make any sense," Nikhil muttered, staring at the email. "We're on schedule. We've been doing everything they asked."

Priya sat down across from him, her eyes filled with worry. "I know. But something's shifted. They're looking at other firms. Nikhil, if they pull out now, we're done. This contract is holding us together."

Nikhil stood up abruptly, pacing the room as the weight of the situation hit him like a freight train. The Verma deal was their lifeline, the one thing that had kept BizBoost afloat through the chaos. Losing it now would mean disaster. The company would collapse.

His mind raced with potential solutions, but none seemed realistic. He had to talk to Mr. Verma—immediately. They couldn't afford to let this slide into uncertainty. The conversation would need to be urgent, but diplomatic. He had to salvage the situation. He grabbed his phone, already dialing Mr. Verma's number.

The phone rang once. Then twice. Then... voicemail.

Nikhil clenched his jaw, trying to steady his breathing. He left a message—polite but firm—asking for an immediate conversation to clarify the email and reassure them that BizBoost was still the right partner for the project.

But even as he left the message, Nikhil felt the gnawing sense of dread settling deeper into his bones. They couldn't lose this contract. Not now. Not after everything they had gone through.

Priya watched him, her expression torn between anxiety and hope. "What do we do?" she asked, her voice quieter now.

Nikhil looked at her, his thoughts racing. "We wait for him to respond. In the meantime, we prepare for a worst-case scenario. We need a backup plan if this deal falls through."

Priya nodded, but Nikhil could see the fear in her eyes. There wasn't a clear backup plan, and they both knew it. Everything was riding on this contract.

That night, Nikhil stayed at the office long after the rest of the team had left. His mind was a storm of worries and calculations, but nothing seemed to add up in their favor. He checked his phone obsessively, waiting for Mr. Verma to return his call, but there was only silence.

Just after midnight, Nikhil's phone buzzed with a notification. He grabbed it immediately, hoping it was Mr. Verma's response. But it wasn't. It was an email—from another client. One they had been courting for months but who had remained frustratingly noncommittal.

Nikhil opened the email, his heart pounding. The message was short, to the point. The client was ready to move forward—on the condition that they could start the project immediately.

Nikhil stared at the screen, a mix of disbelief and cautious optimism running through him. This was the break they needed—a potential new contract that could provide a lifeline. But the timing was a cruel twist of fate. How could they take on another project when they were still struggling to deliver on the Verma deal?

He knew that adding more work to the team's already overwhelming load was risky. But what choice did they have? If the Verma deal fell through, this new client might be the only thing that kept BizBoost from collapsing. It was a dangerous gamble—but one Nikhil knew he had to consider.

The next morning, Nikhil called an emergency meeting with his senior team. Priya, Anuj, and the others filed into the conference room, their expressions filled with unease. They knew something was wrong.

Nikhil wasted no time. "We've got a problem," he said, his voice steady but tense. "The Verma contract is in jeopardy. They're reviewing their options and considering other firms."

The shock in the room was immediate. Anuj sank into his chair, shaking his head. Priya's eyes widened, though she didn't seem surprised—just resigned to the fact that the news she had feared had come true.

"But," Nikhil continued, his voice lifting slightly, "we've got a new opportunity. One of the clients we've been pursuing for months is ready to move forward. They want to start immediately."

Anuj looked up, his expression incredulous. "Immediately? Are we seriously considering taking on more work right now? We can barely handle what we've got!"

Nikhil ran a hand through his hair, the stress of the situation clear in his face. "I know. But if we lose the Verma deal, this new client might be the only thing that keeps us afloat. We don't have the luxury of turning them down."

The room was silent for a moment as the team processed the impossible decision they were facing. More work meant more pressure—pressure they were already struggling to manage. But losing the Verma deal would mean the end.

Priya finally spoke, her voice calm but firm. "Nikhil, I understand the urgency, but we need to be realistic. Taking on another project could break us. We've been on the edge for months, and adding more could push the team too far."

Nikhil sighed, leaning against the table. "I know, Priya. But we don't have a choice. We need to prepare for the possibility that Verma pulls out. We can't afford to wait and see what happens."

Anuj looked at him, his expression filled with doubt. "And what happens if we take on this new client, and the Verma deal still falls apart? We'll be left with twice the workload and no guarantee of survival."

Nikhil met his gaze, his mind racing. He didn't have an answer. Not a good one, anyway. The truth was, there was no perfect solution. They were walking a razor's edge, and every decision felt like a gamble.

"I'm going to talk to Mr. Verma again today," Nikhil said finally. "I'll push to keep the deal intact. But we need to be ready for anything."

As the meeting ended, the team left the conference room, their faces etched with uncertainty. Nikhil stayed behind, staring at the whiteboard filled with project timelines and client deliverables. The weight of everything was suffocating.

He knew what needed to be done. He had to save the Verma contract while onboarding the new client—two impossibly conflicting priorities. But there was no time to second-guess. The survival of BizBoost depended on it.

That afternoon, Nikhil's phone rang. It was Mr. Verma. His heart raced as he answered, bracing himself for the outcome of the most important conversation of his career.

CHAPTER 20

ON THE EDGE OF COLLAPSE

Nikhil's hand shook as he answered the call from Mr. Verma. His mind raced, already spinning with a dozen scenarios of what could unfold in the next few minutes. If Verma confirmed that they were pulling out, it would be a death sentence for BizBoost. Every calculation, every late-night plan, every desperate pitch hinged on this moment.

"Mr. Verma," Nikhil began, his voice as calm as he could muster, "I'm glad you called."

The silence on the other end of the line stretched for what felt like an eternity. Nikhil's heart pounded in his chest. He could almost hear the ticking clock of his company's future.

"Nikhil," Mr. Verma said finally, his tone measured but distant, "we've had some discussions internally. There are concerns about the timeline and your team's capacity to deliver at the scale we need. Our board is hesitant to move forward without stronger assurances."

Nikhil's grip tightened on the phone. Stronger assurances? They had just renegotiated the contract, and now the client was backpedaling, looking for a way out. His pulse quickened, but he kept his voice steady.

"Mr. Verma, I understand your concerns, but I can assure you that we're fully committed to delivering at the highest standard. We've made the necessary adjustments to our processes, and we're bringing in additional resources to ensure that your expectations are not only met but exceeded."

There was another long pause. Nikhil's stomach twisted with the weight of the unknown. This was it. Everything hung on Mr. Verma's next words.

"We're still evaluating other firms," Verma said, his voice clipped. "But I'll give you this—we're not making any final decisions just yet. We'll review your progress over the next two weeks. If we're satisfied with the improvements, we'll move forward as planned. If not, we'll have no choice but to reconsider our options."

Nikhil's heart sank. Two weeks. That was all they had to prove themselves. Two weeks to convince one of their most demanding clients that they were the right choice. He felt the crushing weight of it pressing down on his chest.

"Understood, Mr. Verma," Nikhil said, doing his best to hide the panic creeping into his voice. "We'll make sure the next two weeks demonstrate our full capabilities."

"Good. I'll be watching closely," Verma said before the line went dead.

Nikhil sat there, staring at the phone in his hand. The room seemed to close in around him, the walls tightening as the realization hit: they were on the verge of collapse. One misstep, and it was over.

But he didn't have time to wallow in despair. He had two weeks to turn everything around—to push his team harder than they'd ever been pushed before, to deliver results that would silence any doubts Verma's team had about BizBoost. It was a near-impossible task, but failure was not an option.

He immediately called Priya into his office. She entered quickly, her face etched with worry. "What did he say?" she asked, her voice tense.

Nikhil took a deep breath. "We've got two weeks. They're still considering other firms, but they'll give us a final decision based on our progress over the next fourteen days. If we don't nail it, they'll pull out."

Priya's face paled. "Two weeks? That's... that's barely any time, Nikhil."

"I know," Nikhil said, his voice steady despite the storm inside him. "But we don't have a choice. We have to show them that we're the best option, or we lose everything."

Priya sat down across from him, her eyes filled with worry. "The team's already at their breaking point. If we push them harder... I don't know if they can handle it."

Nikhil leaned forward, his hands clasped tightly together. "I get it, Priya. Believe me, I do. But if we don't deliver, there won't be a team left to protect. We need to find a way to get through this—together."

Priya bit her lip, clearly torn. She had been Nikhil's right hand through all of this, the one who held everything together when it felt like it was falling apart.

But even she had her limits, and Nikhil could see that this situation was pushing her to hers.

"We'll call an all-hands meeting," Nikhil said, already mapping out the next steps in his mind. "I'll be honest with the team—lay it all out. If we work together, we can get through this. We don't have a choice."

Priya nodded slowly, but Nikhil could see the doubt in her eyes. She was holding on, but just barely.

That afternoon, Nikhil gathered his core team in the conference room. The tension in the air was palpable as everyone took their seats. Anuj sat at the far end of the table, his face drawn with fatigue, while the others mirrored his exhaustion. They were all waiting for Nikhil to speak.

"We're in a tough spot," Nikhil began, not sugarcoating the reality. "Mr. Verma's team is reconsidering the contract. We have two weeks to prove ourselves—two weeks to show them that we're the right partner for this project."

The room was silent, the weight of his words sinking in. Nikhil could see the fear and frustration in his team's eyes, but he couldn't let them fall into despair. Not now.

"I know you're all tired," he continued, his voice softening. "I know we've been pushing hard, and the pressure has been relentless. But we're here because we've built something worth fighting for. We've survived setbacks before, and we'll survive this one, too. But it's going to take everything we've got."

Anuj finally spoke, his voice rough. "And if we can't deliver? What happens then?"

Nikhil looked around the room, meeting each of their eyes. "Then we lose everything," he said bluntly. "But we're not going to let that happen. We're going to fight for this. Together."

The team exchanged uneasy glances, but slowly, Nikhil could see the resolve returning to their faces. They weren't ready to give up. Not yet.

"We'll need all hands on deck," Priya added, picking up where Nikhil left off. "This is going to be a sprint, but if we pull it off, it'll be worth it."

Nikhil nodded. "I'm not asking for miracles. I'm asking for focus, for commitment. We can do this. I believe in all of you."

After the meeting, Nikhil retreated to his office, where the enormity of the situation finally caught up with him. Two weeks. That was all they had. Two weeks to salvage everything they had worked for. Two weeks to stave off disaster.

He couldn't stop his mind from spiraling. If they failed, BizBoost wouldn't just be facing a tough time—it would be over. He could feel the weight of every decision pressing down on him, the enormity of what they were trying to achieve crushing him under its force.

As he sat at his desk, staring blankly at the whiteboard filled with project notes and timelines, his phone buzzed. It was a text from the new client—the one they had been courting for months. They wanted a follow-up meeting to finalize the deal.

Nikhil stared at the message, feeling the walls closing in. How could he juggle both? With Verma's project hanging in the balance and the team already stretched to their breaking point, taking on another major project seemed impossible. But turning down the new client could mean missing out on the very lifeline they needed.

He closed his eyes, trying to calm the storm raging inside him. He was walking a razor-thin line, and one wrong move could send everything crashing down.

The next morning, Nikhil stood at the window of his office, watching the city stir to life below him. The weight of the past few days sat heavy on his shoulders, but as the sun rose higher in the sky, a new sense of resolve took hold.

Two weeks. That was all they had. But Nikhil wasn't ready to give up.

He turned back to his desk, grabbing his phone. It was time to fight.

CHAPTER 21
THE EDGE OF DESPERATION

Nikhil sat in his office, staring blankly at his computer screen, the message from the new client still glowing on his screen. They wanted to start immediately. How could they even think about taking on another project with Verma's deal hanging by a thread? The tension in his chest tightened as the reality of his situation settled in. BizBoost was balancing on the thinnest of lines, and one wrong move could send everything crumbling down.

The door creaked open, and Priya walked in, her face reflecting the same exhaustion that Nikhil felt deep in his bones.

"We need to talk," she said, her voice low but urgent.

Nikhil gestured to the chair in front of him. Priya sat down, and for a moment, neither of them spoke. The silence between them felt heavy, like they were both silently bracing themselves for what was to come.

"We've got another problem," Nikhil finally said, breaking the silence. "The new client... they want to start now. Immediately."

Priya's eyes widened, her expression a mixture of disbelief and frustration. "You've got to be kidding me. Nikhil, we're already drowning with the Verma project. How are we supposed to take on more work?"

Nikhil leaned back in his chair, rubbing his temples. "I know. But if Verma pulls out, we'll be left with nothing. This new client... they might be our only lifeline if things go south."

Priya leaned forward, her voice urgent. "And what happens when we can't deliver for either client? We're on the verge of burnout as it is. Adding another project to the pile will break the team, Nikhil. You know that."

"I do know," Nikhil said, his voice strained. "But what choice do we have? If Verma drops us, we're finished. We can't afford to turn this new client away."

Priya shook her head, frustration flashing across her face. "This is playing with fire. If we try to juggle both projects, we could lose everything. Not just Verma, but the new client too. We're stretched too thin."

Nikhil was silent for a moment, his mind racing. Priya was right, of course. They were barely managing the Verma project, and adding more work seemed like a sure way to push the team past their breaking point. But the thought of losing Verma—and having nothing to fall back on—was a risk Nikhil couldn't take. It was a gamble, but what other option did they have?

"I'll talk to the team," Nikhil said finally, his voice firm. "I'll be honest with them. They deserve to know what's at stake."

Priya looked at him, concern etched into her features. "And if the team can't handle it? If they push back?"

Nikhil met her gaze, feeling the weight of the decision pressing down on him. "Then we'll have to find a way.

We don't have a choice."

That afternoon, Nikhil called an emergency meeting. The team gathered in the conference room, their faces lined with exhaustion, their eyes filled with the same uncertainty that weighed on him. They knew something was wrong. The past few weeks had been brutal, and now Nikhil was about to drop another bomb on them.

He stood at the front of the room, gripping the edges of the table as he began to speak.

"I'm not going to sugarcoat this," Nikhil started, his voice steady but tense. "We're in a critical situation. Verma's team is reconsidering our contract. We have two weeks to prove ourselves and save the deal."

The room was deathly silent as his words sunk in. Nikhil could see the fear flicker across their faces. Everyone understood what was at stake.

"That's not all," he continued, his eyes scanning the room. "We've also just received confirmation from a new client. The one we've been chasing for months. They're ready to move forward, but they want to start immediately."

A ripple of disbelief swept through the room. Anuj was the first to speak, his voice laced with frustration. "Nikhil, you can't be serious. We're barely keeping up with Verma. How are we supposed to handle another project on top of that?"

"I know it sounds impossible," Nikhil replied, trying to keep his tone calm. "But if Verma drops us, this new client could be the only thing that keeps us going. I'm not asking for the impossible—I'm asking for focus. For commitment. We've been through tough times before, and we've survived. We can do this."

The team exchanged uneasy glances. They were tired—more tired than ever before. But they were also fighters. Nikhil could see that spark in their eyes, even if it was buried beneath layers of exhaustion.

"We're going to have to pull in extra help," Priya added, jumping in to support Nikhil. "We'll distribute the workload, bring in freelancers if we need to, but we need to act fast. We don't have time to waste."

Anuj shook his head, his frustration barely contained. "You're asking us to risk everything, Nikhil. What happens when we can't deliver on either project? What happens when the team burns out completely?"

Nikhil held Anuj's gaze, feeling the tension crackling in the air. He couldn't deny that the risk was enormous. But what choice did they have? If they didn't fight for both clients, BizBoost would collapse. They were already on the edge—this was a last stand.

"I know it's a lot," Nikhil said, his voice softening. "But we don't have a choice. We either step up and prove ourselves, or we lose everything. I believe in this team. I know we can pull this off. We've come too far to let it all fall apart now."

The room was silent again, the weight of his words pressing down on them all. Slowly, the team began to nod, their expressions still strained but filled with a grim determination. They weren't ready to give up—not yet.

After the meeting, Nikhil lingered in the conference room, his mind racing with the enormity of what he had just asked his team to do. Was it too much? Was he pushing them beyond their limits, risking everything they had built for one last chance?

Priya walked over, her face etched with concern. "Are you sure about this, Nikhil? We're already hanging by a thread."

Nikhil looked at her, the weight of his decision settling in his chest like a stone. "I'm not sure about anything anymore, Priya. But what other choice do we have?"

Priya nodded, though Nikhil could see the doubt in her eyes. "Then we fight."

The next few days were a blur of frantic activity. Nikhil worked around the clock, pulling in every resource he could find, coordinating freelancers, and overseeing both projects with a growing sense of urgency. The office was alive with energy, but it was a frantic, desperate kind of energy. Everyone was pushing themselves to their limits.

As the days passed, the pressure mounted. Every update from Verma's team was scrutinized, every revision nitpicked, every deadline closing in like a vise around their necks. The new client's demands were piling up, and Nikhil found himself running from one fire to the next, trying to keep everything from collapsing.

It was clear that the cracks were beginning to show. Small mistakes turned into bigger ones, and Nikhil knew they were close to breaking. His team was exhausted, and even he was beginning to feel the effects of the relentless pace.

Late one night, long after the office had emptied, Nikhil sat alone at his desk, staring at the endless list of tasks that still needed to be completed. His phone buzzed with a new message from Mr. Verma's team—another request for revisions, another sign that they were losing faith.

aNikhil leaned back in his chair, his heart heavy. How much longer could they keep this up? How much more could they take before it all came crashing down?

His phone buzzed again. This time, it was a message from Priya: "We need to talk. It's urgent."

Nikhil's heart sank as he read the message. What now? He didn't know how much more bad news he could take.

He grabbed his phone and headed for the conference room, bracing himself for whatever new crisis awaited him. As he pushed open the door, he found Priya standing there, her face pale, her eyes filled with worry.

"Nikhil," she said, her voice barely above a whisper, "we have a serious problem."

CHAPTER 22

ON THE VERGE OF SOMETHING GREATER

Nikhil raced down the hallway toward the conference room, Priya's urgent message still buzzing in his mind. He felt his pulse quicken as he pushed open the door, dreading what new crisis might be waiting for him on the other side. Priya stood by the window, her back turned to him, staring out into the dimly lit city beyond. Something was wrong—very wrong.

"Priya," Nikhil said, his voice tight. "What's going on?"

Priya turned slowly, her face pale. She clutched her phone in her hand, her knuckles white from the pressure. "We've got a major problem, Nikhil," she said, her voice barely above a whisper.

Nikhil's stomach dropped. "What happened?" "Verma's team... they've just requested a complete

overhaul of the project. They want changes to the core

framework—something completely different from what we've already delivered. And they want it within the next few days."

Nikhil blinked, his mind struggling to process the information. An overhaul? At this stage? It didn't make any sense. They had been working on the same framework for weeks, refining it down to the smallest detail, and now Verma's team wanted to throw it all out?

"This is impossible," Nikhil muttered, pacing the room. "We've already passed the mid-point. How are we supposed to change the entire framework now?"

Priya nodded, her eyes filled with worry. "It's not just that. They're threatening to cancel the contract if we don't comply. They've been in talks with other firms, Nikhil. I think they're using this as leverage to push us out."

The room seemed to close in around him as Nikhil processed the gravity of the situation. This was more than a simple request—it was a trap. Verma's team had been looking for a way to edge them out, and now they had the perfect excuse. But if they failed to deliver... BizBoost was finished.

"We need to push back," Nikhil said finally, his voice sharper than intended. "This wasn't part of the original contract. We've given them everything they've asked for up to this point."

"I've already tried," Priya said, shaking her head. "They're not budging. It's all or nothing. Either we make the changes, or they walk away."

Nikhil could feel the pressure mounting, the weight of it crushing down on him like a heavy stone. There was no way the team could make the changes in time without collapsing under the strain. They were already working around the clock just to meet the existing deadlines. Piling this on top of them would be a death sentence.

"I don't know if we can pull this off," Priya continued, her voice breaking slightly. "The team is exhausted. Anuj has barely slept in days. If we push them any harder, we'll lose people."

Nikhil stood frozen in place, his mind racing with possibilities. Every path seemed to lead to disaster. If they tried to meet Verma's demands, they would burn out the team and still might fail. But if they didn't try, they would lose the contract, and everything would be over.

His phone buzzed in his pocket, snapping him out of his daze. It was another message from the new client—they wanted to know when the contract would be finalized.

Nikhil stared at the screen, his pulse pounding in his ears. Two ticking time bombs, both threatening to destroy everything he had built. How could they possibly juggle both? The clock was ticking, and every second brought them closer to the edge.

"We need to make a decision," Priya said quietly. "If we're going to try to meet Verma's demands, we need to act now."

Nikhil closed his eyes, trying to block out the panic rising in his chest. This was a no-win situation. But he couldn't afford to freeze—not now. His team needed him to make a choice, and they needed it fast.

"Get the team together," Nikhil said finally, his voice hollow. "We need to discuss this. I'm not making this call alone."

Priya nodded and hurried out of the room, leaving Nikhil alone with the suffocating weight of the decision before him.

A few minutes later, the core team filed into the conference room. Anuj looked worse than Nikhil had ever seen him—dark circles under his eyes, his movements slow and heavy with exhaustion. The others were no better. They sat down around the table, all of them looking to Nikhil for answers.

"We've hit a wall," Nikhil began, his voice tense. "Verma's team is demanding a complete overhaul of the project. They want changes to the core framework—something that will require us to redo almost everything we've delivered so far."

A murmur of disbelief spread through the room. Anuj leaned back in his chair, rubbing his temples. "They can't be serious," he muttered. "We're halfway through the project. How can they expect us to start over?"

"They're using it as leverage," Priya said, stepping in. "They've been talking to other firms, and now they're trying to squeeze us out. But if we don't comply, they'll pull the contract."

Anuj's eyes widened. "They'll what?"

Nikhil nodded grimly. "That's what's at stake. If we don't meet their demands, they'll walk away. And if that happens, we're done."

The room fell silent as the weight of the situation sank in. Nikhil could see the exhaustion in their faces, the fear in their eyes. They had been fighting so hard, for so long, and now everything they had worked for was hanging by a thread.

"What do we do?" Anuj asked finally, his voice barely above a whisper.

Nikhil took a deep breath, steadying himself. "We have two options. We can try to meet their demands, knowing full well that it will push us to our limits and beyond. Or... we push back. We hold the line and tell them this is as far as we go."

Silence filled the room as everyone absorbed the gravity of the decision before them. Priya was the first to speak.

"If we push back, they could cancel the contract.

Are we prepared to take that risk?"

"We might not have a choice," Nikhil said quietly. "The team is already stretched too thin. If we try to do this, we could end up burning out before we even get close to the finish line."

Anuj looked up, his face pale. "But if we push back and they cancel... we lose everything."

Nikhil nodded. "That's the gamble."

The room was tense with uncertainty, everyone waiting for someone else to make the call. This was it—the moment where they had to decide what they were willing to risk. The clock was ticking, and every second brought them closer to a decision that could change everything.

Finally, Priya spoke, her voice steady but filled with conviction. "We push back. If we bend to their demands now, it'll never stop. They'll keep changing the goalposts, and we'll keep burning ourselves out trying to meet them. We've come this far by staying true to what we know. Let's not compromise that now."

Nikhil felt a surge of relief wash over him. Priya was right. They couldn't keep bending. They had built BizBoost on their own terms, and if they were going to go down, they would go down fighting for what they believed in.

He looked around the room, meeting each of their eyes. "Is everyone in agreement?"

Anuj hesitated for a moment, then nodded slowly. "Let's do it. We push back."

The others followed, their faces resolute despite the fear lingering in the air.

Nikhil stood up, feeling a newfound sense of clarity settle over him. "Alright. We're going to hold the line. Priya, set up a meeting with Verma's team. We're going to fight for this—on our terms."

The team dispersed, leaving Nikhil alone in the conference room. The decision had been made, but the real battle was only just beginning. The next few days would determine everything.

As he walked back to his office, Nikhil's phone buzzed again. Another message from the new client, this time more insistent. They needed answers—now.

Nikhil stared at the message, his pulse quickening. Two battles, both raging at the same time.

He couldn't afford to lose either one.

CHAPTER 23

THE LINE IN THE SAND

Nikhil stood at the window of his office, watching the sun set over the city, his mind racing with the gravity of what was about to happen. The decision had been made—they would push back against Verma's impossible demands. But the uncertainty lingered in the air, thick and suffocating.

Priya knocked softly on the door and entered, her face lined with tension. "Verma's team is ready," she said quietly.

Nikhil nodded, steeling himself for what was about to come. This wasn't just another client negotiation—this was a battle for BizBoost's survival. Everything they had worked for was on the line, and the outcome of this meeting could determine whether they lived to fight another day or whether everything came crashing down.

"Let's do this," he said, his voice firmer than he felt.

The core team gathered in the conference room, a mix of tension and determination written across their faces. They had made their decision, but the stakes were clear to everyone. If Verma's team didn't respond well to their pushback, they could lose the contract in an instant. And there would be no second chances.

The video call connected, and Mr. Verma appeared on the screen, his expression as unreadable as ever. His team sat beside him, their faces cool and businesslike, waiting for the conversation to begin.

"Nikhil," Verma said, his voice calm but clipped. "We've received your latest update, and I have to say, it's not quite what we were expecting. We've discussed internally, and we feel that more substantial changes to the framework are necessary if this project is going to succeed."

Nikhil could feel the tension in the room spike as Verma's words sank in. This was exactly what they had anticipated, but hearing it confirmed still sent a wave of anxiety through the team.

"Mr. Verma," Nikhil began, choosing his words carefully, "we've considered your request, but we believe the framework we've developed is solid and in line with the original scope of the project. We're confident it will deliver the results you're looking for, but implementing the changes you've suggested at this stage would be highly disruptive to the project. It would require a complete overhaul of our work to date, which we simply cannot accommodate within the current timeline."

Verma's face remained expressionless, but Nikhil could sense the shift in the energy of the room. This was the moment. The line had been drawn.

"So," Verma said slowly, leaning back in his chair, "what exactly are you proposing?"

"We're proposing that we stick to the agreed framework," Priya jumped in, her voice steady. "It's been carefully designed to meet your objectives. We're open to minor adjustments, but anything beyond that would compromise the integrity of the project—and we're committed to delivering high-quality results."

Verma was silent for a moment, his gaze sharp and assessing. Nikhil's heart raced as the seconds ticked by, each one feeling like a lifetime. They had made their stand, but now it was up to Verma's team to decide if they would fight back—or walk away.

"You're aware that we've been speaking to other firms, yes?" Verma said finally, his tone deliberate.

Nikhil felt the room tighten around him. This was the threat—the hammer they had been waiting to drop. He glanced at Priya, who gave him the slightest nod, urging him to hold the line.

"We're aware," Nikhil said, his voice steady. "But we're confident that BizBoost is the best partner for this project. We've already put significant resources into ensuring that your objectives are met. No other firm will have the same level of commitment to your success."

Verma's lips pressed into a thin line, but he said nothing. The tension in the room was palpable, everyone on both sides waiting for the other to make the next move.

Finally, Verma leaned forward, his eyes narrowing. "Nikhil, let me be clear. We need results. My team is concerned that the current approach is too conservative, and we're looking for something more dynamic, more cutting-edge. If you can't deliver that, we'll be forced to explore other options."

Nikhil's pulse pounded in his ears, but he didn't waver. "We're fully committed to delivering results, Mr. Verma. But we've built this framework based on a deep understanding of your needs. Changing course now would be risky for everyone involved."

Verma's gaze lingered on Nikhil for a long moment, the tension crackling between them. Then, slowly, he leaned back in his chair, a faint smile tugging at the corners of his mouth.

"Alright," he said finally. "We'll continue with the framework as is—for now. But we'll be expecting top-tier results, Nikhil. There won't be any room for errors."

Nikhil exhaled, relief flooding through him. They had done it—they had held the line. But the warning in Verma's words was clear. They had won the battle, but the war was far from over. If they didn't deliver flawless results, Verma wouldn't hesitate to walk away.

"We appreciate your trust, Mr. Verma," Nikhil said, his voice calm. "We won't let you down."

The call ended, and Nikhil slumped back in his chair, his heart still racing. Priya turned to him, her expression a mixture of relief and exhaustion.

"That was close," she said softly.

Nikhil nodded, running a hand through his hair. "Too close. But we bought ourselves some time."

Anuj leaned forward, still looking stunned by what had just transpired. "We actually pulled it off. I can't believe it."

"Neither can I," Nikhil admitted, though the tension in his chest hadn't fully dissipated. "But this isn't over. Verma's going to be watching us like a hawk. We need to be perfect from here on out."

The room fell into a heavy silence as the team processed the enormity of what had just happened. They had narrowly avoided disaster, but the pressure was still suffocating. Every mistake would be magnified, every misstep scrutinized.

As the team dispersed, Nikhil stayed behind, staring at the empty conference room, the weight of the decision still heavy on his shoulders. They had bought time, but at what cost? The team was already close to burning out, and now they were expected to deliver flawless results under even more pressure.

His phone buzzed in his pocket, pulling him out of his thoughts. It was the new client—another demand for immediate action.

Nikhil's stomach churned as he read the message. How could they juggle both? The new client's expectations were just as high, and there was no room for delay. They had barely survived Verma's demands, and now they were staring down the barrel of another massive challenge.

He rubbed his temples, exhaustion pressing in from all sides. There wasn't enough time, enough energy, enough of him to keep everything moving. But there was no turning back now. BizBoost had to deliver on both fronts, or it would all fall apart.

The door opened, and Priya stepped back in, her expression grim. "We've got another problem."

Nikhil looked up, feeling the familiar weight of dread settling over him. "What is it?"

"Two of the freelancers we brought in for the new client just dropped out," she said, her voice tight. "They're overloaded, and they won't be able to meet the deadlines."

Nikhil felt the air leave his lungs. Of course.

Another blow. Another crisis to manage.

"Get Anuj in here," Nikhil said, standing up and grabbing his phone. "We'll need to restructure the team again. We don't have time to waste."

Priya nodded and hurried out, leaving Nikhil alone for a brief moment. He stared at his reflection in the glass window, the weight of the past few weeks etched into his face.

The fight wasn't over.

But as Nikhil walked out of the room, a flicker of doubt crept in. How much longer could they keep this up?

CHAPTER 24

THE BREAKING POINT

Nikhil stayed behind in the office long after the rest of the team had left, staring at his computer screen, unable to focus. The decisions of the last few weeks weighed heavily on him. The team was hanging by a thread, and Priya's words echoed in his mind: *They're breaking.*

The familiar sound of his phone buzzing on the desk brought him out of his thoughts. It was yet another message from the new client: "We need an update on the deliverables. Send us the latest version by tomorrow."

Nikhil clenched his jaw. Tomorrow. Everything was always due "tomorrow," and every delay felt like another step closer to disaster. The clock was ticking, and he was running out of time.

He leaned back in his chair, running his hands over his face. There was no way they could meet both Verma's and the new client's deadlines. Something was going to give—and he didn't know what it would be.

As the hours stretched on, Nikhil was startled by the sound of the office door creaking open. He turned to see Anuj walking in, looking more exhausted than ever. His shoulders were slumped, his eyes rimmed with dark circles, and he moved like a man running on pure adrenaline.

"You're still here," Nikhil said, his voice strained.

Anuj nodded, collapsing into the chair across from him. "Couldn't sleep," he muttered. "Too much on my mind."

Nikhil studied him for a moment, feeling a pang of guilt. Anuj had been working himself to the bone, pushing harder than anyone else. But he was breaking—just like Priya had warned.

"We can't keep doing this," Anuj said after a long silence, his voice thick with fatigue. "We can't keep pulling all-nighters and pretending like we're going to make it through this. The team is exhausted. People are talking about quitting. I'm... I'm not sure I can keep going either."

Nikhil's heart sank. Hearing it from Anuj, his right hand in the company, was like a knife to the chest. If Anuj couldn't hold on, what chance did the rest of the team have?

"You're the glue that's holding this team together," Nikhil said, his voice soft. "I need you, Anuj. BizBoost needs you."

Anuj gave him a tired smile, but there was no humor in it. "I'm just trying to survive at this point, Nikhil. I've given everything I have, and I'm not sure there's anything left."

The weight of his words settled heavily in the room, and for a moment, neither of them spoke.

Nikhil felt his chest tighten. He couldn't lose Anuj. Not now. Not when they were this close to making it—or falling apart completely.

"We'll get through this," Nikhil said, though the words felt hollow. "We'll find a way."

Anuj didn't reply. He just sat there, staring at the floor, as the weight of everything they were facing pressed down on them both.

After a long silence, Anuj stood up, his movements slow and heavy. "I'm going home," he said quietly. "I need sleep. We all do."

Nikhil nodded, watching him leave, feeling more alone than ever. If Anuj was breaking, how much longer could the rest of them hold on?

As the door clicked shut, Nikhil sat alone in the darkened office, his mind racing with the impossible choices ahead of him. He had told the team they would make it through, but as he stared at the endless list of tasks still to be done, the doubt gnawed at him.

He glanced at his phone again. Another message. Another reminder of the expectations hanging over his head. Everyone wanted perfection. And there was no room for mistakes.

Nikhil stood and walked to the window, staring out at the city streets below. The world outside felt so distant from the chaos and pressure that consumed his every waking moment. He closed his eyes, feeling the exhaustion wash over him.

How much longer could they keep this up?

He turned back to his desk, staring at the mountain of work waiting for him. He couldn't afford to break. Not now. Not with everything on the line.

The hours passed in a blur of frantic work, and before he knew it, the first rays of sunlight were creeping through the windows. Nikhil hadn't slept. Again. But there was no time to rest.

As the rest of the team trickled into the office that morning, Nikhil could see the exhaustion in their faces, the tension in the air. They were all running on empty, and the weight of it hung over the office like a dark cloud.

Priya approached him, her expression grim. "We need to talk," she said quietly.

Nikhil's stomach dropped. "What now?"

Priya led him into the conference room, closing the door behind them. "It's Anuj," she said, her voice tight. "He didn't come in this morning. I called him, and he says he's not sure if he can keep going. He's... he's thinking about stepping away."

Nikhil's heart sank. Anuj? Stepping away? He had known Anuj was struggling, but hearing that he was on the verge of quitting hit him harder than anything else.

"He's burned out," Priya continued. "He's been carrying too much for too long, and it's finally catching up to him."

Nikhil rubbed his temples, feeling the full weight of the situation settle on his shoulders. Anuj was critical—he had been there from the beginning, through every challenge and every victory. If Anuj left, it would send shockwaves through the entire team.

"We can't lose him," Nikhil said, his voice barely above a whisper. "Not now."

Priya nodded, her face etched with concern. "I know. But we can't keep pushing people like this, Nikhil. The team is on the edge. If we don't pull back soon, we're going to lose more than just Anuj."

Nikhil slumped into a chair, feeling the exhaustion settle deep in his bones. He knew Priya was right—they couldn't keep running like this. But pulling back meant risking everything. If they didn't meet the deadlines, they would lose both clients, and BizBoost would fall apart.

"What do we do?" Nikhil asked, his voice filled with frustration. "How do we make this work?"

Priya shook her head. "I don't know. But we need to figure it out soon."

As she left the conference room, Nikhil sat alone, staring at the empty table in front of him. How had it come to this? They had been so close to success, but now it felt like everything was slipping away.

His phone buzzed again—another message from the new client. He couldn't ignore it any longer. He had to make a decision.

But what decision could he make? The new client needed immediate attention, but Verma's team was still scrutinizing every detail. There wasn't enough time to juggle everything.

The team was on the edge, Anuj was breaking, and the deadlines were relentless. Nikhil couldn't shake the feeling that they were racing toward something they couldn't escape—a collapse that seemed inevitable.

As the hours ticked by, Nikhil found himself pacing the office, running through every possible scenario. There had to be a way out.

Priya returned later in the day, her face just as weary as before. "I've spoken to the rest of the team," she said, sitting down across from Nikhil. "They're exhausted, but they'll keep going for now. But Nikhil, we can't keep asking this of them. We need a break, or we're going to lose people."

Nikhil leaned back in his chair, rubbing his eyes. She was right. But taking a break meant missing deadlines, and missing deadlines meant losing clients. There was no easy solution.

"Let's get through the next 24 hours," Nikhil said finally, his voice low. "We'll meet the new client's deadline, and then we'll regroup. I'll talk to Anuj, see if we can get him some time off. But for now, we push forward."

Priya gave him a sad smile, the exhaustion evident in her eyes. "Alright. But we can't keep doing this forever."

"I know," Nikhil said, though the words felt empty. "Just one more push."

As the evening wore on, Nikhil found himself alone in the office again, staring at the empty desks around him. The silence was deafening, and the weight of everything they were trying to achieve felt crushing. He had made promises—promises to the team, to the clients, to himself. But could he keep them?

The clock on the wall ticked steadily, reminding him that time was running out. It always was.

As he stared out at the darkened city, Nikhil couldn't shake the feeling that they were on the verge of something—something great, or something catastrophic.

Only time would tell which it would be.

CHAPTER 25

BETWEEN SURVIVAL AND COLLAPSE

The morning sunlight filtered into the office, but there was no energy in the air. The usual buzz of conversation and activity had been replaced with silence. Everyone was exhausted. The long nights, impossible deadlines, and constant pressure had finally taken their toll, and Nikhil could feel it in every corner of the office.

He stood in the middle of the room, watching his team. Priya was at her desk, her eyes red-rimmed from lack of sleep. Anuj's chair sat empty, a glaring reminder that he still hadn't shown up. The others moved slowly, their faces pale, their focus slipping.

Nikhil took a deep breath, trying to shake off the anxiety that clung to him like a second skin. They were on the verge of something—either breaking through or breaking apart. And he wasn't sure which it would be.

Priya walked over to him, her face drawn tight with worry. "We need to talk about Anuj," she said quietly.

Nikhil nodded, already knowing what she was going to say. Anuj hadn't been answering his calls. He had sent a message late last night saying he needed time to think. Nikhil had hoped he would show up this morning, but as the hours ticked by, it became clear that Anuj wasn't coming in.

"Do you think he's really done?" Nikhil asked, though he already knew the answer.

Priya hesitated, glancing toward Anuj's empty desk. "I think he's burned out," she said softly. "He's given everything to this company, and it's finally caught up to him. If we don't let him rest... we might lose him for good."

Nikhil felt a wave of guilt wash over him. Anuj had been with him from the beginning, through every failure and every small victory. He had always been the one to step up, to push harder when things got tough. And now, Nikhil had pushed him too far.

"We can't afford to lose him," Nikhil said, his voice tight. "Not now."

"I know," Priya replied, her voice filled with concern. "But if we keep pushing like this, it's not just Anuj. We're going to lose more people. The team is running on fumes, Nikhil. They're trying their best, but they can't keep going at this pace."

Nikhil ran a hand through his hair, frustration building in his chest. What choice did they have? If they didn't meet the deadlines, they would lose the clients. If they pushed any harder, they would lose the team. It felt like an impossible balancing act—one that was slowly crumbling beneath him.

"We have to get through the next few days," Nikhil said finally, his voice strained. "Once we deliver to the new client, we can reassess. I'll give Anuj whatever time he needs, and we'll pull back on some of the pressure. But right now... we don't have a choice. We can't miss these deadlines."

Priya gave him a long look, her eyes filled with doubt. "Just be careful, Nikhil. You're carrying a lot, and so is the team. There's only so much people can take."

With that, she walked back to her desk, leaving Nikhil standing alone in the middle of the office, the weight of her words pressing down on him. How much could people take? He had been asking himself that same question for days, and he still didn't know the answer.

Later that day, Nikhil sat alone in his office, staring at the latest message from the new client. They were pushing for an accelerated timeline again—demanding the impossible with a smile and a polite email. He had stopped replying immediately to their requests, knowing it would only lead to more demands.

They had to deliver, or it would all fall apart. But how could they meet both clients' needs when his team was falling apart right in front of him?

As if on cue, Nikhil's phone buzzed. It was Anuj.

Nikhil answered immediately, his voice strained with hope. "Anuj. Where are you?"

Anuj's voice on the other end of the line sounded hollow. "I'm at home," he said. "I just... I don't know, Nikhil. I'm not sure I can keep doing this."

Nikhil felt his stomach drop. "Look, Anuj, I know it's been rough. I know we've all been under insane pressure, but we're so close. Once we deliver this project, things will get better. I'll make sure of it."

There was a long pause on the other end of the line before Anuj finally spoke. "I don't know if I have anything left to give. I'm... I'm exhausted, Nikhil. And I don't just mean tired. I don't feel like myself anymore."

Nikhil clenched his jaw, his heart racing. If he lost Anuj now...

"Take a few days," Nikhil said quickly. "Take the time you need to recharge. We'll manage here until you're ready to come back."

Another long pause, then a quiet reply. "I'll think about it."

The call ended, leaving Nikhil feeling more hollow than before. Everything was slipping through his fingers. He had pushed too hard, and now the people he depended on most were starting to crumble.

As the afternoon wore on, the rest of the team kept working, but the energy in the office was flat. There was no spark left, no drive. It was just the mechanical grind of trying to meet deadlines, one after another, without end in sight.

That evening, as the office started to empty, Priya came to Nikhil's office again, her face lined with exhaustion.

"Nikhil," she said, "we need to talk about the Verma project."

Nikhil looked up from his desk, his pulse quickening. The Verma project. It had been simmering in the background while they focused on the new client, but Verma's team was growing more restless by the day.

"What's going on?" he asked, already bracing for the bad news.

"They've requested another meeting," Priya said, her voice tight. "They're concerned about the pace of delivery. They're starting to wonder if we're capable of pulling this off."

Nikhil's stomach clenched. Of course they were concerned. They had already pushed back once, and now they were trying to stay on track, but every day it felt like they were falling further behind.

"When do they want to meet?" Nikhil asked.

"Tomorrow morning," Priya replied. "We need to be prepared to show them progress. Real progress."

Nikhil nodded, his mind racing. Tomorrow morning. As if they didn't have enough to deal with already.

"I'll make sure we're ready," Nikhil said, though even he didn't know how they were going to pull it off.

Priya hesitated, then stepped forward, lowering her voice. "Nikhil... I'm worried about you. You're carrying too much. You've been trying to keep everything going, but it's starting to take its toll."

Nikhil shook his head, trying to push the concern aside. "I'm fine. We just need to get through this."

"No," Priya said, her voice firm. "You're not fine. None of us are fine. We're all running on fumes, and you've been taking the brunt of it. But you can't keep doing that forever."

Nikhil leaned back in his chair, feeling the weight of everything pressing down on him. Priya was right, of course. He had been trying to hold it all together, but how long could he keep this up?

"I'll be fine," Nikhil said finally, his voice quiet. "Once we deliver... things will get better."

Priya gave him a sad smile, but the worry in her eyes didn't fade. "Just promise me you'll take care of yourself."

With that, she left the office, leaving Nikhil alone with his thoughts. The evening stretched on, and as the office finally fell silent, Nikhil sat in the darkness, staring at the computer screen, wondering how much longer they could survive this.

The future of BizBoost was teetering on the edge, and the only thing keeping them afloat was the hope that they could pull off the impossible.

But as Nikhil sat there, exhausted and overwhelmed, he couldn't shake the feeling that they were closer to collapse than they realized.

CHAPTER 26

FLAMES OF DESPERATION

The office was quiet, but it wasn't the calm Nikhil had once cherished. It was the quiet before a storm. Every conversation was whispered, every movement tense. The team wasn't just tired anymore; they were hanging by a thread, and the weight of what they were trying to accomplish was suffocating them all.

Nikhil sat in his office, staring at the list of tasks pinned to the wall in front of him. It felt endless. Verma's project. The new client's deliverables. And now, the unexpected call for yet another meeting with Verma's team—the one thing they couldn't afford to mess up.

Priya had briefed him that morning. Verma was growing more agitated by the day. If they didn't deliver immediate, tangible progress, the contract was in jeopardy. But how could they deliver anything more when they were barely keeping their heads above water?

His phone buzzed on his desk—another email from the new client. Nikhil didn't have to open it to know what it said. More demands. More pressure. More deadlines that felt impossible to meet. He couldn't bring himself to look at it just yet.

Instead, he grabbed his jacket, heading for the door. He needed a breath of air, a moment to think before the day swallowed him whole. As he walked out of the office, he caught sight of Priya. She was on the phone, her face a mask of concentration, but when her eyes met his, she gave him a small, tired nod. They were all tired. They were all running on empty.

Nikhil stepped out into the crisp morning air, but the weight didn't lift. He walked aimlessly down the street, his mind racing. What was he supposed to do? How could he keep holding this together when everything felt like it was slipping through his fingers?

He had fought so hard for BizBoost. He had sacrificed everything—his time, his health, his peace of mind. But now, standing on the edge of the precipice, Nikhil couldn't shake the feeling that it was all unraveling. And he was running out of time.

The Verma meeting loomed like a black cloud over his thoughts. It was scheduled for 11 a.m., just two hours away, and the team wasn't ready. They weren't even close. But cancelling wasn't an option—not if they wanted to keep the contract alive.

Nikhil walked a little farther before turning back toward the office. No time for second-guessing. He had to make a decision, and he had to make it fast.

When he returned, Priya was waiting for him outside his office, her face pale. "We need to talk," she said quietly.

Nikhil nodded, ushering her into the conference room. The tension in the air was thick, and he could see the worry in her eyes.

"Verma's team is on edge," Priya began, sitting down across from him. "They've been in talks with another firm, Nikhil. If we don't deliver something substantial today... we're out."

Nikhil's heart sank. Another firm? He had expected the threat, but hearing it confirmed felt like a punch to the gut. BizBoost couldn't survive without Verma's contract. Not after everything they had invested into it.

"Do we have anything ready to show?" Nikhil asked, though he already knew the answer.

Priya shook her head. "We've made some progress, but it's not enough. Not by their standards."

Nikhil ran a hand through his hair, feeling the pressure building in his chest. They were backed into a corner. If they went into that meeting empty-handed, Verma would drop them without hesitation. But trying to pull something together in the next two hours felt impossible. His team was already stretched to the limit.

"Then we show them what we have," Nikhil said finally, his voice tight. "We spin it. Focus on the progress we've made, frame it as the foundation for the bigger picture. We can buy ourselves some time—just enough to get things back on track."

Priya's expression didn't change, but Nikhil could see the doubt flicker in her eyes. "It's a gamble," she said.

"It's all we have," Nikhil replied.

The next two hours passed in a blur of frantic preparation. Nikhil and Priya pored over every piece of work they had, trying to pull together something cohesive—something that would convince Verma's team that BizBoost was still the right partner for the job.

The weight of it was crushing. Every minute felt like a ticking bomb, counting down to the moment when everything could fall apart.

By the time 11 a.m. rolled around, Nikhil felt like a man on the edge of a cliff, staring down into the abyss. But there was no turning back. He had to face it head- on.

The video conference started, and Verma's face appeared on the screen, stern and expectant. His team sat beside him, their expressions blank but sharp. They were waiting—waiting to see if BizBoost could deliver, or if it was time to cut ties.

Nikhil took a deep breath, his heart pounding in his chest. "Mr. Verma, thank you for taking the time to meet with us," he began, his voice steady despite the turmoil inside. "We're excited to show you the progress we've made on the project."

As he and Priya walked them through the presentation, Nikhil could feel the tension in the room rising. This wasn't their best work—not by a long shot. But they framed it carefully, focusing on the potential, the groundwork they had laid for the bigger picture.

But Verma's expression remained unreadable, his eyes scanning every slide with an intensity that made Nikhil's pulse race.

When they finished, the silence was deafening.

Verma leaned back in his chair, his hands folded in his lap. "I'll be honest with you, Nikhil," he said finally, his voice cool. "This is not where we expected to be at this stage of the project."

Nikhil felt his stomach twist. This was it—the moment of reckoning.

"We've invested a lot in this partnership," Verma continued. "And while I see some potential in the direction you're heading, we need more than potential. We need results."

Nikhil nodded, his mind scrambling for a way to salvage the situation. "I understand, Mr. Verma. And I assure you, we're fully committed to delivering the results you need. What you're seeing today is the foundation of something much bigger, much more impactful. We just need a little more time to bring it to life." Verma was silent for a long moment, his eyes narrowing as he studied Nikhil's face. Then he spoke.

"I'm giving you two weeks, Nikhil. Two weeks to show me real progress. If I don't see significant improvement by then... we'll be exploring other options."

Nikhil exhaled, the relief flooding through him—but it was short-lived. Two weeks. That was all they had. Two weeks to prove themselves, or it would all come crashing down.

"Thank you, Mr. Verma," Nikhil said, keeping his voice steady. "We won't let you down."

The call ended, and Nikhil slumped back in his chair, his heart still racing. They had bought themselves time—but just barely.

Priya turned to him, her face pale. "Two weeks," she said quietly. "That's all we have."

"I know," Nikhil replied, running a hand through his hair. "But it's better than nothing."

As they walked back into the main office, the tension hung in the air like a storm cloud. The team was working, but there was no energy left. They were running on fumes—and now, they had two weeks to pull off the impossible.

Nikhil knew that everything depended on what happened next. Every decision, every step—it had to be flawless, or they wouldn't survive.

As he sat back down at his desk, Nikhil's phone buzzed. Another message from the new client, demanding answers, demanding deliverables. He stared at it for a long moment, feeling the weight of it pressing down on him.

They were fighting on two fronts, and Nikhil wasn't sure if they had enough left to win either battle.

But there was no turning back now. Two weeks. That was all they had. And Nikhil would do whatever it took to make sure BizBoost survived.

CHAPTER 27

RUNNING OUT OF TIME

The moment the call with Verma ended, the weight of the next two weeks crashed down on Nikhil like a tidal wave. He sat at his desk, staring blankly at the screen. Two weeks to turn everything around. Two weeks to deliver the impossible, or Verma would pull the plug.

The noise of the office faded into the background as the enormity of it settled in. The walls seemed to close in, the ticking of the clock in the corner louder than ever. Every second slipping by felt like another step toward disaster.

Priya walked up to his desk, her face set in a mask of calm, but her eyes betraying the tension underneath. "We bought ourselves time," she said quietly, though Nikhil could hear the doubt in her voice. "But we need a plan. A real one."

Nikhil nodded slowly, though the truth was gnawing at him. There wasn't a plan. Not one that would actually work. They were scrambling, patching holes in a sinking ship, and now they were supposed to steer it through a storm.

"What do you think the team's going to say when they hear we only have two weeks?" Priya asked, leaning against his desk.

Nikhil sighed, rubbing his eyes. The team. He didn't even know how they were going to tell them the news. They had been pulling double shifts for weeks, pushing themselves to the brink. What was left to give?

"We'll figure it out," Nikhil said finally, his voice sounding hollow even to himself. "We'll get through it."

But Priya didn't look convinced. Neither was he.

As Nikhil stood to gather the team for yet another emergency meeting, his phone buzzed with a notification from the new client. He hesitated, then glanced at the message. More demands. More pressure.

"Can't focus on them right now," Nikhil muttered under his breath. The new client could wait. They had to.

The team gathered in the conference room, their exhaustion palpable. The faces around the table told the story of a group that had been pushed too far for too long. Dark circles under their eyes, tense postures, the weight of sleepless nights and relentless work hanging heavy on all of them.

Nikhil stood at the front of the room, trying to find the words. How could he ask more of them? How could he tell them they had to dig even deeper when there was nothing left to give?

"We've bought ourselves two weeks," Nikhil began, the words like lead in his throat. "Verma's team wants to see significant progress by then, or they're going to move forward with another firm."

The room fell silent. Nikhil could see the ripple of disbelief and frustration pass through the faces in front of him. Two weeks? It was impossible, and they all knew it.

Anuj, who had finally returned to the office, sat with his arms crossed, staring hard at the table. He didn't look up, but Nikhil could feel the tension radiating from him. Anuj was back, but he wasn't the same.

"How are we supposed to make this happen?" Anuj asked quietly, his voice calm but cold. "We've been burning ourselves out for weeks, and now you're telling us we've got two weeks to pull off a miracle?"

Nikhil's stomach twisted. He had no answers. He didn't even know what to say that wouldn't sound like empty promises. He was asking the impossible, and everyone in the room knew it.

"We're going to have to push harder than we've ever pushed before," Nikhil said, feeling the words fall flat. "This is it. If we can't make this happen, BizBoost is finished."

The silence that followed was suffocating.

Priya broke it first, her voice calm but determined. "I know it sounds impossible," she said, her eyes sweeping the room. "But we've pulled off impossible things before. We've gotten through worse. If we work together, if we focus, we can make this happen."

But even her words, as hopeful as they were meant to be, seemed to hit a wall. The team was running on fumes, and there was nothing left to fuel them.

Anuj shook his head, still not looking up. "What happens if we don't make it?" he asked, his voice low. "If we fail?"

Nikhil looked at him, feeling the weight of that question settle over the room. What happens if they fail?

"We won't," Nikhil said, though the words felt like a lie. "We can't."

But the doubt was there, hanging in the air, thick and suffocating.

That night, Nikhil stayed late at the office, long after everyone else had gone home. The quiet of the empty office felt suffocating. He had pushed his team to the limit, and now he was asking them for more, when there was nothing left to give.

His phone buzzed again. This time it was a message from Verma. He stared at it for a long moment before opening it. "We expect to see substantial progress within the next 10 days. No excuses."

Nikhil felt his pulse quicken, the weight of the pressure pressing down on his chest. Ten days. It wasn't enough time. It was never enough time.

He glanced at the clock. Midnight.

He hadn't eaten. He hadn't slept. But there was no time for either.

Nikhil stood, walking over to the windows and staring out at the dark city below. The office lights from the neighboring buildings flickered like a reminder of the world moving forward, while he stood frozen in place, watching everything slip out of his grasp.

How had it come to this?

His mind raced, a constant churn of doubt and fear. How had everything gone so wrong? He had started BizBoost with so much hope, so much ambition. And now... it was all crumbling.

The sound of his phone buzzing again pulled him out of his thoughts. This time, it was Priya.

"Are you still at the office?" her message read.

Nikhil glanced at the clock again. 12:30 a.m. Of course, she knew he was still here. She always knew.

"Yeah," he replied, his fingers shaking slightly as he typed. "Still here."

Her reply came quickly. "We need to talk tomorrow.

Something's not right."

Nikhil frowned, staring at the message. What now? He didn't think he could handle another crisis, another problem to solve.

"Tomorrow," he replied, slipping his phone back into his pocket. But the knot of anxiety in his stomach didn't ease. Something wasn't right. He knew it. He could feel it in the air, a storm gathering on the horizon, waiting to break.

The night stretched on, and Nikhil sat alone in the quiet, the sound of the clock ticking louder and louder in his ears.

Tick. Tock. Time was running out.

The next morning, Priya was waiting for him at the office, her face pale and tense. She pulled him into the conference room the moment he arrived.

"We have a problem," she said, her voice tight. Nikhil's heart sank. Of course they did.

"What is it?" he asked, though he wasn't sure he wanted to hear the answer.

"It's the new client," Priya said. "They're pulling back. They want to reevaluate the scope of the project."

Nikhil's pulse spiked. Reevaluate? What did that mean? They had been working day and night on this project—had invested everything into making sure it was on track. If the new client pulled out, they were dead in the water.

"Why?" Nikhil asked, his voice sharp. "What happened?"

Priya shook her head, her expression grim. "They're not happy with the pace of delivery. They want a revised timeline, but they're talking about scaling back their investment."

Nikhil felt his stomach churn. Scaling back? That would be the end of it. If they lost the new client now, everything would come crashing down.

"We can't let that happen," Nikhil said, his voice rising. "We've got too much riding on this. We need to fix it."

"I'm trying," Priya replied, her voice tight. "But they're being vague. We need to go in with a clear plan, or we're going to lose them."

Nikhil stared at her, the panic rising in his chest. They were on the brink of collapse—and now, both clients were slipping away. He couldn't lose either of them. Not now. Not when everything was hanging by a thread.

"We have to fix this," Nikhil repeated, his mind racing. "We'll figure it out."

But as he said the words, he felt the weight of it pressing down on him like a crushing force. Time was running out, and they were running out of chances.

Just then, Nikhil's phone rang, vibrating loudly against the table.

He glanced down at the screen, expecting another message from Verma or the new client. But when he saw the name on the caller ID, his blood ran cold.

CHAPTER 28

THE CALL THAT CHANGED EVERYTHING

Nikhil's hand froze above the phone, his heart hammering in his chest. The name on the caller ID shouldn't have been there. Not now. Not like this.

It was Mr. Verma.

For a split second, Nikhil debated letting it go to voicemail. What could he possibly say that Nikhil didn't already know? The pressure, the expectations, the thin ice they were skating on—none of it needed more clarification.

But he knew he couldn't ignore it. Whatever this call was, it couldn't be good.

He hesitated for just a breath longer, glancing at Priya, who stood frozen by the conference table, her eyes wide with unspoken fear. She knew as well as he did—this was the call that could end it all.

Nikhil took a deep breath and pressed answer.

"Mr. Verma," he said, trying to keep his voice steady, though his throat felt tight.

"Nikhil," Verma's voice was smooth, too smooth. It sent a chill down Nikhil's spine. "I wanted to have a quick conversation regarding the progress."

Here it comes. The knife twisting. The final blow. Nikhil braced himself, forcing the words out. "Of course, Mr. Verma. We've been working hard on the adjustments you asked for. There's still some work to be done, but we're on track to show you substantial progress before the deadline."

There was a pause. Nikhil could hear the faint hum of the line, but nothing else. The silence stretched on, long enough to make his pulse quicken.

"Nikhil," Verma said finally, his voice lowering to something almost conspiratorial. "I'm going to be blunt. We've been speaking with another firm. They've made us an offer—one that's hard to ignore."

Nikhil's heart stopped. Another firm? No. Not now. Not when they were so close. This couldn't be happening. They had worked too hard, given up too much to let it all slip away.

"I understand your concerns, Mr. Verma," Nikhil replied, struggling to keep the desperation out of his voice. "But we're committed to delivering exactly what you're looking for. We've made significant progress. I believe we can still meet your expectations."

Verma's sigh crackled over the line. "I'm sure you're trying your best, but business is business, Nikhil. And right now, we need more than promises. We need results."

Nikhil gripped the edge of the table, the words echoing in his mind. Results. They needed results, and they needed them now. But how? How could they deliver when they were already running on empty, with nothing left to give?

Before he could respond, Verma continued. "Look, I'm not pulling the plug—yet. You've got one last chance. I'll give you one more week. If I don't see something concrete by then, we're moving forward with the other firm. This is it, Nikhil. One week."

One week.

Nikhil's mouth went dry. "Thank you, Mr. Verma," he said, barely able to push the words out. "You won't regret this. We'll make sure you see the progress you're expecting."

Verma didn't reply right away. Then, with a clipped tone, he said, "I certainly hope so."

The call ended with a deafening click. Nikhil stood there, staring at the phone in his hand, the words one week echoing in his mind like a death sentence.

He turned to Priya, who was already pacing the room, her face pale. "One week?" she asked, her voice barely above a whisper.

Nikhil nodded, feeling the weight of it settle in his chest. "One week."

Priya stopped pacing, her eyes wide with disbelief. "We're not ready, Nikhil. We're not even close. How are we supposed to pull this off in a week?"

Nikhil didn't have an answer. He didn't have a plan. All he had was the crushing knowledge that they were on the verge of losing everything—and time was slipping away faster than they could keep up.

"We'll figure it out," Nikhil said finally, though even he didn't believe it. How could they possibly figure it out?

But before either of them could say another word, Nikhil's phone buzzed again. Another notification.

This time it wasn't Verma. It was from the new client.

Priya, standing on edge, stared at him as he looked down at the message. Everything froze.

"We're terminating the contract, effective immediately. Our decision is final."

Nikhil felt the air leave his lungs. Terminating the contract? No. No, no, no. This couldn't be happening. Not now. Not when they had just secured another week with Verma.

"What?" Priya's voice broke the silence, her eyes scanning his face for a hint of what was wrong.

"They're pulling out," Nikhil said, his voice barely a whisper. He felt like he was drowning, the walls of the conference room closing in around him.

Priya's hand went to her mouth. "The new client?

They—"

"Terminated. Effective immediately."

The words hung in the air, each one heavier than the last.

Nikhil could feel the weight crushing him from all sides. Everything was falling apart. The new client was gone, and if they didn't meet Verma's impossible demands within a week, BizBoost would collapse.

"How are we supposed to—" Priya began, but Nikhil cut her off.

"I don't know!" he snapped, louder than he intended. He closed his eyes, trying to calm the storm raging inside him. "I don't know," he repeated, softer this time. He didn't have any answers. All he knew was that they were running out of time, and the clock was ticking louder than ever.

There was a long silence between them. Priya was still standing, her hand trembling slightly as she lowered it from her face. The entire team was at their limit, and now the cracks were widening into gaping holes.

"We've got one week, Priya," Nikhil said finally, his voice low but urgent. "One week to save BizBoost."

Priya stared at him, her eyes filled with fear and exhaustion. But there was something else there too—resolve. She nodded slowly, her expression hardening. "Then we'll give everything we have."

Nikhil stood there for a long moment, letting the enormity of it settle in. One week. It wasn't enough time. It was never enough time. But they didn't have a choice.

"Call the team," he said finally. "We need an emergency meeting. We can't afford to lose a single minute."

Priya nodded and left the room, leaving Nikhil alone with his thoughts. One week. That was all they had left. Everything hinged on what they could pull off in the next seven days.

He walked to the window, staring out at the city below, the lights flickering in the distance. How had it come to this? They had been so close—so close to success. But now, everything was unraveling, faster than he could control.

The door to the conference room swung open, and the team began to trickle in. Their faces were grim, their eyes filled with the same exhaustion that had haunted them for weeks.

Nikhil turned to face them, feeling the weight of their expectations pressing down on him like a vice. This was it. Their last chance.

Before he could begin, the door swung open again, and Anuj walked in, his face pale, his eyes locked on Nikhil.

"What is it?" Nikhil asked, his stomach sinking at the look on Anuj's face.

Anuj didn't answer right away. He walked across the room, stopping just in front of Nikhil. His voice, when he finally spoke, was low, barely above a whisper.

"There's something you need to know."

CHAPTER 29

HIGH STAKES AGREEMENT

Nikhil's hand froze over his phone as the name on the screen burned into his mind. This wasn't supposed to happen. Not now.

The name glaring back at him wasn't Verma. It wasn't the new client. It was Anil Bhatia—one of BizBoost's early investors, a man who had taken a significant risk to back Nikhil's startup when it was nothing more than an idea and a vision.

Why was Anil calling?

His heart pounded as he hit the answer button, every nerve on edge. Priya, watching from across the table, had already seen the shift in his expression. She stood motionless, waiting, knowing something was about to happen. Something big.

"Anil," Nikhil said, trying to keep his voice steady. But it cracked, betraying the rising panic he was fighting to contain.

There was a pause on the other end, long enough for the tension to ratchet up another notch. Then, Anil spoke, his voice cool but unmistakably sharp. "Nikhil, we need to talk. And I'm not talking about a catch-up over coffee."

Nikhil swallowed, his throat dry. "What's going on, Anil?"

"You know exactly what's going on," Anil replied, his tone hardening. "We've been patient—more patient than most would have been. But we can't ignore the numbers any longer."

The numbers.

Nikhil's pulse quickened. The financials had been bleeding for months. BizBoost had been burning through cash reserves, trying to keep the team together, trying to meet impossible deadlines. And now, with the new client pulling out and Verma tightening the noose, they were running out of lifelines.

"What are you saying?" Nikhil asked, his voice strained.

Anil didn't mince words. "I'm saying we're running out of reasons to keep supporting you. We've invested heavily, and right now, the only thing we're seeing is red. The board's asking questions, and frankly, so am I. I need to know if you're going to turn this around, or if we need to start considering other options."

Nikhil felt the room spin. Other options? That was code for pulling out—taking what little remained of their investment and leaving BizBoost to fend for itself. If Anil pulled his funding, it wouldn't just be a blow—it would be the death blow.

"Anil, listen to me," Nikhil said quickly, his heart hammering in his chest. "We've hit a rough patch, but we're on the verge of a major breakthrough. Verma's project is almost there. The new client—"

"—has just terminated their contract," Anil cut in sharply.

Nikhil froze. How did he know? How did he know already?

"I've been hearing things, Nikhil. I've got my ear to the ground, and what I'm hearing isn't good. I know about the new client pulling out, and I know Verma's team is losing confidence. So tell me—what exactly is your plan?"

The question hit Nikhil like a sledgehammer. His plan? He didn't have one. Not a real one. Everything he had been doing felt like scrambling, trying to plug holes in a sinking ship while the water kept rising.

He glanced over at Priya, her eyes filled with unspoken fear. She couldn't hear what Anil was saying, but she could see the desperation on Nikhil's face.

"Anil, you know how much this company means to me. I'm not going to let it fall apart," Nikhil said, his voice hoarse. "We've faced challenges before, but we always pull through. We're on the brink of closing a huge deal with Verma. We've bought more time, and in a week, we'll have the progress they need to see. Just... trust me."

"Trust you?" Anil's voice was sharp, cutting through Nikhil's words like a blade. "I've trusted you for years, Nikhil. But my patience isn't infinite. Neither is the board's. If you don't deliver in the next week, we're pulling out. That's your reality now. You've got one week to prove to me and the board that BizBoost is worth saving. Otherwise, we're cutting our losses."

Nikhil gripped the edge of the table, the words sinking in like a weight on his chest. One week. He had one week, and if he failed, it wasn't just Verma who would walk away. It was everyone.

"I understand," Nikhil said, his voice low, barely above a whisper.

"Good," Anil replied, his tone icy. "I hope for your sake you can pull this off. Because if you can't... there won't be anything left to save."

The line went dead, leaving Nikhil standing in the empty conference room, his hand trembling as he set the phone down. One week. That was all the time they had to save BizBoost from complete collapse.

"Nikhil?" Priya's voice was quiet, barely more than a whisper. She had been watching the whole time, reading the fear on his face.

Nikhil looked up at her, his mind racing, his heart pounding in his chest. "That was Anil. He... He gave us an ultimatum."

"What do you mean?" Priya asked, stepping closer.

"I mean we have one week. One week to prove we can turn this around, or the investors pull out. If that happens... we're done. It's over."

The words hung in the air, thick and suffocating.

Priya stared at him, her face pale, the weight of what he'd just said settling over them both. "One week?" she repeated, her voice tight with disbelief.

Nikhil nodded slowly, his mind spiraling. Everything was collapsing. He had thought Verma's deadline was the worst of it, but now it wasn't just Verma. It was the investors, the entire future of BizBoost hanging by a thread.

"We need to talk to the team," Priya said finally, her voice steadying. "They need to know what's at stake."

Nikhil nodded, though his body felt numb. He wasn't sure if he could face them—not now, not when the weight of everything felt like it was crushing him. But he had no choice. This was it. The final push.

The team sat in silence as Nikhil stood in front of them, the tension in the room thick enough to cut with a knife. They already knew things were bad—everyone had been feeling the strain for weeks. But no one was prepared for what Nikhil was about to tell them.

"We have one week," Nikhil began, his voice heavy with the gravity of the situation. "One week to turn everything around. Verma's given us a final deadline, and now the investors have too. If we don't deliver... if we don't show major progress... we lose everything."

A murmur of disbelief rippled through the room. Anuj, who had been sitting with his arms crossed, staring at the floor, looked up sharply. "One week?" he repeated, his voice hard. "How are we supposed to pull that off?"

Nikhil swallowed hard, feeling the weight of their eyes on him. How were they supposed to pull it off? He didn't know. But they had no choice.

"I know it sounds impossible," Nikhil said, his voice tight with emotion. "But this is it. We're out of time, and we're out of options. We have to give everything we've got—push harder than we've ever pushed before. We've pulled off impossible things before. We can do it again."

The room was silent. No one looked convinced. They were exhausted. Burnt out. And now they were being asked to give more than they had ever given before.

"This isn't just about Verma," Priya said, stepping forward. "If we fail, BizBoost collapses. All of it. Everything we've worked for. But if we fight for it—if we push through this—we can save it. We can save all of it."

Anuj leaned back in his chair, staring at the ceiling. "And if we can't?"

Nikhil felt the room shift, the question lingering in the air.

"If we can't..." Nikhil began, his voice quiet, "then we lose it all."

CHAPTER 30

AGAINST THE CLOCK

The clock on the wall ticked like a countdown to disaster. Every minute that passed felt like sand slipping through Nikhil's fingers, and every breath he took seemed heavier than the last. One week. One week to turn everything around, or everything he had built would be destroyed.

The team filed out of the conference room in silence, their faces drained of color. No one had said much after the meeting ended. There was nothing left to say. They all knew what was at stake now—everything.

Priya lingered behind, her arms crossed, watching Nikhil carefully. "They're scared," she said quietly, her voice barely above a whisper.

Nikhil didn't respond. They weren't just scared. They were defeated. He could see it in their eyes, in the way they moved, like they were already bracing for the collapse. But what terrified him more than anything was that a part of him felt the same way. Defeated.

"We're going to lose them if we're not careful," Priya added, stepping closer. "They're running on empty. If we push too hard, they'll crack."

"We don't have a choice," Nikhil muttered, his voice tight. "This is it. We either push, or we die."

Priya looked at him for a long moment, her expression unreadable. "Pushing isn't always the answer," she said softly. "Sometimes... you have to step back and see the bigger picture."

Nikhil wanted to snap back, to tell her there was no time for stepping back. But before he could say anything, Priya's phone buzzed. She glanced down at the screen and her face blanched. "It's Verma," she said, showing him the caller ID.

Nikhil's stomach clenched. Not now. Not again.

Priya answered, her voice steady. "Mr. Verma, good to hear from you."

Nikhil could hear the voice on the other end, sharp and authoritative. He couldn't make out the words, but the tone was enough to send a shiver down his spine.

"Yes, I understand," Priya said, nodding slowly. Her eyes flicked to Nikhil, and he could see the tension tightening in her jaw.

Another few seconds of silence. Then Priya's face fell. "Of course. We'll... we'll address that immediately."

Nikhil's pulse quickened. What now? What had gone wrong this time?

Priya ended the call, her hand trembling as she lowered the phone. "Verma's team isn't happy with the latest update. They said it's not even close to what they expected. They want a full revision by tomorrow."

Nikhil felt the floor drop out from under him. Tomorrow? How were they supposed to pull off a full revision by tomorrow when they were barely holding things together as it was?

"That's impossible," he said, his voice raw. "They can't be serious."

Priya nodded, her face pale. "They are. And they're not just unhappy, Nikhil. They're furious. If we don't deliver something concrete by tomorrow, they're walking."

Nikhil's mind raced, his pulse pounding in his ears. How could they possibly fix everything in less than

24 hours? The team was already on the brink of collapse. If he pushed them any harder, they might break completely.

"We have no choice," Nikhil said, his voice hoarse. "We have to pull an all-nighter. Everyone. We need to get the team back in here."

Priya's eyes widened. "Nikhil, the team is exhausted. They haven't recovered from the last stretch. If you force them to stay here all night—"

"We don't have a choice!" Nikhil snapped, louder than he meant to. The words echoed in the empty conference room, the weight of them hanging in the air.

Priya took a step back, her face hardening. "You can't keep doing this. You can't keep pushing them like this. They're people, Nikhil, not machines."

Nikhil stared at her, the words rattling in his mind. Not machines. But they didn't have time for anything else. They didn't have time to stop and care.

"We'll lose everything if we don't push through this," Nikhil said quietly. "If we don't get Verma back on our side, there won't be a company left to save."

Priya held his gaze for a long moment, then shook her head, exhaling slowly. "Fine," she said finally, her voice low. "But if you push too hard and they break, that's on you. You're the one who has to live with that."

Nikhil didn't reply. He couldn't. She was right. But what other choice did he have?

The team trickled back into the office, one by one, their faces heavy with exhaustion and frustration. They didn't ask questions. They didn't argue. They just went to their desks and started working, knowing that tonight would be another battle in the war they were slowly losing.

Nikhil moved between them, checking on progress, offering words of encouragement, but he could see it in their eyes—the weariness, the doubt. They were running out of steam.

By midnight, the office felt like a pressure cooker, the tension thick and suffocating. Anuj had his headphones in, staring at his screen with a look of grim determination, while Priya sat across the room, her fingers flying over the keyboard, the lines of stress etched into her face.

But even as they worked, Nikhil could feel the cracks widening. Something was going to give. He could feel it in the air.

Around 2 a.m., Nikhil's phone buzzed again. Anil.

His heart dropped. Not again.

He stepped outside, the cool night air hitting his face as he answered the call. "Anil," he said, trying to keep his voice steady.

"We're cutting it too close," Anil's voice came through, laced with frustration. "The board's starting to panic. They want to know if you're making any progress with Verma."

Nikhil swallowed hard. "We're working on it. We're pulling an all-nighter to get everything ready. We'll have what they need by tomorrow."

"You better," Anil replied, his voice cold. "Because if Verma pulls out, it's not just BizBoost that's finished—it's your reputation. No one will trust you with another investment. Ever."

The words hit Nikhil like a punch to the gut. His reputation. His future. If BizBoost collapsed, it wouldn't just be a company that died—it would be his career, his name, everything he had spent his life building.

"I understand," Nikhil said, his voice barely above a whisper.

"Good," Anil replied. "I'm giving you one more day.

After that, I'm stepping in personally."

The call ended with a click, leaving Nikhil standing in the empty parking lot, the cold air swirling around him. One more day. That was all the time he had left before everything came crashing down.

He turned back toward the office, his heart pounding in his chest. One more day to save everything.

Inside, the tension had reached a breaking point. Nikhil could see it in the way people moved, the way they looked at him, the way their fingers slowed on the keyboard. They were nearing the edge.

But he couldn't stop now. Not when they were this close.

At 3 a.m., it happened.

Anuj slammed his laptop shut, the sound echoing through the quiet office. Everyone turned to look at him, their eyes wide.

"I'm done," Anuj said, his voice flat, his face pale. "I can't do this anymore."

Nikhil's heart stopped. "Anuj, wait—"

"No." Anuj shook his head, standing up. "You keep telling us to push harder, to give more, but there's nothing left to give, Nikhil. We're done. I'm done."

Priya stood up slowly, her face tense. "Anuj, you're tired. Let's just take a break—"

"A break?" Anuj laughed bitterly. "There's no break. There's just more work, more deadlines, more impossible expectations. Nikhil keeps telling us we're going to pull this off, but we're not. We're just spinning our wheels, pretending like we can save this company when we all know it's already dead."

Nikhil felt the weight of Anuj's words hit him like a sledgehammer. Was he right? Was it already over?

"Anuj, please," Nikhil said, his voice shaking. "Just... just give it a little more time. We're so close."

Anuj stared at him for a long moment, his eyes filled with something Nikhil hadn't seen before—pity.

"I'm sorry, Nikhil," Anuj said quietly. "But I'm done."

He turned and walked out of the office, leaving Nikhil standing frozen in place, watching the door slowly close behind him. The sound of Anuj's footsteps echoed down the hallway, fading into the silence. Gone. Just like that, one of Nikhil's most loyal, hardworking teammates had walked away—and he didn't blame him.

Priya stood beside Nikhil, her face pale, her hands trembling as she watched Anuj disappear. The room was suffocating, the weight of his exit hanging over them all like a dark cloud. The rest of the team sat in stunned silence, too tired and too shocked to speak. Anuj was their rock, the one who had held everything together during the worst of it—and now he was gone.

Nikhil turned away, unable to look at the empty spot where Anuj had been. His mind raced, his pulse pounding in his ears. He couldn't think. He couldn't breathe.

"This is it, isn't it?" Priya's voice cut through the thick silence, shaking him from his spiraling thoughts.

"What do you mean?" Nikhil asked, though the answer was already clawing at the back of his mind.

Priya sighed; her eyes heavy with the same weight that was crushing Nikhil. "You heard him. We're running on fumes. The team is breaking, Nikhil. If Anuj—Anuj—walked out, how long until the rest of us follow?"

Her words cut deep, like a knife twisting in his gut. How long until the rest of them follow? He knew they were all close to the edge, that he had been pushing them harder than they could handle. But there was no way out. No escape. They either kept pushing or everything they had built would collapse around them.

"We're not there yet," Nikhil said, though his voice was hoarse, the words weak. "We still have time."

Priya shook her head slowly, her eyes filled with an unbearable sadness. "Do we? Because I don't know how much more I can give, either."

Nikhil stared at her, his heart hammering in his chest. Priya too? She had always been the one who stayed strong, the one who held the team together when things got bad. If even Priya was close to breaking, what hope did they have?

"I'll talk to him," Nikhil said, his voice barely a whisper. "I'll talk to Anuj. I'll make him understand—"

"He understands," Priya cut him off, her voice sharp with frustration. "We all do. You're asking us for more than we can give, Nikhil. You keep telling us that we're close, that we're going to pull this off. But you've seen the same numbers we have. The project is a mess. Verma's about to walk. And now we've got one week left to save everything? It's not enough."

Nikhil clenched his fists, his chest tightening. "It's all we have."

Priya stepped closer, her voice softening. "Nikhil, we can't keep pretending that everything's going to be okay. It's not. The team can't take much more of this. You're asking them to push beyond their breaking point."

Nikhil shook his head, the panic rising in his throat. He couldn't accept that. He couldn't accept that they were this close to losing everything.

"We can still do this," he said, his voice shaking with desperation. "We just need to hang on a little longer."

Priya's eyes softened, the hard edge in her voice fading. She reached out and put a hand on his shoulder. "We're human, Nikhil. We're not machines. We can't keep this up."

Nikhil stared at her, his chest heaving, the weight of her words pressing down on him like a ton of bricks. Human. Not machines. But he needed them to be machines. He needed them to push harder, to go further than they thought they could. Because if they didn't...

"Take a break," Priya said quietly, her eyes filled with sympathy. "You need it as much as the rest of us."

Nikhil shook his head again, faster this time. "No. I can't. Not now."

But Priya didn't argue. She just watched him, her expression unreadable, before turning and walking out of the room, leaving him alone with the crushing silence.

Nikhil sat in his office, the dim light of the computer screen casting long shadows across his face. The hours were slipping by, and with each minute, the sense of impending doom grew heavier. Anuj's words haunted him, echoing in his mind. *We're spinning our wheels... pretending like we can save this company...*

His phone buzzed on the desk. Anil. Again.

He knew what was coming. More pressure. More threats. More reminders that they were out of time. But Nikhil couldn't bring himself to answer. He couldn't hear it right now.

Instead, he stared at the spreadsheet on his screen, the numbers blurring together. The project was a mess. Priya was right about that. Verma wasn't going to be satisfied with anything they gave him. Not in its current state. But they had no time left to fix it.

He rubbed his eyes, exhaustion clawing at him. His mind felt foggy, his thoughts tangled in a web of fear and frustration. There had to be a way out. There had to be a way to pull this off.

But every path he saw led to a dead end.

The door to his office creaked open, and Nikhil looked up, expecting Priya. But it wasn't her.

It was Anuj. Nikhil's heart skipped a beat. Anuj stood in the doorway, his face pale, his eyes filled with an unreadable emotion.

"What are you doing here?" Nikhil asked, his voice tight.

Anuj didn't answer right away. He stepped into the office, closing the door softly behind him, before turning to face Nikhil. "I needed to talk to you."

Nikhil sat up straighter, hope flickering in his chest. "Anuj, listen. I know things are bad, but we're not done yet. We can still—"

"I didn't leave because I was tired," Anuj interrupted, his voice low but steady. "I left because I've seen something. Something you need to know."

Nikhil frowned, confusion swirling in his mind. "What are you talking about?"

Anuj took a deep breath, his hands trembling slightly. "Nikhil... Verma's already made a deal with the other firm."

Nikhil's heart stopped. What?

"They've been working with them behind the scenes for weeks," Anuj continued, his voice tight with anger. "Verma's been playing us. They were never going to stick with BizBoost."

Nikhil's pulse raced, his mind spinning. "How do you know this?"

"I have a contact," Anuj said, his voice hardening. "Someone on Verma's team. They confirmed it. Verma's been stringing us along, keeping us distracted while they finalized their deal with the other firm. They're pulling the plug on us, Nikhil."

The room tilted, the walls closing in. This couldn't be happening. After everything they'd done, everything they'd sacrificed, Verma had been playing them all along?

"They're walking away," Anuj said quietly, the words like a dagger in Nikhil's chest. "It's over."

Nikhil stared at him, the weight of the truth crashing down on him like a tidal wave. Over. The word echoed in his mind, hollow and final.

"All of this," Anuj continued, his voice filled with quiet rage, "the all-nighters, the pressure, the sacrifices... it was all for nothing."

Nikhil couldn't breathe. His chest felt tight, his vision blurring. No. This couldn't be real. This couldn't be how it ended.

But it was.

Verma had already made his choice. And they had lost.

CHAPTER 31

A CRUMBLING FOUNDATION

Nikhil sat frozen, his mind spiraling in the wake of Anuj's revelation. Verma had already made his choice. The hours, the sleepless nights, the sacrifices—all for nothing.

His hands trembled as he gripped the edge of the desk, staring at Anuj, the weight of the truth crushing him. How could this be happening? Everything they had been fighting for was gone. Verma had played them like pawns, stringing them along while quietly finalizing a deal with another firm. BizBoost was hanging on by a thread, and now even that thread was frayed beyond repair.

Anuj's words echoed in his mind: *It's over.*

Nikhil shook his head, refusing to believe it. "We... we can still fix this," he stammered, his voice barely audible. "Maybe if we—"

"There's nothing left to fix," Anuj interrupted, his tone flat, but beneath the calmness, there was a seething anger. "They've moved on, Nikhil. Verma's just waiting for the right moment to drop us officially. We're not even in the game anymore."

Nikhil's chest tightened as reality sank in. He had lost. The sinking feeling in his stomach was undeniable, but some part of him—a part built on years of resilience—wasn't ready to give up.

He stood up suddenly, his movements abrupt. "No.

We still have a chance. We need to fight."

Anuj's eyes flickered with something between disbelief and pity. "Fight for what? A contract that's already been handed to someone else? You're in denial, Nikhil. I know you've always fought for BizBoost, but sometimes fighting isn't enough. Verma played us—and we lost."

Nikhil felt his pulse quicken, his thoughts racing as he paced the room. "There has to be something we can do. Maybe... maybe we can confront them. Expose what they did. If they've been negotiating behind our backs—"

"Stop!" Anuj's voice boomed, cutting through the air like a whip. The force of it made Nikhil freeze in place. "This isn't about exposing them or saving face. This is about survival. And right now, BizBoost is dead in the water. The longer you pretend otherwise, the harder it's going to be to pick up the pieces."

Silence fell between them, thick and suffocating. Nikhil's heart raced, the weight of Anuj's words crashing over him like a tidal wave. He wanted to argue, to fight back, to keep clinging to the belief that there was still something to salvage. But the look in Anuj's eyes—tired, frustrated, defeated—told him otherwise.

Anuj had always been the realist. The one who saw things as they were, not as they should be. And in this moment, Nikhil could see that Anuj had already accepted what he was desperately trying to deny.

"What do we do now?" Nikhil asked, his voice cracking.

Anuj took a deep breath, the tension in his shoulders finally releasing. "We regroup. We cut our losses and start thinking about damage control."

"Damage control?" The words felt foreign to Nikhil, like a language he didn't understand. "We're not just talking about a project, Anuj. We're talking about the entire company. Everything we've built."

Anuj nodded slowly. "I know. And that's why we need to stop chasing ghosts and start figuring out how to move forward—without Verma."

Nikhil stared at him, his mind whirling. How could they move forward without Verma? The Verma deal had been their lifeline. Without it, the company was on the verge of collapse. The investors would pull out, and everything would unravel faster than they could react.

"There's no moving forward without this deal," Nikhil said, his voice strained. "If Verma walks, so do our investors. Anil's already breathing down our necks." Anuj sighed, running a hand through his hair. "I know. But chasing after something that's already gone isn't going to save us. We need to be smart about this."

Nikhil turned toward the window, staring out into the night. Smart. Was that what he had been all this time? Or had he been reckless, pushing too hard, betting everything on one deal while the rest of the business slowly fell apart?

His phone buzzed on the desk again—another message from Anil. Nikhil didn't have to read it to know what it said. More pressure. More threats. Anil had already given them a final warning, and now, with Verma out of the picture, Nikhil knew exactly what would happen next.

The investors would pull the plug. And BizBoost would collapse.

By the time Nikhil stepped out of his office, the team was already in the trenches—working late, yet again, oblivious to the full weight of what was happening behind the scenes. Priya caught his eye from across the room, her face tense with concern. She knew something was wrong.

Nikhil motioned for her to join him, and the moment they stepped into the hallway, the dam broke.

"What is it?" Priya asked, her voice hushed but urgent. "What happened in there with Anuj?" Nikhil rubbed his temples, the exhaustion finally catching up with him. "Verma's gone. They've already signed with another firm."

Priya's eyes widened, shock flashing across her face. "What?"

"They've been stringing us along, waiting for the right moment to drop us. It's over, Priya. We've lost the contract."

For a moment, Priya stood frozen, disbelief washing over her. Then, slowly, her expression shifted to something darker—a mix of anger and resignation. "So, what now?"

Nikhil exhaled sharply, the weight of it pressing down on him like a lead blanket. "I don't know. Anuj says we need to regroup. Figure out a way forward without Verma."

"Without Verma?" Priya's voice was sharp, incredulous. "How? That deal was the only thing keeping us afloat. If they walk, Anil and the other investors will follow. We're finished."

"I know," Nikhil said, his voice barely above a whisper. "But Anuj's right. We can't chase something that's already gone. We have to figure out what comes next."

"What comes next?" Priya repeated, her voice rising. "Nikhil, we don't have time to figure out what comes next. The investors aren't going to give us more time. They'll shut us down before we can even—"

She stopped, catching herself, her eyes locking with Nikhil's. They both knew the truth. BizBoost was hanging by a thread, and that thread was unraveling faster than either of them could control.

"We're out of time," Priya said quietly. "We've been out of time for a while now."

Nikhil nodded slowly, his throat tight. "I know."

The silence between them was heavy, filled with the weight of everything they had built and everything they were about to lose. The hum of the office behind them felt distant, like a ghost of the company that had once thrived.

Priya looked away, her voice softening. "What are we going to tell the team?"

Nikhil closed his eyes, the question swirling in his mind like a storm. What could they tell them? The truth? That everything they had been working for was about to collapse? That no matter how hard they worked, no matter how many hours they put in, it wouldn't be enough?

"I don't know," he said finally, his voice barely a whisper. "I don't know what to say."

Priya turned back toward the office, the weight of the situation etched into every line of her face.

"We can't keep this from them for long, Nikhil. They deserve to know what's coming."

Nikhil nodded, though every fiber of his being resisted the thought of breaking the news to his team. Telling them would make it real. It would mean acknowledging that BizBoost was on the verge of collapse, that there was no last-minute miracle waiting to save them.

"I'll figure it out," Nikhil said finally, though the words felt hollow. "But for now... we just keep moving forward."

Priya gave him a long, searching look before nodding slowly. "Okay."

But as she walked back into the office, Nikhil couldn't shake the gnawing feeling in his gut. Moving forward to what? A slow death? Or the moment when the investors finally pulled the rug out from under them?

His phone buzzed again. Another message from Anil.

Nikhil didn't read it.

Instead, he turned and walked back into his office, closing the door behind him.

CHAPTER 32

THE EDGE OF THE ABYSS

The office felt colder than usual. The kind of cold that had nothing to do with the temperature but everything to do with the atmosphere. Nikhil could feel it—the weight of what was about to happen.

Sitting at his desk, he stared at his phone, which had been vibrating non-stop with emails and messages from Anil and other investors. He couldn't bring himself to open any of them. What more could they say that he didn't already know? The clock was ticking, and time was running out. Any minute now, everything could come crashing down.

The knot in his stomach tightened, and his chest felt heavy, like someone had tied weights around his heart. He had promised his team, his investors—everyone—that he would make BizBoost a success. But here he was, staring down the barrel of failure.

The door to his office creaked open, and Priya stepped inside, her face etched with concern. "Nikhil, we need to talk."

He looked up at her, his thoughts still clouded by the whirlwind of emotions he was trying to suppress. "What is it?"

Priya glanced back toward the door, as if checking to make sure no one was listening, before walking over to his desk. She leaned in, her voice barely above a whisper. "There's a problem with payroll."

Nikhil's heart skipped a beat. "What kind of problem?"

She sighed, running a hand through her hair. "We don't have enough to cover the next round of salaries. The cash flow... it's dried up. Between the money we spent on trying to keep Verma happy and the new client's termination, there's nothing left."

Nikhil stared at her, his blood running cold. No money for payroll? That was the last thing they needed. If the team found out they weren't getting paid, the few who had stuck around would walk out for good.

"How long do we have?" he asked, his voice hoarse.

Priya hesitated, biting her lip. "We can delay payments for a week, maybe two at most. But after that..."

She didn't need to finish. After that, there would be nothing left.

Nikhil leaned back in his chair, the weight of the situation pressing down on him even harder. No payroll. No Verma deal. No investors willing to stick around. The walls were closing in, faster and faster, and he couldn't see a way out.

"What do we do?" he asked, his voice barely audible.

Priya shook her head, her eyes filled with a mixture of sympathy and frustration. "I don't know, Nikhil. I really don't. We've pushed this as far as we can, but the truth is, without a miracle, BizBoost is going under."

Her words hit him like a sledgehammer. Going under. That was it, wasn't it? The end of everything. The years of work, the sleepless nights, the sacrifices—all of it crumbling before his eyes.

For a long time, neither of them spoke. The silence was deafening, filled with the weight of the unspoken truth. Nikhil could feel his hands trembling, his mind racing for solutions that simply weren't there.

"We have to tell the team," Priya said softly, breaking the silence. "They deserve to know."

Nikhil's chest tightened. Tell the team? How could he look them in the eye and tell them that everything they had worked for was about to disappear? That they wouldn't be getting paid, and that their jobs were hanging by a thread?

He swallowed hard, trying to push down the rising panic. "Let me... let me think for a minute. There has to be something we can do."

Priya watched him carefully, her eyes searching his face for any sign of hope. But there was none. Finally, she nodded, her voice soft. "Alright. But we don't have much time."

As she turned to leave, Nikhil felt a surge of desperation rise in his chest. This couldn't be how it ended. There had to be a way out. There had to be something he hadn't thought of.

But what?

The truth hit him like a tidal wave: He had nothing. No backup plan, no secret weapon, no lifeline. BizBoost was teetering on the edge of the abyss, and he was powerless to stop it.

The next few hours passed in a blur of frantic emails, tense phone calls, and more bad news. Every conversation seemed to end the same way—with no solution in sight. The investors were getting restless, demanding answers that Nikhil didn't have. The pressure was mounting, and with every passing minute, the walls seemed to close in tighter.

By late afternoon, Nikhil was running on pure adrenaline, his nerves frayed, his body aching from exhaustion. He hadn't slept in days, and it was starting to show. His mind felt foggy, his thoughts jumbled, and yet he couldn't stop. He had to keep pushing forward, even though he knew, deep down, that it was futile.

As he sat at his desk, staring blankly at the screen, his phone buzzed again. He didn't have the energy to check it. Another message from Anil, no doubt. More threats. More pressure.

Suddenly, there was a knock on the door. Nikhil looked up, his vision blurry, and saw Priya standing in the doorway again, her face pale.

"Nikhil," she said quietly, "they're here."

Nikhil frowned, his mind struggling to catch up. "Who's here?"

She hesitated for a moment, her hands gripping the doorframe. "The investors. Anil and the others. They want to talk. In person."

Nikhil's heart dropped. In person? That could only mean one thing—they were here to shut him down.

He stood up slowly, his legs feeling weak beneath him. "How long have they been here?"

"They just arrived," Priya said, her voice trembling slightly. "They're in the conference room."

Nikhil nodded, his mind reeling. This was it. The final confrontation. The moment he had been dreading for weeks. He glanced around his office, the reality of the situation finally hitting him with full force. This could be the last time he stood in this room.

Without a word, he walked past Priya and headed toward the conference room, his heart pounding in his chest. With every step, the walls seemed to close in tighter, the weight of everything pressing down on him like never before.

When he reached the door, he paused, taking a deep breath. Anil and the other investors were waiting on the other side. Waiting to deliver the final blow. Nikhil's hands trembled as he reached for the door handle, his mind racing with a thousand thoughts, none of them helpful.

This was it. The end of BizBoost. And there was nothing he could do to stop it.

With a final breath, Nikhil opened the door and stepped inside.

The room was eerily quiet. Anil sat at the head of the table, flanked by two other investors, their faces set in cold, stony expressions. The tension was thick, almost suffocating, and Nikhil felt the weight of their eyes on him the moment he entered.

He forced a smile, though it felt hollow, and walked to the opposite end of the table. "Anil," he said, his voice tight. "I didn't expect to see you in person."

Anil didn't return the smile. His eyes were hard, unyielding. "We thought it was time for a face-to-face discussion," he said, his voice sharp.

Nikhil swallowed hard, trying to keep his composure. This was it. The moment of reckoning. He could feel the walls closing in around him, the pressure building to a breaking point.

"We need to talk about the future of BizBoost," Anil continued, his voice cold and formal. "Specifically, whether there is a future."

Nikhil's heart sank. Whether there is a future. The words echoed in his mind, hollow and final.

He had known this moment was coming, but that didn't make it any easier. He sat down slowly, his mind scrambling for something—anything—that could change the course of the conversation. But there was nothing.

Anil leaned forward, his eyes locked on Nikhil. "You've run out of time. The Verma deal is gone. The new client pulled out. We've been patient, but we're not seeing any return on our investment. The board wants to know what your plan is to turn this around—or if it's time to cut our losses."

Nikhil stared at him, his mind blank. A plan. They wanted a plan. But how could he give them a plan when everything had already fallen apart?

His throat tightened, his chest aching with the weight of the impossible situation. He had always been the one with the answers, the one who found a way out. But now, he was staring down the barrel of defeat, with no lifeline in sight.

"I... I don't have a plan," Nikhil said quietly, his voice shaking. Anil's expression didn't change. If anything, his eyes grew colder.

"We invested in you, Nikhil, because we believed in your vision," Anil said, his voice sharp but controlled. "But belief only takes you so far. At some point, it has to translate into results—and we're not seeing those results. The numbers don't lie."

Nikhil's heart pounded. Results. That was what they wanted, and it was the one thing he couldn't deliver. Not now. Not with everything crumbling around him.

Anil leaned forward, his elbows resting on the table, his eyes locked on Nikhil's. "So, let me ask you again—what's your plan?"

The silence that followed was suffocating. Nikhil glanced at the other investors, hoping to find a glimmer of understanding, of patience. But their faces were hard, unyielding, and the pressure mounted with every second.

Finally, Nikhil spoke, his voice barely more than a whisper. "I... I don't have one."

For a moment, no one said anything. Anil's gaze remained fixed, unwavering. Then, leaning back in his chair, he folded his arms across his chest. "Then we have a problem."

Nikhil's heart sank. A problem. That was putting it mildly. The truth was, this was more than a problem—it was the end of the road.

"We've been more than patient," one of the other investors, Suresh, said from across the table. His tone was measured, but the edge in his words was unmistakable. "We've given you time, resources, and support. But it's clear that BizBoost isn't moving in the direction we'd hoped."

Nikhil felt the words like punches to his chest, each one hitting harder than the last. They were right. The numbers weren't there. The Verma deal had fallen apart, the new client had pulled out. And now, they were done with waiting.

"I need more time," Nikhil said, his voice trembling with desperation. "If I can just—"

"We've run out of time," Anil interrupted, his voice cold. "We're not sinking any more money into a sinking ship."

Nikhil flinched at the harshness of his words. A sinking ship. That's what BizBoost had become. And there was nothing he could do to stop it from going under.

"The board has decided to pull out," Anil continued, his voice emotionless. "Effective immediately."

Nikhil's world stopped. Pull out? The words hit him like a physical blow, leaving him breathless.

"You can't," Nikhil said, his voice cracking. "If you pull out now, BizBoost won't survive."

Anil's expression didn't change. "I know."

The finality of his words crushed Nikhil. This was it. The moment he had feared. The moment when everything would come crashing down. Everything he had worked for, sacrificed for—it was all gone.

"I've given everything for this company," Nikhil said, his voice barely above a whisper. "Everything."

Anil's eyes softened for a brief second, but it was fleeting. "I know you have," he said quietly. "But sometimes, giving everything isn't enough."

The silence in the room was suffocating. Nikhil sat there, staring at the faces of the men who had once believed in him, who had once trusted him to lead BizBoost to success. And now, they were walking away.

"We'll give you time to wind things down," Suresh said, his voice emotionless. "But effective immediately, we're pulling our investment."

Nikhil wanted to scream, to beg, to do something—anything—to stop this from happening. But he knew it was pointless. It was over.

He nodded slowly, his heart heavy. "I understand." Anil stood up, signaling the end of the conversation.

"It's never easy to let go," he said, his tone softer. "But sometimes, it's the only choice."

Nikhil couldn't respond. He watched in silence as the investors gathered their things and walked toward the door, leaving him alone in the room with nothing but the weight of his failure.

As the door clicked shut behind them, the silence was deafening.

Nikhil sat there for a long time, staring blankly at the table. His mind was numb, his body exhausted. Everything was gone. The company he had poured his heart and soul into, the dream he had chased for so long—it had all crumbled to dust.

And there was nothing left to fight for.

For the first time in years, Nikhil felt truly, utterly defeated.

CHAPTER 33

AFTER THE FALL

The air in the room felt thick, almost suffocating. Nikhil stared at his hands, the tremor in his fingers betraying the storm swirling inside him. Everything had led to this moment—the final collapse.

How had it come to this?

The once bustling office that hummed with the energy of ideas and innovation was now silent, almost abandoned. He could hear the distant sounds of a few remaining employees, but even they seemed like ghosts, drifting aimlessly through a ship that was sinking fast.

He felt like he was drowning, each breath heavier than the last. The vision of BizBoost, of everything he had worked for, now seemed like a distant dream, slipping away faster than he could catch it.

Priya's knock on the door felt like a distant echo. When she entered, her face showed the kind of sadness reserved for funerals.

"Nikhil," she said softly, her voice barely above a whisper. "We need to talk."

Nikhil didn't respond. He couldn't. His mind was trapped in a loop, replaying the moment Anil delivered the final blow. We're pulling out. It's over.

"Nikhil, please," Priya pressed, taking a step closer. "The team... they're waiting. They need answers."

He finally looked up at her, his eyes red and heavy with the weight of failure. "What do I tell them, Priya? That everything they've worked for is gone? That I failed them?"

The words left his mouth, but they felt like someone else's. Failure. The one word that had haunted him his whole life. And now it was staring him in the face, mocking him, daring him to rise again—but what was left to rise to?

Priya's eyes softened. She had always been his rock, the steady force that held things together when the pressure mounted. But even she looked defeated now, her eyes darkened by the truth they both didn't want to face.

"You didn't fail them, Nikhil," she said, her voice calm but firm. "You gave everything you had."

"Everything," Nikhil whispered, staring into space. "And what good did it do? We're still sinking."

The silence between them hung heavy, the gravity of the situation pressing down on both of them. Finally, Priya spoke again, her voice barely more than a breath. "You need to tell them, Nikhil. They deserve to hear it from you."

He nodded slowly, knowing she was right. His team, the people who had believed in him, followed him through sleepless nights, through all the impossible deadlines, all the pain, the sacrifices—they deserved more than this. They deserved the truth.

Nikhil rose to his feet, the weight of a thousand failures dragging him down. Every step toward the conference room felt like wading through quicksand. His heart pounded in his chest, the finality of it all looming like a dark cloud.

The team sat in silence, the room unnervingly still. Their faces were a mix of confusion, fear, and the faintest glimmer of hope—a hope Nikhil wasn't sure he could deliver on. They were waiting for him, looking to him for answers. Answers he didn't have.

Nikhil stood at the front of the room, his mouth dry, his hands clenched tightly at his sides. He could feel Priya's presence next to him, her quiet support the only thing keeping him from breaking.

"I..." His voice cracked. This was harder than he thought. His vision blurred, but he forced himself to push through it. "I wish I had better news."

The weight of his words settled over the room like a heavy fog. The team shifted uncomfortably, their eyes wide, searching his face for some shred of optimism, a light at the end of this dark tunnel.

But there was none. "The investors have pulled out," Nikhil continued, each word like a dagger to his own heart. "BizBoost... BizBoost is over."

A stunned silence filled the room, the disbelief hanging in the air like a dark cloud. It felt as if someone had punched the breath out of everyone at once.

"I don't understand," someone muttered from the back of the room. "How... how did this happen?"

Nikhil felt his chest tighten. How had it happened? He had been asking himself the same question over and over again, but there were no easy answers. He had made mistakes. Pushed too hard. Taken too many risks. And now, the consequences were crashing down on him like an avalanche.

"We lost the Verma deal," Nikhil explained, his voice barely audible. "The new client pulled out. We ran out of cash. And... the investors lost faith."

He could see the disbelief in their eyes, the silent anger, the devastation. He had let them down. All of them. And it tore him apart inside.

"What happens to us now?" one of the team members asked, their voice trembling with fear.

Nikhil took a deep breath, the heaviness in his chest almost unbearable. "I don't know."

The words felt like they weren't enough. He wanted to say more, to offer some kind of hope, but the truth was, he didn't have any. There was no road map for this kind of failure.

The room fell silent again, the weight of the situation sinking in. Nikhil could feel the eyes of his team on him, searching for something—anything—that could make this nightmare go away.

But there was nothing left to give.

"I'm sorry," Nikhil whispered, his voice cracking with emotion. "I'm so sorry."

Some of the team members exchanged looks, others stared blankly ahead, unable to process the finality of it all. They had followed him through thick and thin, trusted him to lead them to success, and now they were staring at the wreckage of everything they had worked for.

"I gave everything," Nikhil continued, his throat tight. "But it wasn't enough."

The words hung in the air, heavy and suffocating. They were broken. He could see it in their faces. The disbelief had morphed into something deeper—a profound sense of betrayal.

People began to stand, gathering their things in silence. One by one, they filed out of the conference room, their footsteps echoing through the empty space.

No one said a word.

The door clicked shut behind the last person, leaving Nikhil standing alone in the empty room. His chest felt tight, his hands shaking as the reality of it all finally set in.

This was it. The end.

Priya stepped up beside him, her voice quiet but steady. "It wasn't your fault, Nikhil."

Nikhil shook his head, his voice hoarse. "They trusted me, Priya. And I let them down."

Priya sighed, her hand resting gently on his arm. "You did everything you could. Sometimes, things don't work out, no matter how hard you fight."

Nikhil clenched his fists, his mind racing with a thousand thoughts. What now? What was left for him after this? He had built his life around BizBoost, poured every ounce of himself into it. And now, it was gone.

"I don't know what to do," he admitted, his voice breaking. "I don't know how to move forward from this."

Priya gave him a soft, reassuring smile. "You'll figure it out. You always do."

But for the first time in his life, Nikhil wasn't sure if that was true. He wasn't sure if he had anything left to give.

Understood! We'll stay focused on the core challenges, the intensity of Nikhil's professional downfall, and his inner struggles as he tries to rise from the ashes. I'll make sure we keep the emotional and dramatic tension high, centered around his journey of overcoming the collapse of BizBoost and the personal and professional turmoil that follows.

CHAPTER 34

THE FIGHT WITHIN

The collapse of BizBoost felt like a storm that refused to end. Days passed, but Nikhil could feel the weight of failure pressing harder on his chest. It was no longer just about the company. It was about him. Every plan he had, every vision he had clung to, had shattered in front of him. And now, all he had left was the bitter taste of defeat.

The office, once bustling with activity, was now a ghost town. The desks that had been filled with creative minds and energy were abandoned. The few remaining staff members were only here to collect their things or say their final goodbyes. He had let them all down.

As he stood by the window, watching the dark clouds gather outside, Nikhil felt like he was standing at the edge of something far worse than failure. Hopelessness.

But that wasn't what terrified him the most. What scared him more was the growing realization that he didn't know who he was without BizBoost. For years, his identity had been tied to this company, to the idea that he could build something meaningful. And now that it was gone, what was left of him?

He was empty. The familiar knock on the door pulled him out of his thoughts. Priya entered, her face a mirror of exhaustion and concern.

"Nikhil, we need to talk," she said, her voice quiet but firm.

He nodded, motioning for her to sit, though he remained by the window, his back to her.

"They're closing the office," she continued after a moment of silence. "The lease is up next month, and there's no money to renew it. We have to clear out in two weeks."

Nikhil felt a lump form in his throat. Closing the office. The last physical piece of BizBoost that remained. It shouldn't have hurt so much, but it did. The walls of this office had witnessed his dreams and ambitions, and now, they would witness his downfall.

"I figured," Nikhil said, his voice strained.

"There's more," Priya added hesitantly, the silence thick between them. "Anil... he's asked to meet with you."

Nikhil turned sharply, a bitter laugh escaping him. "Anil? Now? After he pulled the plug, what does he want to talk about?"

Priya shrugged, though her expression was filled with empathy. "Maybe it's about the final financial settlements. Maybe he wants to see how you're handling things. I don't know."

Nikhil clenched his jaw, anger flaring in his chest. How I'm handling things? It felt like a cruel joke. Anil, the man who had watched everything crumble and walked away without looking back, now wanted to check in on him? The thought of facing him made Nikhil's blood boil, but at the same time, he knew there was no avoiding it.

"Set it up," Nikhil muttered, turning back toward the window, his voice cold. "Let's get it over with."

Priya nodded, sensing his anger, and stood up. Before leaving, she placed a hand on his shoulder, her touch warm and reassuring. "You'll get through this, Nikhil. I know you will."

He didn't respond. He wasn't sure if he believed it.

The meeting with Anil was scheduled for the next morning. Nikhil barely slept the night before, his mind racing with a thousand thoughts, none of them good. He kept replaying the past few months in his head, trying to pinpoint the exact moment when everything had started falling apart. Was it the Verma deal? The investors losing faith? Or had it been doomed from the start?

By the time he arrived at the cafe where they had agreed to meet, his hands were trembling. He hated this. He hated the feeling of powerlessness, of being the one who had failed. The once-confident, driven entrepreneur was now a shadow of his former self, walking into a meeting that felt more like a final judgment.

Anil was already there, sitting at a table near the window, casually sipping a coffee as if nothing had changed. The ease with which he moved through life infuriated Nikhil.

"Ah, Nikhil," Anil greeted, standing up to shake his hand. "Good to see you."

Nikhil forced a tight smile, though his insides churned with resentment. "You too."

They sat, the tension between them palpable. Nikhil could feel his pulse quicken as Anil studied him, his calm demeanor contrasting sharply with the storm raging inside Nikhil's head.

"So," Anil began, placing his coffee cup down. "I know the past few weeks have been rough. I wanted to check in and see how you're holding up."

Holding up? The question almost made Nikhil laugh. Holding up was for people who had suffered minor setbacks, not for people whose entire world had collapsed.

"I'm managing," Nikhil replied, his tone clipped.

Anil nodded, though he didn't seem convinced. "I understand this has been hard for you. But you're a resilient guy, Nikhil. I know you'll bounce back." Nikhil's hands tightened into fists under the table.

Bounce back. It sounded so simple when Anil said it,

as if he was talking about recovering from a bad day at work, not the loss of years of effort and sacrifice.

"I didn't call you here to talk about that," Anil continued, his voice shifting to a more serious tone. "There's something I need to tell you."

Nikhil's heart skipped a beat. What now? Another blow?

Anil leaned forward slightly, his expression unreadable. "There's been some interest in BizBoost."

The words hit Nikhil like a slap in the face. Interest?

What interest? The company was dead, wasn't it? "What do you mean?" Nikhil asked, his voice sharp.

"Some investors have expressed interest in acquiring what's left of the company. Not the whole thing, of course, but certain assets, the tech framework, and your customer base. It's not a huge deal, but it's something. They think there's potential to rebuild, under new leadership."

The blood drained from Nikhil's face. Rebuild?

Under new leadership?

"So what are you saying?" Nikhil asked, his voice tight with anger. "You want to sell off the remains of BizBoost to someone else and let them take over?"

Anil raised his hands in a gesture of peace. "It's not about taking over, Nikhil. It's about salvaging what's left. I wanted to run it by you first, see how you felt."

How I felt? Nikhil's mind was reeling. He had built BizBoost from the ground up, poured his heart and soul into it, and now Anil wanted to sell it off like a piece of junkyard scrap?

His vision blurred with rage, his pulse pounding in his ears. He had failed, yes, but this... this felt like the ultimate betrayal.

"I'll think about it," Nikhil said finally, his voice cold.

Anil nodded, clearly sensing the tension in the air. "Take your time. It's not an easy decision, but sometimes letting go is the best option."

Nikhil's jaw tightened, his fists clenched beneath the table. Letting go. That's what Anil was suggesting. Letting go of everything he had built, everything he had sacrificed for. And for what? A few scraps?

The meeting ended with a handshake, but as Nikhil walked out of the cafe, his mind was spinning. He wasn't sure what he was angrier about—the collapse of his company, or the fact that others were already circling, ready to pick apart the remains.

The storm inside him was far from over.

CHAPTER 35

THE OFFER THAT BURNS

The cold morning air hit Nikhil like a slap as he walked back from the café, his mind swirling with the weight of Anil's proposal. Sell the remnants of BizBoost. Let go. Hand over what little was left of his dream and watch someone else take the reins.

The anger simmered beneath the surface, rising with every step. How dare they? They'd pulled the rug from under him, forced his company into the ground, and now they wanted to pick through the scraps as if nothing had happened.

His phone buzzed in his pocket, breaking through his thoughts. It was Priya.

"Did you meet with Anil?" she asked, her voice steady, though he could sense the tension.

Nikhil clenched his jaw. "Yeah. You're not going to believe what he offered."

Priya was quiet for a beat. "Tell me."

"They want to sell off BizBoost—what's left of it, anyway. The tech, the customer base... they think there's something there worth salvaging." The words felt bitter on his tongue.

He could hear Priya exhale slowly on the other end of the line. "Are you serious? After everything?"

"Yeah," Nikhil muttered, his hands tightening into fists. "After everything."

There was a pause, long enough for Nikhil to know that Priya was weighing the situation, trying to figure out how to respond. She was always the practical one, the one who could see things clearly when emotions ran high. But even she couldn't fix this.

"What are you going to do?" Priya asked finally.

Nikhil stared at the street ahead, his mind buzzing with too many thoughts to make sense of. "I don't know. Part of me wants to walk away. But another part of me... I don't know if I can let them take it."

"They're not taking it, Nikhil. They're scavenging it," Priya said, her voice sharper than usual. "They're vultures picking at the bones of your company."

The words hit him hard. Vultures. That's exactly what it felt like. Like they were circling, waiting for him to fall so they could swoop in and claim whatever was left.

"I just need time to think," Nikhil said, his voice low.

"Of course. But don't let them push you into something you'll regret," Priya added gently. "This is still your legacy, no matter what's left."

Her words settled over him like a blanket, bringing a small measure of comfort. My legacy. That's what it was, wasn't it? Even if BizBoost was dead, it was still something he had built, something he had poured his soul into.

But was his pride worth more than the opportunity to salvage whatever remained?

Back at his apartment, Nikhil sat at his kitchen table, staring at the small mountain of papers scattered across it. Financial reports, contracts, termination letters—a graveyard of everything that had gone wrong.

His mind wandered back to the early days of BizBoost, when he had first had the idea, when the excitement and optimism fueled every decision. Back then, everything had seemed possible. The vision had been so clear, the path forward so full of potential. And now, sitting amidst the wreckage, it felt like a lifetime ago.

He reached for a bottle of water, taking a long sip as the weight of it all settled on his shoulders again. He had always been able to bounce back, to fight through the setbacks and find a way forward. But this time... this time was different. This time, it felt like the fight was gone.

Nikhil's phone buzzed again, pulling him from his thoughts. It was a text from one of his former team members, Shweta. She had been with him from the very beginning, one of the few who had believed in the vision of BizBoost when it was nothing more than an idea on paper.

"Hey Nikhil, just wanted to check in. I know things have been rough, but I want you to know we're all still rooting for you. You're not alone in this."

The message hit him harder than he expected. He hadn't realized how much he needed to hear that. You're not alone. The words echoed in his mind, breaking through the wall of isolation he had been building around himself.

He typed a quick response, thanking her for the support, but the knot in his stomach only tightened. The truth was, he did feel alone. The weight of the decisions in front of him felt like more than he could bear, and no amount of support from friends or former colleagues could change that.

Nikhil stood up, pacing the length of his small apartment, the walls closing in on him. What was he supposed to do? Sell off BizBoost's assets and walk away, or hold on to whatever scraps of his dream remained, even if it meant prolonging the agony?

He could feel the anger rising again, a familiar burn in his chest. Anger at Anil, at the investors, at the system that had pushed him into this corner. But more than anything, anger at himself. For not seeing the cracks sooner, for not being able to save the company when it mattered most. He grabbed his jacket and stormed out of the apartment, the need to escape overwhelming him. He couldn't sit in that small space, suffocating under the weight of his thoughts.

The city was alive with noise, but Nikhil barely heard it as he walked aimlessly down the streets, his mind churning. Every step felt heavy, as if the ground itself was trying to pull him down. He needed clarity, some kind of sign, but all he could see was a tangled mess of broken dreams and uncertainty.

As he passed a small park, he stopped, staring at the empty benches and the quiet stillness of the place. He found himself sitting down, the exhaustion washing over him. He was tired. Tired of fighting. Tired of pretending that he had it all together when everything was falling apart.

In the silence of the park, Nikhil finally allowed himself to feel the full weight of his loss. The dream he had worked so hard for was gone, and no amount of anger or frustration could change that. BizBoost was dead, and no matter how much he tried to resist, he couldn't bring it back.

He thought about the offer again—Anil's offer to sell off what was left. Was it worth holding on? Or was it time to let go, to walk away from the wreckage and start a new?

The thought of starting over felt like an impossible task. He didn't have the energy for it. He didn't even know where to begin. But the idea of letting someone else take over his vision, his creation, felt like a betrayal of everything he had fought for.

A gust of wind rustled the leaves around him, and Nikhil closed his eyes, feeling the chill in the air. What would happen if he let go? Would it be the end of his dream? Or was it the first step toward something new?

He didn't have the answers yet. But as he sat there, the weight of the decision pressing down on him, Nikhil knew one thing for sure: He couldn't run from it anymore.

He had to face it. One way or another.

221

CHAPTER 36

THE BREAKING POINT

The next morning, Nikhil woke up with a sense of dread lingering in his chest. His body felt heavy, his mind clouded with exhaustion, but he knew he couldn't stay in bed any longer. Today was the day he had to face the choice he had been avoiding—whether to sell what remained of BizBoost or to keep fighting a losing battle.

His phone buzzed on the nightstand. He didn't need to look to know it was Priya, checking in to see what he had decided. She was right to push him, but the pressure only made the decision harder.

Nikhil swung his legs out of bed, the cold floor sending a jolt through him. He glanced at the phone but ignored the message. Today, he needed space to think.

As he got ready for the day, the weight of everything he had to do sat like a stone in his gut. He wasn't ready for any of this. How could he be? The idea of letting go of BizBoost, of everything he had built, was more than just a financial decision—it felt like a surrender. And Nikhil wasn't the kind of person who surrendered easily. He found himself pacing again, his small apartment feeling even smaller. The walls were closing in, the pressure building. How had his life spiraled to this point? How had the dream of building something great turned into this nightmare of uncertainty?

With a deep breath, he grabbed his jacket and left the apartment, determined to clear his head before facing the meeting with Anil.

The city was a blur as Nikhil walked through the crowded streets, his mind racing with conflicting thoughts. How could he let it go? How could he give up on something he had poured years of his life into?

But what other choice did he have? There was no money left, no investors willing to take a chance on a failed company. BizBoost had burned through its resources, and now, all that was left were ashes.

As he walked past a row of shops, a sign caught his eye: *"Rebuild. Renew. Restart."* It was a motivational poster in the window of a small business, the kind of thing Nikhil would have scoffed at a few years ago. But now, it felt like a slap in the face.

Restart. That was the last thing he wanted to do. He was tired, beaten down by the relentless grind of the past few years. The thought of starting over from scratch was terrifying.

But what was the alternative? Hold on to the ruins of BizBoost and watch them crumble even further?

He found himself standing in front of a coffee shop, the familiar aroma of coffee and baked goods wafting through the air. Without thinking, he stepped inside, needing the warmth and comfort of a simple cup of coffee. It was a small act of normalcy in a world that felt anything but normal.

As he waited in line, his phone buzzed again. This time, he checked it. Another message from Priya.

"Nikhil, I'm meeting with Anil at noon. We need an answer."

He sighed, running a hand through his hair. Noon. The deadline was looming, and he still didn't have a clear answer.

After ordering his coffee, Nikhil found a seat near the window, the hum of the café providing a brief escape from the chaos in his mind. He stared out at the street, watching people go about their lives, oblivious to the storm inside him.

As he sipped his coffee, he felt the weight of the decision settle on him again. This wasn't just about BizBoost. This was about who he was. For years, his identity had been tied to the company, to the idea that he was building something bigger than himself. And now, without it, he wasn't sure who he was anymore.

He thought back to the early days, when BizBoost was just an idea, a spark of inspiration that had turned into something real. Those days had been hard, too, but there had been hope. There had been excitement. Now, all that remained was a hollow sense of loss.

Nikhil took a deep breath, his chest tight. Maybe Priya was right. Maybe it was time to let go. Maybe the only way to move forward was to close this chapter and start again, no matter how painful it was.

But the thought of someone else taking over BizBoost, someone else building on the foundation he had laid, made his stomach turn. Wasn't it better to go down fighting than to hand over his legacy to strangers?

He stared at his phone, the clock ticking closer to noon. The decision was coming, whether he was ready or not.

By the time Nikhil reached the office for his meeting with Anil and Priya, his mind was still a storm of uncertainty. He had spent the entire walk trying to find clarity, but all he felt was the crushing weight of indecision.

Anil was already there, sitting at the conference table with a calm, unreadable expression. Priya sat beside him, her eyes flickering with concern as Nikhil walked in.

"Nikhil," Anil greeted him with a nod. "I'm glad you're here."

Nikhil forced a tight smile, though his insides churned. This was it. The moment of truth. "Have you made a decision?" Anil asked, his voice even, though there was a subtle urgency behind the words.

Nikhil sat down, his hands gripping the edge of the table. His mind raced with a thousand thoughts, each one pulling him in a different direction. He could feel the tension in the room, the weight of the decision pressing down on all of them.

For a long moment, he didn't speak. The silence hung heavy in the air, the only sound the distant hum of the city outside.

Finally, Nikhil took a deep breath, his voice barely above a whisper. "I don't know if I can do it."

Priya's eyes softened, her expression full of understanding. She had seen him struggle, seen him fight tooth and nail to keep BizBoost alive. She knew how much this company meant to him, how much of himself he had poured into it.

But Anil remained calm, his gaze steady. "I get it, Nikhil. I do. But you need to understand something—there's no more time. If you don't make this decision now, the opportunity will be gone."

Nikhil's heart pounded in his chest. The opportunity. That's what Anil called it. But to Nikhil, it didn't feel like an opportunity. It felt like a surrender. "I built this company from nothing," Nikhil said, his voice tight with emotion. "I put everything I had into it. And now, you're asking me to let it go."

Anil nodded, his expression softening slightly. "I'm not asking you to let go of the work you've done. I'm asking you to think about what's best for your future. Sometimes, letting go of one thing opens the door to something better."

Nikhil clenched his fists under the table, his anger bubbling just beneath the surface. Letting go. It sounded so simple when Anil said it, as if walking away from the company he had built was just another business decision.

But for Nikhil, it wasn't that simple. BizBoost wasn't just a company—it was his dream. It was his identity. And now, Anil was asking him to walk away from it.

"I'll need more time," Nikhil said, his voice strained. "I'm not ready."

Anil's jaw tightened, but he nodded slowly. "I understand. But Nikhil, we don't have much more time. Think it over, but don't take too long."

As the meeting ended, Nikhil felt more conflicted than ever. He had thought he would find clarity in this conversation, but instead, the decision seemed even more impossible.

Priya stayed behind as Anil left, her eyes full of concern. "Whatever you decide, Nikhil, I'm with you. But you need to think about yourself too. You can't keep fighting forever."

Nikhil nodded, though her words didn't bring him the comfort he needed. Fighting forever. That's what it felt like. A never-ending battle. And now, he was starting to wonder if he had anything left to give.

CHAPTER 37

ON THE EDGE

The cold, clinical walls of the boardroom felt suffocating. Nikhil sat at the far end of the long conference table, staring blankly at the documents spread in front of him. This was it. The moment he had fought against for months. The moment that marked the end of everything he had built.

Priya sat beside him, her presence a silent comfort, though it did little to ease the storm inside him. Anil sat across from them, calm and composed as always, the perfect image of someone who knew he had won. He leafed through the papers, unbothered by the gravity of what was happening. For him, it was just another transaction—another business deal.

But for Nikhil, it was everything. BizBoost was his life. It had been more than just a company. It was the physical manifestation of his ambition, his blood, his sleepless nights. And now, he was about to sign it all away.

"You're making the right decision, Nikhil," Anil said, his voice smooth, almost patronizing. "This is the best outcome for everyone involved. The investors, the team... and you."

Nikhil's stomach churned. How could this be the best outcome? How could this be anything but the death of everything he had worked for?

He stared down at the pen in his hand, his grip tightening around it. All he had to do was sign his name, and it would be over. The pressure mounted, each second stretching painfully as he debated whether to go through with it.

"I can't," Nikhil muttered, his voice low but firm. Priya glanced at him, her eyes wide with shock.

"Nikhil..."

"I can't do this," he repeated, louder this time. He pushed back from the table, the chair scraping against the floor as he stood. "This isn't right."

Anil raised an eyebrow, though his expression remained composed. "What do you mean? Nikhil, we've gone over this. This is the only way to salvage anything."

But Nikhil couldn't hear him. The roaring in his ears drowned out the rational voice telling him to accept defeat. This wasn't just about salvaging a company. It was about salvaging himself. And in this moment, signing that paper felt like signing away everything that made him who he was.

"I need more time," Nikhil said abruptly, pushing the papers toward Anil. "I'm not ready to give up."

Anil's composure faltered for a brief moment, a flicker of frustration crossing his face. "Nikhil, we've already agreed to the terms. There's no more time to—"

"There's always time," Nikhil snapped, his voice louder than he intended. He glanced at Priya, his eyes pleading for her to understand. "I'm not walking away from this without a fight."

Priya stood, her expression a mix of confusion and concern. "Nikhil, I know how hard this is, but—"

"No," Nikhil cut her off, his voice trembling with emotion. "We're not done yet. I'm not done yet."

Anil sighed, leaning back in his chair. "You need to be realistic, Nikhil. There's no coming back from this. The investors have moved on, the clients have moved on. The company is bankrupt. What are you holding on to?"

Nikhil's mind raced, his pulse pounding in his ears. What was he holding on to? The dream? The identity? The idea that he could still claw his way back from the brink?

But underneath it all, there was something else—a flicker of hope, small and fragile, but there. Maybe he couldn't save BizBoost as it was, but that didn't mean he couldn't rebuild. Maybe not the same company, but something new. Something stronger.

"I don't know what comes next," Nikhil admitted, his voice quieter now. "But I'm not going to let you take what's left of my legacy and strip it for parts."

Anil's eyes narrowed, his tone hardening. "You don't have the luxury of playing the hero, Nikhil. You're out of options."

Nikhil met his gaze, his jaw clenched. "Then I'll find another way."

The tension in the room was thick, the silence deafening as the weight of Nikhil's decision settled over them. Priya looked between them, her expression conflicted. She had stood by Nikhil through every step of this journey, but now, even she wasn't sure what to make of his sudden refusal.

"Nikhil," she began, her voice soft, "if you walk away from this deal, there might not be another one. You know that, right?"

"I know," Nikhil said, his voice steady now. "But I'm not going to let them tear it apart. Not like this."

Anil stood up slowly, his expression cool but his eyes flashing with irritation. "You're making a mistake. A big one."

Nikhil stared him down, the fire in his chest growing. "Maybe. But I'd rather go down fighting than sell my soul."

The room fell into an uneasy silence. Anil didn't respond right away, but the tension in his jaw was visible. He picked up his briefcase, his movements slow and deliberate.

"Alright, Nikhil," he said finally, his voice tight with barely concealed frustration. "You want to fight? Fine. But remember, this was your chance. When you come back, there won't be any more offers."

Without another word, Anil turned and walked out, the door closing behind him with a sharp click that echoed through the room.

Nikhil stood frozen, his heart pounding in his chest. He had just walked away from the deal. He had walked away from the safety net that could have softened the blow of BizBoost's collapse.

For a moment, panic surged through him. What had he done? Was this the moment where he finally pushed too far? Had he just sealed his own fate?

But as the panic ebbed, something else took its place. Resolve.

Priya stepped up beside him, her voice quiet but steady. "That was... intense."

Nikhil let out a shaky breath, nodding. "Yeah. It was."

Priya hesitated for a moment, then placed a hand on his arm. "So... what's the plan now?"

Nikhil didn't have a plan. Not yet. But for the first time in weeks, he felt something stirring inside him. He had chosen to fight, even if it meant standing alone.

"We rebuild," he said finally, his voice firmer than he felt. "I don't know how yet, but we rebuild."

Priya smiled faintly, though there was uncertainty in her eyes. "Then I'm with you."

As they stood together in the empty room, Nikhil realized that the fight was far from over. In fact, it was just beginning. Walking away from the deal with Anil wasn't just a decision—it was a declaration. A statement that he wasn't ready to let go of everything he'd worked for, not yet.

But with that declaration came the weight of reality. The challenges ahead were immense, and the resources were gone. The investors had moved on, the team was scattered, and the company's reputation was in tatters. Rebuilding would require more than just willpower. It would require a miracle.

Priya's hand on his arm grounded him for a moment. "We'll figure it out," she said softly, as if reading his thoughts.

Nikhil nodded, though the certainty he had felt just moments before was starting to waver. Rebuilding wasn't going to be easy. There was no money left, no team to rely on, no clients waiting in the wings. He had walked away from the one lifeline he had left, and now, he was facing the prospect of starting from scratch, with nothing but his conviction.

But deep down, Nikhil knew that this wasn't just about BizBoost anymore. It was about him. This fight was personal now. He had spent years building this company, pouring everything he had into it, and if he was going to go down, it wouldn't be without exhausting every last option. This wasn't just about pride—it was about proving to himself that he still had the fire, the drive to build something from the ashes.

"I can't fail," he muttered, almost to himself. "You won't," Priya said firmly. "We won't."

As they left the office, Nikhil's chest felt lighter, but his mind was racing with the daunting reality of what lay ahead. The stakes were higher than ever, and the road forward was uncertain.

But he had made his choice. Now, it was time to fight.

CHAPTER 38

THE REBUILDING BEGINS

The office felt emptier than usual as Nikhil sat in front of his laptop, the glow of the screen casting a faint light across his tired face. He had spent the last few hours poring over old documents, trying to find some thread to pull, some piece of his past work that could serve as a foundation for his next move. But nothing seemed to stick.

Priya, sitting across the table, was equally engrossed, though her energy was visibly waning. "We're going to need a solid pitch, something different, something that stands out," she said, rubbing her eyes.

Nikhil nodded, though his mind was elsewhere. What could they offer that was different? They had tried everything before—new ideas, tech-driven solutions, innovative approaches to business. And still, BizBoost had crumbled. The weight of the failure loomed over him, a constant reminder of the high stakes they were facing.

"We need more than just a pitch," Nikhil said, leaning back in his chair. "We need a new identity."

Priya looked up, confused. "You mean a rebrand?"

Nikhil shook his head. "Not just that. We need to shift the way we operate, the way we present ourselves. If we're going to rebuild, we can't do it the same way we did before."

Priya frowned, her pen tapping the edge of her notebook. "So, what's the plan? You want to pivot? Focus on something different entirely?"

Nikhil stared at the screen, the words blurring as exhaustion set in. "We need to focus on people—on building relationships, not just chasing profits. That's where we went wrong before. We built something great, but we didn't have the trust or the loyalty of the people we needed."

There was a pause as Priya considered his words. "So you want to focus on community building?"

Nikhil nodded. "Exactly. We need to connect with our clients on a deeper level. Understand their needs, their challenges, and then build solutions that speak directly to them. No more flashy pitches. No more chasing investors who don't care about what we're trying to do."

Priya smiled faintly. "It's a bold move. But it's risky."

"Everything is risky now," Nikhil said, his voice firmer. "But we've already lost everything. What's left to lose?"

Priya leaned back, the tension in her shoulders easing slightly. "You're right. If we're going to go down, let's go down fighting."

Nikhil's phone buzzed, snapping him out of his thoughts. It was a message from one of his old clients—someone he hadn't heard from in months. Could this be the opportunity he had been waiting for?

He opened the message, his heart pounding as he read the brief note.

"Nikhil, heard you're back at it. Let's talk. I might have something for you."

It wasn't much, but it was a start. And right now, that's all Nikhil needed—a glimmer of hope in the darkness.

He looked up at Priya, a small smile forming on his lips. "I think we've got our first lead."

The meeting was set for the following afternoon, and Nikhil could feel the familiar mix of anxiety and excitement building in his chest. This wasn't just a casual conversation—it was a lifeline. One wrong move, one misstep, and the fragile foundation he was trying to build could collapse before it even had a chance to form.

As he walked into the sleek café where they had agreed to meet, Nikhil spotted his old client, Raghav, seated by the window. Raghav had been one of BizBoost's first supporters, back when the company was just starting out. His business had grown over the years, and now, he was a major player in the industry. Nikhil approached the table, his heart racing. This was his chance.

"Nikhil," Raghav greeted him with a warm smile, standing to shake his hand. "It's been too long."

"It really has," Nikhil replied, though his mind was focused on the task at hand. He couldn't afford to let this slip through his fingers.

They sat down, and after some small talk, Raghav got straight to the point. "I've been hearing about what happened with BizBoost," he said, his tone sympathetic. "It's a tough market. But I think there's something we can do together."

Nikhil felt his pulse quicken. "What do you have in mind?"

Raghav leaned forward, his expression serious. "I've been looking to expand into new markets, but I don't have the infrastructure or the network to make it happen. That's where you come in. You've built connections before, and I think you can do it again—this time with a more targeted approach."

Nikhil's mind was already racing with possibilities. This was exactly what they needed—a foot in the door, a way to rebuild with the support of someone who believed in what they were trying to do.

"I'm interested," Nikhil said carefully. "But what's the catch?"

Raghav smiled. "The catch is that I need results—and fast. We don't have time to slowly build up momentum. If you're in, I need to see progress within the first few months."

The pressure hit Nikhil like a wave, but he didn't back down. This was his shot.

"I can deliver," he said, his voice steady. "We'll make it happen."

Raghav nodded, satisfied. "Then let's get started."

As they shook hands to seal the deal, Nikhil couldn't help but feel a surge of optimism. It wasn't going to be easy, and the road ahead was filled with uncertainty, but for the first time in a long time, he felt like he was moving in the right direction.

CHAPTER 39

THE PRESSURE COOKER

The moment Nikhil stepped out of the café, the weight of the commitment he had just made settled on his shoulders. The handshake with Raghav felt final, like signing a contract without any safety net beneath him. He had promised results—and fast. But now, the reality of that promise began to sink in.

Raghav's trust wasn't something to be taken lightly. He had been one of BizBoost's earliest backers, and Nikhil knew that failing him again could burn a bridge he desperately needed. The pressure was suffocating, but there was no room for doubt now. This was the break he'd been waiting for, and he couldn't afford to fail.

As Nikhil headed back to his office, Priya met him at the door, her expression expectant. "How did it go?" she asked, her tone a mix of hope and concern.

"We have a deal," Nikhil said, his voice steady, but his mind still racing. "Raghav's giving us a shot to help him expand into new markets. But he wants to see progress fast."

Priya nodded, though her brow furrowed slightly. "How fast?"

Nikhil exhaled sharply, rubbing the back of his neck. "A few months."

The concern on Priya's face deepened. "A few months? We're barely set up to handle what we have now. Do we even have the resources to pull this off?"

"We don't," Nikhil admitted. "But we're going to make it work. We have no other choice."

Priya fell silent for a moment, the weight of the situation sinking in. "Okay," she said finally, her voice firm. "Then we start now."

They spent the next several hours huddled over their laptops, sketching out strategies, outlining goals, and setting up meetings with potential partners and clients. It was an all-hands-on-deck situation, and Nikhil could feel the familiar burn of adrenaline coursing through him. This was what he thrived on—the pressure, the challenge, the race against time.

But even as they worked late into the night, Nikhil couldn't shake the nagging voice in the back of his mind: What if it's not enough?

The stakes had never been higher. If they failed to deliver, it wouldn't just be another blow to their reputation. It could mean the end of everything.

The days blurred into each other as Nikhil and Priya worked tirelessly, their focus narrowing in on the goal in front of them. Every meeting, every call, every email was a step closer to proving themselves again.

But the pressure was relentless. Nikhil barely slept, and when he did, it was with his phone by his side, ready to jump into action the moment an opportunity presented itself.

He could feel the strain taking its toll—on his body, his mind, and even his relationship with Priya. They had always worked well together, but now, the constant grind was wearing them both thin.

"Nikhil, you need to take a break," Priya said one evening, her voice strained as she massaged her temples. "You're going to burn out if you keep going like this."

"We don't have time for breaks," Nikhil replied, his tone sharper than he intended. "You know what's riding on this."

Priya frowned, her patience fraying. "I do know. But if you collapse, what then? We can't afford to lose you halfway through this."

Nikhil sighed, the tension in his shoulders intensifying. He knew she was right. He was pushing too hard, but he didn't know how to stop. Every minute felt like it could make or break their chances. And the thought of losing everything again was unbearable.

"I'll slow down," he said finally, though they both knew it was an empty promise.

Priya gave him a look, her worry evident, but she didn't push the issue. Instead, she refocused on the task at hand, her determination matching his. They were in this together, for better or worse.

As the deadline with Raghav approached, Nikhil found himself at a crossroads. They had made progress—significant progress—but it still wasn't enough. The expansion plans were in motion, but delays, complications, and unforeseen roadblocks were slowing them down. It felt like every step forward was met with two steps back.

Nikhil sat at his desk, staring at the list of tasks that still needed to be completed. It was overwhelming. The clock was ticking, and he could feel the weight of failure looming over him again.

His phone buzzed with a message from Raghav: "How's it coming along? Looking forward to seeing the results."

Nikhil's heart pounded. He had no choice but to deliver good news, even if it wasn't fully accurate. He typed a quick response: "We're on track. Final stages coming together."

It wasn't a lie, exactly. But it wasn't the full truth either.

Priya, sensing his anxiety, glanced over. "What did Raghav say?"

"He wants an update," Nikhil replied, his voice tight. "We're running out of time." Priya bit her lip, her own stress visible. "We'll get there," she said, though her words sounded more like an attempt to reassure herself than him.

But Nikhil wasn't so sure. They were running out of time, and the cracks were starting to show. If they didn't pull this off, everything could come crashing down—again.

Nikhil walked out of the café feeling like the ground was slipping beneath him. He had just promised Raghav results within months, but as the reality of the deal settled in, so did the weight of that commitment. This wasn't just about delivering a project. This was life or death—the line between salvaging his reputation or losing everything for good.

The air outside felt heavy, thick with the pressure that now enveloped him. He checked his watch—already late. Priya would be waiting at the office. She deserved to know what they were up against, but the thought of telling her made his stomach churn.

He arrived to find Priya pacing, her nerves clearly on edge. "How did it go?" she asked, not even bothering to sit down.

Nikhil dropped into the nearest chair, running his hands through his hair. "We've got a deal," he said, his voice tight. "But there's a catch."

Priya's eyebrows shot up. "What kind of catch?"

"We have a few months to deliver," Nikhil said, looking up at her. "And if we fail... it's over. Raghav won't give us another chance."

Priya sank into a chair opposite him, her face paling. "A few months? We're barely holding it together as it is. Do we even have the capacity to make this happen?"

"No," Nikhil said bluntly. "We don't. But we don't have a choice."

For a moment, there was nothing but silence between them, the enormity of what they were facing sinking in. Priya leaned forward, her voice barely above a whisper. "If we screw this up..."

"We won't," Nikhil interrupted, though even he wasn't convinced. The odds were stacked against them—the time frame was impossible, the resources were thin, and the cracks in their team were already starting to show. But what choice did they have? This was their only shot.

Priya nodded slowly, though her eyes betrayed the anxiety coursing through her. "Then we have to start now. No breaks. No second-guessing."

"We've got to give it everything we've got," Nikhil agreed, though the words felt hollow. Could they really pull this off?

The next few days blurred into a haze of late nights, frantic phone calls, and endless strategy sessions. Every hour seemed to slip through their fingers faster than the last. Nikhil and Priya threw themselves into the project with everything they had, but with each passing day, the deadline loomed closer, and the weight on Nikhil's chest grew heavier.

The pressure was unbearable. Nikhil could feel it creeping into every corner of his life, robbing him of sleep and eroding the confidence he had fought so hard to rebuild. This wasn't just business anymore—it was personal. Raghav's deal represented everything Nikhil had lost, everything he was fighting to regain. If he failed now, there would be no coming back.

As the days wore on, the cracks in their plan began to widen. Delays in communication with potential partners, missed deadlines, and mounting tension within the team threatened to derail everything. Every time they managed to solve one problem, another seemed to spring up in its place.

Priya was doing her best to hold things together, but Nikhil could see the toll it was taking on her too. She snapped more often, her patience fraying as the stress mounted. One evening, after a particularly grueling day of back-to-back meetings, she threw down her phone in frustration.

"Nikhil, we can't keep doing this," she said, her voice shaking. "We're barely treading water, and we're running out of time."

Nikhil stared at the documents scattered across the desk, the weight of her words pressing down on him like a ton of bricks. She was right.

"I know," he admitted, rubbing his tired eyes. "But we don't have any other options."

Priya shook her head, her voice rising. "This isn't sustainable. We can't keep putting out fires every day and expect everything to magically come together."

"I'm aware, Priya!" Nikhil snapped, his frustration boiling over. "But what do you want me to do? We're in too deep to back out now."

The silence that followed was deafening. Priya's shoulders sagged, her eyes clouded with exhaustion and anger. "I don't want to watch this all fall apart again," she said quietly. "I don't think I can go through that a second time."

Nikhil's heart twisted at her words. He knew what that felt like—the feeling of everything slipping through your fingers, of watching your dreams crumble before your eyes. And now, he was dragging Priya through it with him.

"I'm sorry," Nikhil said softly. "But I can't let this fail."

Priya didn't respond right away. She sat back, closing her eyes for a moment, trying to gather herself. "Then we push harder," she said finally, her voice steadier now. "But we need a miracle." Two weeks passed, and the miracle they were hoping for still hadn't arrived. Nikhil was running on fumes, barely sleeping, eating whenever Priya reminded him to. His inbox was a constant barrage of problems—delayed shipments, unresponsive partners, and Raghav's increasingly frequent check-ins.

Each message from Raghav was like a ticking time bomb, a reminder that they were running out of time. One morning, as Nikhil read another impatient email from him, he felt his chest tighten. They weren't going to make it.

He didn't tell Priya, but the fear gnawed at him. He was trying to keep up the facade of control, but inside, the panic was setting in. Every day, it seemed more likely that they were headed for disaster.

One afternoon, just as Nikhil was about to leave for yet another meeting, his phone buzzed. It was a call from Raghav.

His heart skipped a beat as he answered. "Raghav, hey—"

"I don't have time for pleasantries, Nikhil," Raghav cut him off, his tone icy. "I need an update. Now."

Nikhil's throat went dry. He knew Raghav wasn't going to like what he had to say. "We're making progress," he said, his voice steady but forced. "There have been some delays, but we're on track."

"On track?" Raghav repeated, his voice dripping with disbelief. "You're running out of time. I can't keep waiting for results. If you don't have something concrete soon, I'm pulling the plug."

Nikhil's pulse quickened. This was the moment he had been dreading. If Raghav pulled out now, everything they had worked for would collapse. Everything.

"I just need a little more time," Nikhil said, his voice tightening as panic set in. "We're almost there."

"You have two weeks, Nikhil," Raghav said coldly. "If I don't see progress by then, we're done."

The line went dead, and Nikhil stared at the phone in his hand, his mind racing. Two weeks. That's all they had. Two weeks to pull off the impossible.

CHAPTER 40
THE TWO-WEEK DEADLINE

Two weeks.

The number echoed in Nikhil's mind like a relentless countdown, each day ticking away faster than the last. Every time he glanced at the calendar, the knot in his stomach tightened. Fourteen days to deliver what seemed like an impossible project, and the pressure was becoming unbearable.

Sitting at his desk in the office, Nikhil stared at the endless tasks piling up in front of him. The lists on his laptop were overwhelming—emails unanswered, calls that needed to be made, partnerships to finalize, and a million other loose ends. Where to start? No matter what he prioritized, it felt like something else was crumbling beneath him.

Across the room, Priya was pacing. She had the same harried expression she'd worn for the past week, her usual calm and collected demeanor now replaced by thinly veiled panic.

"Nikhil," she started, her voice strained, "We're not going to make it at this pace. We need help. We need... something."

He looked up at her, seeing the same stress and exhaustion that plagued him. "Help?" Nikhil's laugh was dry, almost hollow. "There's no help, Priya. This is it.

Just you and me, and the clock ticking."

Priya stopped pacing, her eyes narrowing. "That attitude isn't going to get us anywhere. We need a solution, not more pressure. Can we outsource? Bring in some freelance talent, someone who can handle the technical load?"

Nikhil sighed, rubbing his temples. "With what money? Everything we had went into this. Outsourcing costs more, and we're already running on fumes. We just have to push harder."

Priya threw her hands up in frustration. "Push harder? We're already running at full capacity! I haven't slept more than four hours in days, Nikhil. This isn't sustainable."

He knew she was right. They were burning out, both of them. But there was no way to stop. Stopping meant failure, and failure meant losing everything. They had no choice but to keep pushing, even if it was killing them.

"We'll make it," Nikhil said, though the confidence in his voice was forced. "We have to."

The days that followed were a blur of chaotic energy. Nikhil and Priya worked around the clock, fueled by adrenaline and caffeine. Meetings were held late into the night, emails were fired off in rapid succession, and any semblance of balance in their lives had completely disintegrated.

But the cracks were starting to show.

One evening, as they sat huddled in the office, Priya suddenly slammed her laptop shut with a force that made Nikhil jump.

"I can't do this anymore," she said, her voice shaking. "This isn't working."

Nikhil turned to her, his own frustration bubbling up. "What are you talking about? We're close! We're almost there!"

"No, we're not!" Priya snapped. "We're running in circles, Nikhil. Everything is a mess. We're not moving forward fast enough, and you know it."

Nikhil felt the familiar wave of panic rise in his chest, but he forced it down. "We've hit roadblocks before. We always figure it out."

Priya's eyes flashed with anger. "This isn't like before. We don't have time for miracles. We need to face reality. We're out of time, out of resources, and you're running us both into the ground."

Nikhil stood up, frustration coursing through him. "So what? You want to quit? You want to just walk away after everything we've done?"

Priya's expression softened, but there was a weariness in her eyes that Nikhil hadn't seen before. "I don't want to quit, Nikhil. But we need to be honest with ourselves. We're failing."

Her words hit him like a punch to the gut. Failing. He had spent years clawing his way back from failure, trying to prove that he could succeed again, that

BizBoost wasn't the end of his story. And now, it felt like everything was slipping through his fingers once more.

Nikhil sank back into his chair, his energy drained. "I don't know what else to do," he admitted, his voice barely above a whisper. "We're so close, but it feels like we're miles away."

Priya sat down across from him, her voice gentler now. "We need to rethink our approach. Maybe we're focusing on the wrong things. What if we simplified the project? Cut back on the things that are slowing us down and focus on what we can deliver in the next two weeks?"

Nikhil looked at her, a spark of hope flickering inside him. Could they simplify? Would scaling back give them a chance to meet the deadline and save the project?

"It's risky," Nikhil said, considering her suggestion. "If we strip too much, we might not deliver what Raghav is expecting."

"It's a bigger risk to do nothing and hope we somehow finish everything," Priya countered. "We can't let perfection be the enemy of progress. Let's focus on what we can control."

Nikhil leaned forward, nodding slowly. She was right. This was their last chance, and they had to be strategic. The scope of the project had ballooned out of control, and it was time to reign it back in.

"Okay," he said finally. "We cut down, we simplify.

Focus on the core deliverables. It's the only way."

Priya exhaled, relief visible on her face. "Let's do it."

The next few days were a whirlwind of last-minute changes and recalibrations. Nikhil and Priya worked tirelessly to refocus their efforts, cutting back on the unnecessary and doubling down on the essential parts of the project. The workload was still immense, but by narrowing their focus, they began to see some progress.

But the clock was ticking, and with each passing day, the deadline loomed closer. Raghav was still in the dark about their pivot, and Nikhil knew they were gambling everything on this final push. Would it be enough?

One night, as they were finalizing the last of their updates, Nikhil's phone buzzed. It was Raghav.

Nikhil's heart skipped a beat as he answered. "Raghav, hey... I was just about to send you an update."

"Cut the small talk, Nikhil," Raghav said, his voice sharp. "Where are we? I need something concrete by tomorrow."

Nikhil swallowed hard. Tomorrow. They weren't ready. Not yet.

"We're almost there," Nikhil said, forcing a calm tone. "We've made some adjustments to streamline the project. You'll have the first phase of deliverables tomorrow."

There was a long pause on the other end of the line, and Nikhil's pulse quickened. Finally, Raghav spoke. "Tomorrow. If it's not on my desk, we're done. No more excuses."

The call ended, and Nikhil stared at his phone, his hands trembling. Tomorrow.

He looked over at Priya, who had been listening in on the call. She didn't say anything, but her expression said it all.

This was it. The final stretch.

CHAPTER 41

JUDGMENT DAY

The early morning light filtered through the office blinds, casting long shadows across the floor. Nikhil sat hunched over his laptop, his fingers flying across the keyboard. It was the day. The final day. Everything came down to this.

He hadn't slept. Neither had Priya. The two of them had worked through the night, fueled by nothing but adrenaline, caffeine, and sheer determination. The deadline was only hours away, and they were still fine-tuning the project's final details, making sure there were no loose ends before sending it off to Raghav.

"Nikhil," Priya's voice cut through the tense silence. "I've double-checked the financials. Everything lines up. We're good to go."

Nikhil nodded, but his focus was on the screen. One last task, one final hurdle. His heart pounded in his chest as he clicked through the presentation files. "Okay, that's done," he muttered, his voice tight with tension. "Let me run through the summary one more time."

Priya's exhaustion was visible, but she nodded and turned her chair to face him. "We've cut it as close as we can. We don't have time for any more changes."

"I know," Nikhil said, exhaling sharply. "But this has to be perfect. If we mess up now..."

He didn't need to finish the sentence. They both knew what was at stake. One mistake, one misstep, and the entire deal could crumble.

Nikhil's fingers hovered over the send button, a bead of sweat trickling down his temple. This was it. Months of sleepless nights, endless meetings, and constant pressure—all leading to this single moment.

"You ready?" Priya asked quietly, her voice softer now.

Nikhil took a deep breath, his hand shaking slightly as he hovered over the button. "Yeah," he said, though he wasn't sure if that was true. "Let's do this."

With one final click, the email was sent. The files were on their way to Raghav. There was no turning back.

The next few hours passed in a blur of nervous energy. Nikhil and Priya stayed glued to their phones, waiting for a response. Every minute that passed felt like an eternity. The office was eerily quiet, the usual hum of activity replaced by a suffocating stillness.

Nikhil paced back and forth, his nerves fraying with every second of silence. Priya, who had been glued to her laptop, finally leaned back in her chair and closed her eyes, exhaustion written all over her face.

"Do you think he's seen it yet?" she asked, her voice barely above a whisper.

Nikhil stopped pacing, glancing at his phone for what felt like the hundredth time. Still nothing.

"I don't know," he said, his frustration mounting. "It's been hours. He should've at least acknowledged it by now."

Priya sighed, her eyes still closed. "He's probably going over every detail. Raghav's thorough—he won't respond until he's sure."

"Or he's already decided we failed," Nikhil said, the words escaping before he could stop himself.

Priya's eyes snapped open, and she gave him a sharp look. "Don't go there. Not yet."

Nikhil ran a hand through his hair, the weight of the situation pressing down on him like never before. He couldn't shake the fear gnawing at him. If they failed today, all of their efforts would be for nothing. They would be back at square one—worse off, even.

Just as he was about to check his phone again, it buzzed.

Nikhil froze, his pulse quickening. He stared at the screen, his heart pounding in his ears. It was Raghav.

With shaking hands, Nikhil answered the call. "Raghav—hey, did you get the files?"

There was a long pause on the other end of the line, and Nikhil's heart felt like it might explode from the tension.

"I got them," Raghav said finally, his tone unreadable. "I've been going through them all morning."

Nikhil's breath caught in his throat. He shot a glance at Priya, who was watching him with wide eyes. "And?"

Another pause. Longer this time.

"I'm impressed," Raghav said slowly. "You two pulled it off."

Nikhil felt his knees go weak, relief flooding through him. He leaned back against the desk, closing his eyes for a moment. "Thank you," he breathed, his voice shaky with exhaustion.

"But," Raghav added, and Nikhil's heart skipped a beat again. "There's still a lot to be done. The project isn't over yet. This is just the beginning."

Nikhil opened his eyes, adrenaline still coursing through him. "We're ready. Whatever comes next, we'll handle it." Raghav's voice softened, though it still held a note of caution. "I hope so, Nikhil. Because this is the big leagues now. There's no room for mistakes."

After a few more details were discussed, the call ended, and Nikhil slowly lowered the phone from his ear. For a moment, he just stood there, letting the relief wash over him.

Priya sat up straight, her expression hopeful. "Well?"

Nikhil smiled for the first time in what felt like weeks. "We did it. He's impressed."

Priya let out a long, shaky breath, her shoulders sagging in relief. "We did it."

That night, for the first time in weeks, Nikhil and Priya left the office before midnight. The exhaustion clung to them both, but there was a sense of triumph in the air. They had done it.

As they walked down the quiet street outside the office, the tension that had weighed them down for so long finally began to lift. Nikhil glanced at Priya, who looked as worn out as he felt, but there was a faint smile on her lips.

"You know," she said, breaking the silence, "I didn't think we were going to make it."

Nikhil laughed softly, though there was no humor in it. "Neither did I." They walked in silence for a while, the night air cool against their skin. Nikhil's mind raced with thoughts of what was next. Raghav had been clear—this was just the beginning. The real work was still ahead of them. But for tonight, they had earned a moment of peace.

As they reached the corner of the street, Priya turned to him. "We should celebrate. You know, while we still have the chance."

Nikhil grinned. "I'll take you up on that."

For the first time in a long time, Nikhil allowed himself to feel a flicker of hope. They had survived the worst of it. And though the challenges ahead were daunting, tonight, they had won.

CHAPTER 42

A TEMPORARY VICTORY

The next morning, Nikhil woke up with a rare sense of lightness. For the first time in months, he hadn't been consumed by the dread of looming deadlines. They had done it. The crushing weight of failure had been lifted, even if just temporarily. He allowed himself to savor the victory—one that had been so hard-fought.

As he stepped into the office, the energy in the air was different. Priya was already at her desk, her focus sharp but not burdened by the frantic tension of the last few weeks.

"How are we feeling this morning?" Nikhil asked, setting down his coffee and flashing her a rare smile.

"Like I can finally breathe," Priya said, smiling back, though the exhaustion was still evident in her eyes. "I don't think I've slept that well in years."

Nikhil chuckled, feeling a strange sense of calm. "Well, we've earned a break."

But the reality of their situation wasn't far from their minds. Raghav had made it clear—this was just the beginning. The real challenge lay ahead, and while they had bought themselves some time, the stakes were about to get much higher.

"Speaking of which," Priya said, glancing at her phone, "I got an email from Raghav this morning. He wants to set up a call to discuss next steps."

Nikhil nodded, the weight slowly returning to his shoulders. "Right. Next steps."

The short-lived victory suddenly felt fragile. They couldn't afford to get comfortable.

A few hours later, Nikhil and Priya were back in their usual positions—laptops open, notes scattered across the desk—preparing for the call with Raghav. The euphoria of their success had been replaced by a familiar sense of pressure, the kind that lingered in the pit of their stomachs.

"This time, we need to be ready for anything," Nikhil said as he scribbled down potential discussion points. "He's going to want more than just progress. He'll want a vision, a roadmap for the next six months."

Priya nodded, her expression serious. "We've already pushed ourselves to the limit just to get this far. What happens if he asks for more?"

Nikhil didn't have an answer. "We can't think like that. We'll just have to figure it out. Like we always do."

As they logged into the video call, Nikhil's heart rate picked up again, the familiar nerves settling in. Raghav appeared on the screen, his usual stoic expression giving nothing away.

"Morning," Raghav said, his tone businesslike. "Let's get straight to it. The initial phase went well, but I'm expecting a lot more in the coming months. I want to scale up—fast."

Nikhil's pulse quickened. Scale up? They were barely holding it together as it was.

"What do you have in mind?" Priya asked, her voice calm, though Nikhil could see the tension in her posture.

Raghav leaned forward, his gaze sharp. "We're looking to move into international markets within the next quarter. The domestic success was a good start, but it's time to think bigger. I need a plan for global expansion—Europe, Southeast Asia, and North America. We need market research, partnerships, and execution strategies, all in place within the next three months."

Nikhil's stomach dropped. Global expansion? In three months?

"Three months?" Priya said, trying to keep her voice steady. "That's... ambitious. We'll need to significantly ramp up our resources to make that happen."

Raghav didn't blink. "Ambitious is what we do. I've already lined up some potential investors and partners overseas. I need you two to deliver on the ground. If you can't handle it, let me know now, and I'll find someone who can."

The threat hung in the air, unspoken but clear.

Nikhil's mind raced. How could they possibly deliver on something of this scale? The domestic rollout had already stretched them thin. Going international would require a whole new level of effort, resources, and time—time they didn't have.

But saying no wasn't an option.

"We can handle it," Nikhil said, forcing confidence into his voice. "We'll start working on the plan immediately."

Priya shot him a look, but didn't contradict him.

Raghav nodded. "Good. I'll be expecting updates every two weeks. Don't make me regret this."

The call ended, leaving Nikhil and Priya sitting in stunned silence.

The office felt suffocating after the call, the weight of Raghav's demands bearing down on them. Priya broke the silence first.

"Are you out of your mind?" she snapped, standing up and pacing. "Global expansion in three months? How are we supposed to pull that off?"

Nikhil sighed, rubbing his temples. "What choice did we have? If we said no, he would've walked. We can't afford that."

"And what makes you think we can afford this?" Priya shot back, her frustration spilling over. "We're barely managing with what we have. Scaling up internationally is a whole different beast. We need more people, more money, more time—none of which we have!"

Nikhil stood up, his own frustration boiling to the surface. "I know! But what do you want me to do,

Priya? Say we can't handle it and lose everything we've worked for? This is the only way forward."

Priya shook her head, her hands on her hips. "This isn't just about working harder, Nikhil. This is about knowing when we've hit our limit."

Her words hung in the air, and for a moment, Nikhil felt the full weight of them. Had they hit their limit?

"We haven't hit it yet," Nikhil said, though the certainty in his voice was wavering. "We'll find a way."

Priya sighed, her anger fading into exhaustion. "We need help, Nikhil. We can't do this alone anymore. We have to bring in more people, hire some freelancers, something. We can't just keep pushing ourselves like this." Nikhil knew she was right. They had reached the point where their two-person operation wasn't enough anymore. If they were going to take on something as massive as international expansion, they needed backup.

"You're right," he said finally. "We need to expand the team. Start looking for freelancers who can help with the research and market analysis. I'll start reaching out to potential partners. We can't do this alone."

Priya nodded, relief washing over her. "Okay. We'll make it work. But we need to be realistic about what we can handle."

Nikhil sat back down, his mind already racing with ideas. The stakes had just been raised, and the pressure was back on. But there was no turning back now. This was the next phase, and they had to rise to the challenge.

265

CHAPTER 43

GATHERING THE TROOPS

The morning light streamed through the windows of the office, casting a warm glow over the desk where Nikhil sat. He stared out at the world outside, trying to take in the quiet before the storm. The deadlines, the expectations, the mountain of work ahead—it all loomed over him like a shadow. But for now, the silence was comforting.

Priya entered the room, holding two cups of coffee. "Peace before the chaos, huh?" she said, handing him one of the cups.

Nikhil nodded, offering a small smile. "Yeah. Let's enjoy it while it lasts."

They sipped their coffee in silence for a moment, neither of them ready to dive into the madness that was coming. It felt good to just pause for a second—to sit back and acknowledge the calm before the next big storm.

"Feels strange, doesn't it?" Priya said, breaking the silence. "We spent so much time fighting just to get that last project done. And now, we're back at the start of something even bigger."

"Strange doesn't even cover it," Nikhil replied. "It feels... heavy. Like, there's no room for mistakes anymore."

Priya gave him a sidelong glance. "You know, we don't have to take everything on our shoulders. That's what today's about, right? Bringing in more people?"

Nikhil nodded slowly. She was right, of course. They needed help. If they were going to make this global expansion work, they had to stop trying to do everything themselves. The weight of responsibility was too much for just two people to carry.

"I've already reached out to a few freelancers for research and market analysis," Priya said, taking a seat at her desk. "We should be hearing back from them today."

"That's good," Nikhil replied, setting his coffee aside. "I've been putting out feelers to potential partners overseas. We need solid people on the ground in Europe and Asia to get things moving."

Priya sighed, leaning back in her chair. "It still feels like we're about to climb Everest without enough oxygen."

Nikhil laughed softly. "We've done crazier things." "True," Priya said, smiling. "But this... this is next level. We're playing in the big leagues now." They exchanged a look—one that spoke of shared exhaustion, uncertainty, but also a glimmer of excitement. The challenge was huge, but so was the opportunity.

By mid-morning, the quiet start to their day had been replaced by a flurry of activity. Emails were coming in, responses from freelancers and potential partners who were interested in collaborating on the project. Nikhil and Priya quickly fell into their usual rhythm, juggling meetings, answering questions, and sorting through proposals.

As the day wore on, it became clear that they were making progress, even if it felt like they were still at the base of a mountain. The freelancers they brought on were sharp, efficient, and eager to prove themselves. Their market research was coming together, and there was a steady flow of communication between them and the potential overseas partners.

At around 2 p.m., Priya received a message from one of the freelancers—an analyst named Sanya, who had been helping them with European market trends. Priya quickly scanned the report, her expression brightening as she read.

"Nikhil, look at this," she said, standing up and walking over to his desk.

Nikhil took the tablet from her, reading through the data. "This is solid," he said, his tone surprised. "Looks like Sanya really knows her stuff."

Priya nodded. "She's great. I think she'll be a real asset."

Nikhil set the tablet down, feeling a small sense of relief. For the first time in days, it felt like they were gaining ground.

"Okay," Nikhil said, his mind already racing ahead. "We need to keep building on this momentum. Let's have a meeting with Sanya and the other freelancers this evening. I want to get everyone on the same page."

Priya smiled, nodding. "Let's do it."

The meeting later that evening felt different than the frantic ones they had been holding for weeks. There was a sense of control, of direction. Sanya, along with two other freelancers, was on the video call, walking Nikhil and Priya through their findings and ideas for the next phase of the expansion.

"This is great work," Nikhil said at the end of the meeting. "But we're on a tight timeline, and there's a lot more to do. I'll be sending out updated tasks later tonight, so be ready."

The freelancers nodded, their faces filled with determination. It was clear they were excited about the project, and that energy was infectious.

After the call ended, Priya leaned back in her chair, exhaling deeply. "I think we're actually starting to build something here."

Nikhil smiled, a quiet confidence settling in his chest. "Yeah. We might actually pull this off."

But as he turned back to his laptop, a message notification appeared—one from Raghav.

Nikhil opened it, his brow furrowing as he read. "Good progress so far, but I need to see a concrete

timeline by the end of the week. Investors are getting anxious. No more delays."

The sense of calm that had settled over the office evaporated in an instant. The pressure was back.

Nikhil closed the message, rubbing his temples. Raghav was pushing harder. The expectations were higher than ever, and the room for error was shrinking by the day.

"We're back in the fire," Priya said softly, reading the tension in his face.

Nikhil nodded. "Yeah. It was nice while it lasted."

CHAPTER 44

WALKING THE TIGHTROPE

The hum of the office had shifted. What was once a place of pure chaos was now becoming something of a controlled storm. The freelancers Nikhil and Priya had brought on were proving to be more than just helpful—they were essential. The weight that had pressed down on both of them for weeks seemed to lift, if only slightly, as their team began to take shape.

The deadline for the concrete timeline Raghav had requested was approaching, and with every passing hour, the tension in the office ticked up a notch. Nikhil stared at his screen, tapping his fingers against the desk as he waited for the latest report from one of their overseas contacts. Everything was riding on this next move.

"We've made a lot of progress," Priya said, standing at the corner of his desk, scrolling through her notes. "But I'm worried we're missing something."

Nikhil looked up, his face etched with concern. "What do you mean?"

Priya sighed, setting her phone down. "It feels like we're moving too fast. We've been so focused on meeting Raghav's demands that I think we're cutting corners. If this goes wrong, it won't just be on us—it'll be on our whole team. We've got to make sure that we're solid before we move forward."

Nikhil rubbed his eyes, leaning back in his chair. She was right. They had been racing toward the deadline without taking a moment to breathe, to reflect on whether or not their foundation was strong enough. They were walking a tightrope, and one misstep could send everything crashing down.

"I know," Nikhil said finally. "But we're out of time. If we stop to double-check everything, we'll miss Raghav's deadline. We can't afford that."

Priya crossed her arms, her expression hardening. "I get that, but this isn't just about pleasing Raghav anymore. We've built something here. It's not perfect, but it's something. And if we rush it, we could lose all of it."

Nikhil exhaled slowly. He knew she was right. The last thing they wanted was to create something that collapsed under its own weight. They needed to be sure that what they were building could stand the test of time, but the ticking clock was relentless. Every day brought them closer to the moment of truth.

"We'll make it work," Nikhil said, though his voice lacked the confidence it once had. "We always do.

That evening, after another marathon day of calls and emails, Nikhil sat alone in the office, staring out the window at the darkened skyline. The city buzzed with life, but inside, everything felt unnervingly still.

He glanced at the project board, the task list glaring back at him. They had made incredible progress in such a short time, but it didn't feel like enough. The scope of the global expansion was growing, and the more they built, the more cracks seemed to form.

His phone buzzed with another message. Raghav. "How's the timeline coming along? I'll need it by

tomorrow afternoon. Investors are anxious."

Nikhil's heart sank. The pressure from Raghav was mounting by the minute, and Nikhil couldn't shake the feeling that they were balancing on the edge of disaster. He quickly typed back a response: "We're on track. You'll have it tomorrow."

But as he set his phone down, a thought gnawed at the back of his mind: What if they weren't on track? What if they were rushing toward something that wasn't ready?

Priya's words echoed in his head. They had created something meaningful—a team, a vision, a plan for the future. But they were skating dangerously close to losing it all if they didn't slow down and make sure they had everything in place.

The next morning, Nikhil arrived at the office early, the weight of the timeline heavy on his shoulders. Priya was already there, reviewing the latest reports from their overseas contacts. Her face was drawn with concentration, but there was a tension in the air between them that hadn't been there before.

"I sent Raghav a draft of the timeline," Priya said, her voice clipped. "We've got everything lined up for the first phase of the expansion, but there are still a few gaps. We're going to need more time to solidify the partnerships in Asia."

Nikhil nodded, sitting down at his desk. "We'll figure it out. Raghav knows we're under pressure."

Priya shot him a glance. "You said that last week, and here we are. What happens when we run out of things to figure out?"

Nikhil didn't respond. He could feel the tension building between them again, and the last thing he wanted was another argument. They were both exhausted, both stretched thin, and the looming deadline wasn't helping.

The day flew by in a blur of activity—more calls, more reports, more emails. But as the hours passed, the pressure mounted. Nikhil could feel it in the pit of his stomach, the familiar weight of impending failure.

As evening approached, Priya walked over to Nikhil's desk, her expression softening. "I think we need to take a step back," she said quietly. "We've been running ourselves into the ground, and it's not sustainable." Nikhil sighed, leaning back in his chair. She was right again.

"We've been through a lot, Nikhil," Priya continued. "We've built something here, and I don't want to see it fall apart because we're too focused on hitting deadlines. Let's take a breath, regroup, and make sure we're doing this the right way."

Nikhil looked at her, the exhaustion in her eyes mirroring his own. They had been running on fumes for so long, and now it was catching up with them. The cracks were starting to show, not just in the project, but in them.

"You're right," Nikhil said finally, his voice heavy with resignation. "We need to slow down. Let's take tonight to breathe, and tomorrow we'll regroup."

Priya smiled faintly, the tension between them easing. "We'll make it through this."

CHAPTER 45

THE CALM BEFORE THE NEXT STORM

Nikhil sat at his desk in the early morning light, the empty office around him providing a rare moment of peace. The decision to regroup and take a step back had been the right one, but as the quiet settled in, he couldn't help but feel the tension brewing just beneath the surface. There was still so much to do, and time was quickly running out.

Priya arrived a short while later, her expression a little more relaxed than the day before. "Morning," she said, setting her coffee down on her desk. "Ready to dive back in?"

Nikhil nodded, though the calm they had embraced last night was already starting to fray. The looming deadlines were still there, and though they had taken a step back, it wouldn't be long before the pressure began to mount again.

"I think we made the right call," Priya said, taking a seat across from Nikhil. "We were headed for burnout. Slowing down was the only way to keep this thing going."

"Yeah," Nikhil replied, though his voice was distant. "But we can't slow down for long. Raghav's expecting results."

Priya leaned forward, her tone soft but firm. "We'll give him results. But we'll do it on our terms this time. No more running ourselves into the ground. If we're going to expand globally, we need to be strategic. No more cutting corners."

Nikhil knew she was right, but the pressure weighed heavily on him. How were they supposed to find the balance between moving fast enough to meet Raghav's demands and slow enough to build something sustainable?

Before he could answer, his phone buzzed with a notification—an email from Raghav.

"Speak of the devil," Nikhil muttered, opening the email.

The message was brief but direct: "Need progress report by end of the week. Investors are growing impatient."

Nikhil sighed, running a hand through his hair. "Of course they are."

Priya frowned as she read the email over his shoulder. "They always are. But that doesn't mean we have to rush back into chaos."

Nikhil stared at the email, feeling the familiar weight of expectation settling on his chest. They needed to deliver, and soon. But how could they meet Raghav's timeline without falling into the same trap they'd just climbed out of?

That afternoon, they sat down with the team—Sanya and the other freelancers they had brought on board. The small conference room felt cramped, the tension palpable as they began outlining their strategy for the next few weeks.

"We need to refocus," Nikhil said, addressing the team. "We've been moving fast, but it's time to make sure we're building something solid. We're going to scale back on a few non-essential tasks and double down on what's most important—our partnerships in Europe and Asia."

Sanya nodded, her usual calm demeanor reassuring. "I've already started refining the market research. I think we'll be able to identify the key partners we need to focus on within the next couple of days."

"That's good," Priya added. "Once we have that, we can start narrowing our focus and streamline our approach. No more scrambling to do everything at once."

The team seemed to relax a little, the clarity of their new approach offering some relief from the chaos of the last few weeks. But the weight of the timeline still loomed large.

As the meeting wrapped up, Nikhil felt a flicker of hope. They had a plan, one that was more focused and deliberate. But as they walked out of the conference room, he couldn't shake the feeling that time was slipping away.

That evening, Priya stayed late, working through some of the final details for the progress report they needed to send to Raghav. Nikhil sat across from her, poring over the latest data from their partners in Europe. The silence between them was comfortable but heavy with the knowledge of what was still left to do.

"Do you ever wonder if we're in over our heads?" Priya asked suddenly, her voice cutting through the quiet.

Nikhil looked up, surprised. Priya rarely voiced doubts, even when things were tough.

"All the time," Nikhil admitted, leaning back in his chair. "But it's too late to back out now. We've come too far."

Priya nodded slowly, her fingers still tapping on the keyboard. "I know. It's just... we've worked so hard to get here, but sometimes it feels like no matter what we do, it's never enough."

Nikhil understood exactly what she meant. The higher they climbed, the more precarious it felt. The pressure to succeed was overwhelming, and the stakes only seemed to get higher with every step they took.

"I guess that's just part of the deal," Nikhil said, though the words didn't bring much comfort. "We wanted to build something big, and this is what comes with it."

Priya gave a half-smile. "I just hope we don't lose ourselves in the process."

The words hung in the air between them, and for a moment, Nikhil didn't know how to respond. Were they losing themselves? They had poured everything into this project, sacrificing sleep, relationships, and any sense of balance. The drive to succeed had consumed them, and now, with the global expansion on the horizon, the stakes were higher than ever.

"We won't," Nikhil said finally, though he wasn't sure if he believed it. "We'll figure it out. We always do."

Priya didn't respond, but the doubt lingered in her eyes.

The next morning, Nikhil sat at his desk, staring at the draft of the progress report they were about to send to Raghav. It was solid—clear, concise, and backed up with real progress. But there was an uneasiness in Nikhil's chest that he couldn't shake.

Was this enough?

He glanced over at Priya, who was busy reviewing the last-minute updates from their freelancers. They had done everything they could, but the feeling of uncertainty loomed large. What if Raghav wasn't satisfied? Taking a deep breath, Nikhil hit "send" on the email. The report was on its way to Raghav, and now, all they could do was wait.

CHAPTER 46

THE WAITING GAME

The sound of the email's *whoosh* as it was sent seemed to echo in the office, filling the silence that followed. Nikhil sat back in his chair, staring at the screen as if expecting Raghav's response to appear instantly. But he knew better than that. Now came the hardest part—the waiting.

Priya didn't say anything as she finished reviewing her notes, her focus on the project files in front of her. The silence between them had become more frequent lately, a growing tension that neither of them wanted to address directly.

"I guess now we wait," Nikhil muttered, his voice breaking the silence.

Priya glanced up, her eyes tired but focused. "Yeah. But not for long. You know how Raghav is—he'll want a response out of us just as quickly as we're waiting on one from him."

Nikhil nodded, feeling the weight of her words. Raghav was demanding, and he wasn't known for giving long periods of grace. If he wasn't satisfied with the report, they'd know soon enough, and they'd have to scramble—again.

Priya leaned back in her chair, rubbing her temples. "We've done everything we can for now. We need to rest, Nikhil. We're no good to the project if we're running on empty."

Nikhil knew she was right, but the anxiety gnawing at him wouldn't let up. He kept replaying the past few weeks in his mind, wondering if they had missed something, if there was more they could have done. Was it enough?

"We can't lose momentum," Nikhil said, standing up from his desk and walking to the window. The city stretched out below them, bustling with life, oblivious to the storm brewing in their little office. "If we let up now, even for a moment, we could lose everything."

Priya didn't respond immediately. She watched him in silence, her brow furrowed with concern. "Nikhil, we're going to burn out if we don't take a break. We've been running nonstop for weeks. If we don't recharge, there won't be anything left of us to keep this going."

Nikhil sighed, pressing his forehead against the cool glass of the window. How had it come to this? The dream of building something great had consumed them both, leaving little room for anything else. Now, they were holding on by a thread, desperate not to fall apart under the pressure.

"I know," Nikhil admitted, his voice softening. "But I'm not sure how to slow down anymore. Every time I try, all I can think about is the next deadline, the next task we need to complete."

Priya stood up, crossing the room to stand beside him. "You're not alone in this, you know. We're in it together. But we can't keep pushing ourselves like this.

At some point, we're going to break."

Nikhil turned to her, seeing the exhaustion in her eyes, the weariness that matched his own. She was right, of course. They had both been running on empty for far too long, and the cracks were starting to show.

"What if we don't make it?" Nikhil asked, his voice barely above a whisper.

Priya's expression softened, and for a moment, she didn't answer. "We've made it this far, haven't we? We'll find a way to keep going. But we need to take care of ourselves too. Otherwise, what's the point?"

The words hung in the air between them, and Nikhil felt a pang of guilt. He had been so focused on the project, on delivering results, that he had lost sight of everything else. The long nights, the constant pressure—he had pushed them both to the limit, and now they were teetering on the edge.

Priya gave him a small smile, her voice softening. "Why don't we take the afternoon off? Just a few hours. We can clear our heads and come back fresh."

Nikhil hesitated, the idea of taking time off feeling almost foreign. But as he looked at Priya, he could see the strain in her expression, the exhaustion weighing on her. She was right. They needed a break, even if just for a little while.

"Okay," Nikhil said finally. "Let's take the afternoon off."

The afternoon passed in a blur. Nikhil and Priya had left the office, heading out to the nearby park for a walk, trying to clear their heads and put some distance between themselves and the project that had consumed them.

For the first time in weeks, the fresh air felt like a relief. The constant noise in Nikhil's mind quieted down, if only slightly, as they walked in silence. The weight of the deadlines, the pressure to succeed, and the fear of failure still lingered, but it felt more manageable now.

As they walked, Priya spoke up, breaking the silence. "Do you ever think about what comes next? After all of this?"

Nikhil glanced at her, surprised by the question. "After this project? I don't know. I guess I've been so focused on getting through it that I haven't thought much about what comes after."

Priya smiled faintly. "Yeah, me neither. But I wonder sometimes... what's the point of all of this if we don't stop to enjoy it? If all we do is work ourselves to the bone, where does it leave us?"

The question hit Nikhil harder than he expected. What was the point? They had worked so hard to build something, to prove themselves, but in the process, they had lost sight of everything else. Was it worth it?

"I don't know," Nikhil said, his voice quiet. "But I'd like to figure it out."

Priya nodded, her smile widening slightly. "Maybe that's something we can work on—after all of this."

Nikhil smiled too, the tension between them easing for the first time in days. There was more to life than just the project, and for the first time in a long time, he allowed himself to think about what might come next.

That evening, back in the office, the sense of calm lingered. Nikhil sat at his desk, feeling more centered than he had in weeks. The project was still looming, but now it felt like something they could handle—if they worked together.

As they wrapped up for the night, Priya glanced at her phone and raised an eyebrow. "Raghav hasn't responded yet."

Nikhil felt a flicker of anxiety, but it was quickly replaced by a sense of calm. "He will. And whatever he says, we'll figure it out."

Priya smiled, nodding. "Yeah. We will."

For the first time in a long time, Nikhil felt like maybe—just maybe—they could make it through this.

CHAPTER 47

THE RESPONSE

The office felt unusually quiet as Nikhil and Priya settled back into their desks after their brief respite. The calmness of the walk had offered them a sliver of peace, but it hadn't lasted long. Raghav's response still hung over them like a storm waiting to break.

Nikhil glanced at his phone every few minutes, expecting it to buzz with an email notification at any moment. But the silence stretched on, and with it, a growing sense of unease.

Priya broke the quiet first. "It's like waiting for a bomb to go off," she muttered, tapping her pen against the edge of her desk. "The longer we wait, the worse it feels."

Nikhil nodded, unable to shake the feeling of dread that had settled in the pit of his stomach. "Yeah, I know. But we did everything we could. We've shown real progress."

"Progress isn't always enough," Priya replied softly, her eyes fixed on her computer screen. "Especially with someone like Raghav."

They both knew what she meant. Raghav wasn't just looking for progress—he was looking for something exceptional. Anything less, and they risked losing his confidence, his investment, and everything they'd worked so hard to build.

Just as the tension in the room reached its peak, Nikhil's phone buzzed.

He stared at it for a moment before reaching for it, his heart pounding in his chest. This was it.

"It's from Raghav," Nikhil said, his voice tight. Priya straightened in her chair, her eyes locked on

Nikhil as he opened the email. The silence in the room was deafening as he began to read.

The message was short and to the point, typical of Raghav's style.

"I've reviewed the progress report. We're not where we need to be. There are gaps in the partnerships you've established in Asia and Europe, and the timeline isn't aggressive enough for my investors. You need to push harder. I expect an updated plan by the end of the week."

Nikhil's stomach dropped. He read the email again, hoping he'd missed something, but the words were clear. It wasn't enough.

He glanced at Priya, her expression already mirroring his own. "He wants more. He says the partnerships aren't solid enough, and the timeline isn't aggressive enough."

Priya closed her eyes, leaning back in her chair with a frustrated sigh. "Of course he does. He wants us to keep pushing, but we're already stretched to the limit."

Nikhil stared at the email, the familiar weight of pressure settling back on his shoulders. They'd given everything they had, but somehow, it still wasn't enough for Raghav.

"What do we do now?" Priya asked, though her tone was more resigned than questioning.

Nikhil rubbed his temples, his mind racing. "We have to deliver. We don't have a choice. We need to reach out to more partners in Asia and Europe, tighten up the timeline, and figure out how to move faster."

Priya shook her head. "But faster means cutting corners. And if we do that, we risk the whole thing falling apart."

"I know," Nikhil said, his voice strained. "But what else can we do? Raghav's not going to wait. If we don't give him what he wants, he'll pull the plug. And then all of this—everything we've worked for—will be gone."

Priya didn't respond right away, her eyes fixed on the floor. They were trapped, caught between Raghav's impossible demands and the limits of what they could realistically deliver. After a long pause, Priya spoke, her voice barely above a whisper. "We can't keep doing this, Nikhil. We've been chasing deadlines, pushing harder and harder, but at some point, it's going to break us. We can't keep sacrificing everything for Raghav's approval."

Nikhil stared at her, the exhaustion in her eyes mirroring his own. She was right. They were burning themselves out, giving more than they had, and it still wasn't enough.

"What are you saying?" Nikhil asked, though he already knew the answer.

"I'm saying that maybe it's time to draw the line," Priya said, her tone steady but firm. "Maybe it's time to tell Raghav that this is it. That we can't keep pushing like this. If he wants more, he's going to have to invest more—give us more resources, more time, more support. Otherwise, we're just running ourselves into the ground."

Nikhil's first instinct was to argue. How could they tell Raghav no? How could they risk losing his backing, his connections, his investment? But as he looked at Priya, he realized that she was right. They couldn't keep doing this.

They had sacrificed too much already—time, energy, their own well-being. If they kept pushing at this pace, they wouldn't just lose the project. They'd lose themselves.

Nikhil exhaled slowly, the tension in his chest easing ever so slightly. "Okay," he said finally. "Let's push back. We'll tell Raghav that if he wants us to move faster, he needs to meet us halfway."

Priya looked at him, a flicker of relief in her eyes. "You think he'll go for it?"

"I don't know," Nikhil admitted. "But it's our only option."

The next morning, Nikhil sat at his desk, drafting the email to Raghav. It was one of the hardest emails he'd ever written. Pushing back against Raghav felt risky, like stepping into unknown territory. But it was necessary.

As he typed, his mind raced with thoughts of what could go wrong. What if Raghav refused? What if he pulled his investment? What if this was the end?

But then he thought of Priya's words, of the toll this project had taken on both of them. They couldn't keep sacrificing everything for the sake of progress. There had to be a limit.

The email was clear but firm, outlining the need for more resources and support if Raghav expected them to accelerate the timeline. Nikhil took a deep breath as he hovered over the send button.

"Ready?" Priya asked, standing beside him.

Nikhil glanced up at her, giving a small nod. "Ready."

With a final click, the email was sent.

CHAPTER 48

THE GAMBLE

The office felt unnaturally still after Nikhil hit send. He leaned back in his chair, staring at the blank screen, as if waiting for something to happen. But nothing did—at least not yet. The ball was in Raghav's court now.

Priya sat across from him, watching him carefully. "How do you feel?" she asked, her voice soft.

Nikhil shook his head, rubbing the back of his neck. "Honestly? I don't know. Part of me feels like we just took a huge risk, and the other part feels like we had no choice."

Priya nodded, the tension still visible in her posture. "We did what we had to do. If Raghav doesn't see that, then maybe this whole thing was doomed from the start."

Nikhil didn't respond right away. What if Priya was right? What if no matter how hard they worked or how much they sacrificed, Raghav was never going to be satisfied? Maybe his expectations had been impossible from the beginning, and they had been too focused on pleasing him to see it.

But now, everything felt different. For the first time, they had pushed back, drawn a line in the sand. And now they waited.

Hours passed, and still no response from Raghav. Nikhil tried to focus on other tasks, but his mind kept wandering back to that email, to the possibility that they had just torpedoed their project and everything they had worked for.

As the afternoon dragged on, Priya broke the silence. "Do you think he's going to walk away?"

Nikhil's fingers paused over the keyboard, the thought lingering in the back of his mind. "I don't know," he admitted. "But if he does, I think we'll be okay. We've built something real here, and it's bigger than Raghav's approval."

Priya's eyes softened as she leaned back in her chair. "You're right. We've put so much into this, and it's ours now. If he walks, we'll find another way."

Nikhil smiled faintly, though the knot of anxiety in his stomach hadn't loosened. Was it really theirs? Or had they been chasing Raghav's approval so hard that they'd forgotten what they were building for themselves?

Suddenly, Nikhil's phone buzzed, snapping him out of his thoughts. His pulse quickened as he grabbed it, seeing Raghav's name on the screen. Priya sat up, her eyes wide with anticipation.

"It's him," Nikhil muttered, opening the message.

The words on the screen were brief, but they hit like a hammer.

"Meet me tomorrow. We need to talk in person."

Nikhil felt his stomach drop. This wasn't the response he'd expected. An in-person meeting with Raghav meant only one thing: this was about to get serious.

Priya leaned over to read the message, her expression tight with concern. "What do you think that means?"

"I don't know," Nikhil said, his voice low. "But it's not good."

The next morning, Nikhil and Priya sat in the lobby of the sleek, glass-walled office building where Raghav's headquarters were located. The air was thick with tension, both of them knowing that whatever happened in this meeting would shape the future of their project—and possibly their careers.

"Whatever happens in there," Priya said, glancing at Nikhil, "we stand our ground. We can't go back to the way things were."

Nikhil nodded, though the tightness in his chest hadn't loosened. They had made a stand, and now they had to see it through.

A few minutes later, Raghav's assistant called them in. The room they entered was as imposing as ever—floor-to-ceiling windows, a massive table, and Raghav seated at the far end, his expression unreadable.

"Sit," Raghav said, his voice clipped.

Nikhil and Priya exchanged a quick glance before taking their seats. The tension in the room was palpable.

Raghav didn't waste time on pleasantries. "I got your email," he began, his tone sharp. "And I have to say, I'm not used to being told how things are going to go. I run the show here. Not you."

Nikhil felt his pulse quicken, but he forced himself to remain calm. "We understand that, Raghav," he said carefully. "But we've been working nonstop to deliver what you've asked for. We've put everything into this project, but if we keep going at this pace without more resources, it's going to fall apart. We need more support."

Raghav leaned back in his chair, his eyes narrowing. "And what makes you think I'm going to just give you more resources because you're asking for them?"

Priya spoke up, her voice steady but firm. "Because if we keep going like this, we'll fail. And I don't think that's what you want either. We're not asking for anything unreasonable. We're asking for the tools we need to make this project a success."

Raghav stared at them for a long moment, the tension in the room thickening with every passing second. Finally, he leaned forward, folding his hands on the table.

"I'll give you what you're asking for," he said slowly. "But understand this—if you don't deliver, you're done. No second chances. No excuses. You either meet my expectations, or I walk."

Nikhil felt a wave of relief wash over him, but it was tempered by the weight of Raghav's words. This was their last shot.

"We'll deliver," Nikhil said, his voice steady. "We just need the support to make it happen."

Raghav's gaze remained intense, but after another long moment, he nodded. "Fine. You'll have the resources you need. But don't disappoint me."

As they left the building, the weight of what had just happened began to sink in. They had pushed back against Raghav, and it had worked. But the stakes had never been higher. This was their last chance—if they didn't deliver, they'd lose everything.

"We did it," Priya said, her voice filled with cautious relief. "He's giving us more support."

Nikhil nodded, though the pressure in his chest hadn't fully eased. "Yeah. But now we have to prove we can deliver. This is it, Priya. No more mistakes."

Priya smiled, though her expression was serious. "We've got this, Nikhil. We've made it this far. We'll figure it out."

Nikhil wanted to believe her. They had fought hard to get here, and they had just secured the support they needed. But the weight of what lay ahead was enormous, and the clock was ticking faster than ever.

CHAPTER 49

The Final Push

The moment they stepped back into their office, Nikhil felt the shift in the atmosphere. The stakes had always been high, but now there was no more room for error. Raghav had given them what they asked for, but he had made it clear: failure wasn't an option. This was their last shot.

Priya set her bag down and sat at her desk, her eyes scanning the tasks laid out in front of her. "It feels different now, doesn't it?" she said, glancing up at Nikhil.

Nikhil nodded, the weight of the next few weeks already settling heavily on his shoulders. "Yeah. It's like we're on a tightrope, and the net's been taken away."

Priya gave him a small, tight smile. "But we've got more tools now. We've got the support we need."

"Tools are good," Nikhil replied, "but we still have to make them work. And fast."

They both knew what that meant—longer hours, more meetings, and the kind of laser focus that left no room for distractions. They had to deliver, and this time, there would be no safety net if they failed. That afternoon, Nikhil and Priya gathered the team together. Sanya and the freelancers had been instrumental in helping them with the first phase, and now they were about to embark on the most critical part of the project: expanding into the new markets Raghav wanted—Europe and Asia.

"We've secured more resources," Nikhil said, addressing the team. "That means we're bringing in additional partners and ramping up efforts in the international markets. But it also means the clock is ticking. We have to move fast and efficiently. There's no room for delays."

Sanya nodded, her expression serious. "We've been preparing for this. I'll get the market research finalized by the end of the week, and we'll be ready to reach out to key contacts."

Priya chimed in, her voice steady. "We're also going to bring on a few more freelancers to help with the logistics of the expansion. We can't afford to get bogged down by the details, so we'll delegate as much as possible. Our focus has to stay on the bigger picture."

The team seemed energized, ready to take on the challenge. But Nikhil could still feel the pressure building inside him. Everything was riding on this.

The next week passed in a blur of activity. Nikhil and Priya worked around the clock, managing meetings with new partners, overseeing the expanded team, and ensuring that every piece of the puzzle was coming together. It was relentless, and as the days wore on, the exhaustion began to creep back in.

One evening, after a particularly long call with their partners in Asia, Nikhil slumped into his chair, rubbing his eyes. They were making progress, but it still felt like they were running on the edge of a cliff.

"We're getting there," Priya said from across the room, though her voice was thick with fatigue.

Nikhil glanced at her, noticing the dark circles under her eyes. "Barely," he muttered. "Raghav's going to expect an update soon. I'm not sure we're as far along as he wants us to be."

Priya leaned back in her chair, letting out a slow breath. "We're doing everything we can. That has to be enough."

Nikhil wasn't so sure. They had brought on more freelancers, expanded their network of partners, and pushed harder than ever before. But the project felt like a race against time, and with every day that passed, the deadline loomed larger.

"We'll get there," Priya repeated, though the strain in her voice was hard to ignore.

Two days later, Nikhil received the message he'd been dreading—Raghav wanted another update. He sat at his desk, staring at the email as if it might change on its own. It hadn't been long since their last meeting, and yet, Raghav was already growing impatient. "What do you think?" Priya asked, reading over his shoulder. "Are we ready to show him the progress we've made?"

"We don't have a choice," Nikhil said, his voice tight. "He's expecting an update, and if we don't give him something concrete, he's going to pull the plug."

They spent the next few hours finalizing their reports, gathering the data from their new market research, and compiling everything into a presentation that would satisfy Raghav's demands. It had to be perfect.

When the report was finally ready, Nikhil stared at the file on his screen, hesitating before hitting send. He felt like a gambler, betting everything on a hand he wasn't sure was strong enough.

"Do you think this is enough?" Nikhil asked, glancing at Priya.

Priya looked up from her laptop, her expression unreadable. "It has to be."

With a deep breath, Nikhil hit send.

The next morning, Nikhil and Priya waited for Raghav's response. It was like being stuck in limbo, every hour that passed filled with the weight of uncertainty.

"He's going to ask for more," Priya said, her voice resigned. "No matter what we give him, it's never enough."

Nikhil didn't respond. What if she was right? What if no matter how much they delivered, it would never satisfy Raghav? He had pushed them to their limits, and now, they were teetering on the edge.

Suddenly, Nikhil's phone buzzed. His heart skipped a beat as he reached for it. It was a message from Raghav.

He opened it, his pulse racing.

"Progress looks good. But we need to move faster. The investors want to see results by the end of the month."

Priya read the message over his shoulder, her face paling. "The end of the month? That's impossible."

Nikhil felt the air leave his lungs. The end of the month was only a few weeks away. They had barely finished laying the groundwork, and now Raghav was expecting results in a matter of days.

"This is insane," Priya said, shaking her head. "There's no way we can deliver that fast."

"We don't have a choice," Nikhil said quietly, the weight of the deadline crashing down on him. "We have to figure out a way to make it happen."

Priya stared at him, her eyes wide with disbelief. "Nikhil, we can't do this. We're already stretched thin, and now he's asking for something that's not even possible."

"I know," Nikhil said, his voice tight with frustration. "But if we don't deliver, we lose everything. There has to be a way."

Priya stood up, pacing the room. "I don't know how much more we can take. This is beyond pushing—it's impossible."

Nikhil didn't respond. They were stuck, trapped between Raghav's impossible demands and the reality of their limits.

For the first time, Nikhil felt like they might not make it. The clock was ticking, and time was running out.

301

CHAPTER 50

ON THE EDGE

The next few days were a blur of activity. Nikhil and Priya were running on fumes, pushing themselves harder than they ever had before. The end of the month was only two weeks away, and the weight of Raghav's demand was crushing them.

Every meeting, every email, every conversation felt like a race against time. They had to show results, but how could they produce something tangible in such a short period? The pressure was relentless, and with every passing hour, the stress mounted.

Priya had taken to pacing the office, her frustration bubbling beneath the surface. "This isn't going to work, Nikhil," she said one afternoon, her voice tight with exhaustion. "We're going to burn out before we even get close to what Raghav wants."

Nikhil sat at his desk, staring at the endless list of tasks in front of him. His eyes burned from lack of sleep, and his body felt heavy with fatigue, but he couldn't stop. There was too much at stake.

"We don't have a choice," Nikhil muttered, running his hand through his hair. "If we don't deliver, it's over." Priya stopped pacing, her eyes narrowing. "And if we keep going like this, we're going to destroy ourselves. Raghav is asking for the impossible. We're running on empty, and he's just going to keep pushing."

Nikhil knew she was right. They were both at their breaking point. But what could they do? They couldn't afford to stop, not now. They had fought so hard to get here, and to walk away now would be to admit defeat.

"There's got to be a way," Nikhil said, though the words felt hollow. "We'll find a way to make it work."

Priya stared at him, her face tight with frustration. "And if we don't? What then?"

Nikhil didn't have an answer. Failure wasn't an option, but the path to success was looking more impossible with every passing minute.

Later that evening, Nikhil found himself alone in the office. Priya had left hours earlier, her exhaustion finally catching up with her. He had told her to go home and get some rest, but he couldn't bring himself to do the same. The clock was ticking, and the pressure was suffocating.

He stared at the project board, the tasks and deadlines blurring together in front of him. How had they ended up here? They had started with a vision, a dream of building something great, but now it felt like they were chasing something they could never catch.

His phone buzzed, pulling him out of his thoughts.

It was a message from Raghav.

"Checking in. Investors want to see the results by next Friday. Are we on track?"

Nikhil's heart sank. Next Friday? That was less than a week away. He felt the weight of the deadline crash down on him again, and for the first time, he wasn't sure if they could make it.

He quickly typed back: "We're working on it. We'll have something to show by Friday."

As soon as he sent the message, he regretted it. What would they have to show? They were barely holding everything together, and now the pressure to deliver in such a short time was overwhelming.

Nikhil leaned back in his chair, closing his eyes. The weight of it all was too much. He had pushed himself harder than ever before, but now, he was starting to see the cracks. Was this what success looked like? Was this constant pressure and fear of failure what they had been working toward?

The next morning, Priya arrived at the office, looking as exhausted as Nikhil felt. She dropped her bag on the desk and sat down heavily, rubbing her eyes.

"How are we going to make this work?" she asked, her voice thick with fatigue.

Nikhil didn't have an answer. He had spent the entire night trying to come up with a solution, but nothing felt right. They were running out of time, and no matter how hard they pushed, it felt like they were falling further behind.

"We'll figure it out," Nikhil said, though his voice lacked conviction.

Priya looked at him, her eyes filled with frustration. "We keep saying that, but nothing's changing. We're not making progress, Nikhil. We're just spinning our wheels, trying to meet Raghav's impossible demands. When does it stop?"

Nikhil didn't know how to respond. He felt like he was on autopilot, moving forward simply because he didn't know how to stop. Was Priya right? Were they chasing something they could never reach?

Before he could answer, Sanya walked into the office, her usual calm demeanor replaced by visible tension. "I've got the latest report from the European partners," she said, handing Nikhil a file. "But it's not great. We're behind schedule, and they're starting to get concerned."

Nikhil flipped through the report, his heart sinking.

It was worse than he thought.

"We can't afford any more delays," Priya said, her voice filled with urgency. "We're running out of time." Nikhil set the report down, feeling the weight of the situation pressing down on him like never before. They were in trouble, and no matter how hard they pushed, they weren't making the progress they needed.

"We need to make a decision," Priya said, her voice calm but firm. "Either we tell Raghav we can't meet his deadline, or we keep pushing and risk losing everything."

Nikhil looked at her, feeling the pressure of the decision weighing heavily on him. It was a no-win situation. If they told Raghav they couldn't meet the deadline, they risked losing his support. But if they kept pushing, they risked burning out completely.

"What do we do?" Priya asked, her eyes filled with concern.

Nikhil stared at the project board, his mind racing. There had to be a way out of this. But for the first time, he wasn't sure what that was.

Later that evening, Nikhil sat in the darkened office, the weight of the decision pressing down on him like a heavy cloak. This was it. The moment that would define everything.

He glanced at his phone, seeing another message from Raghav.

"Update?"

Nikhil stared at the message, his fingers hovering over the screen. What could he say? They weren't ready. They were far from ready. But how could he admit that now, after everything they had done?

He typed a response, his heart pounding. "We need more time."

The words felt like a defeat, but they were the truth. They couldn't keep pushing at this pace without risking everything.

A few moments later, his phone buzzed again. "Not an option. Make it happen, or we're done." Nikhil's heart sank. Raghav wasn't going to budge.

He set his phone down, feeling the weight of Raghav's ultimatum crush him. This was it. They had pushed as hard as they could, but now, it felt like they were standing at the edge of a cliff, staring into the abyss.

"What do we do?" Priya asked again, her voice barely above a whisper.

Nikhil looked at her, feeling the full weight of the decision pressing down on him. He didn't know.

CHAPTER 51

THE BREAKING POINT

The office was quiet, but it wasn't a peaceful silence. It was the kind of stillness that settled in right before something broke. Nikhil sat at his desk, staring at the same spot on the wall he had been looking at for the last hour. His mind was racing, but he couldn't focus on any one thought for long. Everything felt like it was slipping away.

Across the room, Priya sat with her head in her hands, the weight of exhaustion and frustration bearing down on her. Neither of them had spoken in a while. There wasn't much left to say.

Nikhil closed his eyes, his breath coming out in short, shaky bursts. How had it come to this? They had started this project with so much hope, so much energy, and now it felt like they were drowning, pulled under by the impossible demands of Raghav and their own fear of failure.

Priya broke the silence first. "We can't do this anymore," she said, her voice trembling with frustration. "Not like this."

Nikhil opened his eyes and looked at her. There was a weariness in her face that he hadn't noticed before, or maybe he had been too wrapped up in his own panic to see it. She was just as worn down as he was.

"I know," Nikhil said, his voice barely above a whisper. "But what do we do? If we stop now..."

Priya shook her head, cutting him off. "It's not about stopping. It's about changing. We're doing everything wrong, Nikhil. We're killing ourselves trying to meet Raghav's impossible deadlines, and we're losing sight of what we're actually trying to build."

Her words hit Nikhil harder than he expected. She was right. They weren't just burning out—they were losing the essence of why they had started this journey in the first place. They had become so focused on pleasing Raghav and hitting his arbitrary targets that they had forgotten what mattered: building something real, something that could last.

Nikhil rubbed his eyes, the weight of her words settling deep inside him. How had they let it get this far? They had been so sure of themselves in the beginning, so confident that they could build something great. But somewhere along the way, they had lost their path, chasing approval instead of vision.

"We need to refocus," Priya said, her voice firm but gentle. "If we keep going like this, we're going to crash. And it won't just be the project—we'll lose everything we've worked for, everything we've sacrificed."

Nikhil nodded slowly, the fog in his mind beginning to clear. Priya was right. They had been sprinting toward a goal that kept moving, trying to hit every deadline, check every box, without stopping to consider whether any of it was even necessary.

"What if we stop trying to do it all?" Nikhil asked, his voice gaining strength. "What if we focus on the parts of the project that matter? The parts we know we can deliver, the ones that will actually build something sustainable?"

Priya looked at him, her eyes searching his face for a moment before she smiled faintly. "That's exactly what we need to do. We've been running ourselves ragged trying to meet someone else's idea of success. It's time to take control."

Nikhil sat back in his chair, the tension in his chest loosening for the first time in weeks. Priya was right. They needed to take control. They couldn't keep living under the pressure of Raghav's expectations, constantly scrambling to meet his impossible demands. They needed to focus on what they were good at, on building something they could actually be proud of.

"We need to pivot," Nikhil said, the words coming out with more conviction than he had expected. "We need to narrow our focus, stop trying to expand so fast, and focus on the core of the project. The things we can actually deliver."

Priya nodded, her expression softening as she sat up straighter. "Exactly. We need to cut back on the noise and get back to what we're good at. We've been chasing too much."

They both sat in silence for a moment, the weight of the decision sinking in. It was a risk, stepping back from the aggressive pace Raghav had set for them. But what other choice did they have?

The clock on the wall ticked loudly in the silence of the office. Nikhil's thoughts were a swirl of what-ifs, doubts, and fears. What if Raghav didn't accept the change? What if pulling back was seen as a sign of weakness? What if everything they had worked for crumbled because of this decision?

But then, there was another side to the coin. What if continuing as they were was the real mistake?

The memory of Raghav's last conversation echoed in his mind. The tension in the room, the pressure in his voice, and the unyielding demand for results. No matter how much they delivered, Raghav would always want more. Nikhil realized that pleasing Raghav had become the goal, rather than delivering something meaningful.

"What's the worst that could happen?" Priya asked quietly, almost as if she were reading his thoughts.

Nikhil blinked and turned to her. "He could pull the plug. We could lose everything."

Priya shook her head. "No. The worst that could happen is that we continue down this path, and we burn out. We lose more than just the project. We lose ourselves."

Her words cut through Nikhil's fear. She was right. They had already sacrificed too much. Sleepless nights, strained friendships, and a growing distance between the dream they had started with and the reality they were living in. If they didn't make this change, the project wouldn't be the only casualty.

"We need to be bold, Nikhil," Priya said, her voice steady. "This is our vision. We started this to create something that would last, not just to meet a quarterly report. If we're going to take a risk, it might as well be on something we believe in."

Nikhil sat back in his chair, her words settling over him like a calming blanket. This was the right move. The fear didn't completely disappear, but it began to shift, making room for something else—clarity.

The rest of the evening was a blur of action. Nikhil and Priya began reworking the project with renewed focus. They stripped away everything that wasn't essential, cutting out the tasks and deliverables that had been weighing them down. The aggressive expansion plan into Asia was paused, and they decided to prioritize Europe, where they already had traction.

"We'll focus on building a strong foundation here," Priya said as she typed notes into the new project plan. "Once we've proven this model in Europe, we can expand into Asia with more confidence."

Nikhil nodded, his fingers flying across the keyboard as he updated the timeline. It wasn't about scaling as fast as possible anymore. It was about scaling smart. They had been running at full speed without a clear direction, and now, for the first time in weeks, they were setting their own pace.

The office grew quieter as the night wore on. The oppressive weight that had hung over them for so long was starting to lift, though the pressure still lingered. They had made the decision to pivot, but the real test was still ahead.

"We're going to have to sell this to Raghav," Priya said, her voice breaking the silence. "We can't just change the plan and hope he goes along with it."

Nikhil felt a familiar knot form in his stomach at the thought of confronting Raghav. It was never easy dealing with him—his demands, his impatience, his relentless pursuit of results. But this time felt different. They weren't coming to him with excuses or desperation. They were coming to him with a solid plan, one that was grounded in reality and their expertise.

"He'll have to listen," Nikhil said, more to himself than to Priya. "If he wants this to succeed, he'll have to trust us."

Priya smiled, though it was tinged with exhaustion. "Let's hope you're right."

CHAPTER 52

THE PIVOT

The next morning, Nikhil walked into the office with a heaviness he couldn't shake. The conversation with Priya the night before had lingered in his mind, challenging everything he had been telling himself for months. For the first time in a long time, he wasn't sure if pushing harder was the right answer.

Priya was already at her desk when he arrived, her face set in a serious expression. She looked up when he entered, but there was no greeting, no small talk. They both knew what they had to talk about.

"I've been thinking," Nikhil said, breaking the silence as he sat down across from her. "You're right. We can't keep doing this."

Priya sighed, a mix of relief and exhaustion on her face. "We're at the breaking point, Nikhil. If we don't change something, we're not going to make it. Not just the project—us."

Nikhil nodded, the words settling deep inside him. He had been so focused on Raghav's approval, on hitting impossible deadlines, that he had lost sight of why they started this journey in the first place. He had forgotten that their strength didn't come from chasing every task, but from the core of what they were trying to build.

"What if we stop chasing the deadlines and refocus on what we're really good at?" Nikhil asked, his mind racing with the idea that had been forming since the night before. "What if we take a step back and focus on the parts of the project that actually matter, the things that will make this sustainable in the long run?"

Priya looked at him, a flicker of hope in her eyes. "You mean... stop trying to do everything? Focus on what we're best at?"

Nikhil nodded, feeling a new kind of energy building inside him. "Exactly. We've been trying to meet every demand Raghav throws at us, but we're not built for that. We started this because we had a vision, a real strategy for creating something meaningful. Maybe it's time we get back to that."

For a moment, Priya said nothing, her expression unreadable. Then, slowly, a smile tugged at the corners of her lips. "That sounds like something we can actually manage. But what about Raghav? He's not exactly known for his patience."

Nikhil leaned forward, the determination returning to his voice. "We'll have to sell it to him. Show him that our approach is the only way to make this work in the long term. If he wants something real, something that can last, he'll have to trust us." The rest of the day was spent reworking the project. Nikhil and Priya sat side by side, going over the details, cutting back on the tasks that had been dragging them down, and refining the core elements that they knew they could deliver. It was a pivot—not abandoning the original vision, but refocusing on what made the project strong to begin with.

"We've been trying to expand too fast," Priya said, scanning over the latest market research. "Instead of rushing into every market, we should double down on the partnerships that are already showing real promise. Europe is coming along, but we need to focus our resources there first before spreading ourselves too thin in Asia."

Nikhil nodded, the pieces falling into place in his mind. This was the clarity they had been missing. "Agreed. Let's prioritize Europe for now. Asia can wait until we've solidified our position."

They spent hours refining the plan, making sure that everything they presented to Raghav was sharp, clear, and achievable. It wasn't about over-promising anymore—it was about delivering something they could be proud of.

By the time they finished, the exhaustion they had been carrying for weeks began to lift, replaced by a cautious sense of hope.

The next morning, Nikhil sat in front of his computer, the revised plan ready to send to Raghav. It was a risk—pushing back and showing him that they had changed their approach. But Nikhil felt a calm confidence that hadn't been there before. This was the right move.

"I'm ready," Nikhil said, glancing at Priya, who was sitting beside him.

"Let's do it," Priya replied, her voice steady. With a deep breath, Nikhil hit send.

A few hours later, the response came.

Nikhil's phone buzzed, and his pulse quickened as he saw Raghav's name on the screen. He opened the message, feeling Priya's eyes on him as he read.

"Interesting shift in strategy. Meet me tomorrow to discuss."

Nikhil exhaled, a mix of relief and anxiety flooding through him. Raghav hadn't dismissed it outright. That was a good sign.

"He wants to meet tomorrow," Nikhil said, looking up at Priya.

She raised her eyebrows. "Is that a good thing?" Nikhil smiled faintly. "It's not a 'no,' so I'll take it."

Priya nodded, though her expression was still cautious. "Now we just have to convince him."

The following day, Nikhil and Priya found themselves once again in the sleek, imposing office building where Raghav held court. The stakes felt different this time—they weren't coming in as desperate. They had a plan, a solid strategy that they believed in.

Raghav was already seated at the far end of the table when they entered, his expression unreadable. He motioned for them to sit, wasting no time on pleasantries.

"I reviewed your revised plan," Raghav said, his tone as sharp as ever. "It's more focused, but you're pulling back on the timeline. Why?"

Nikhil leaned forward, his voice calm but firm. "Because the timeline was unrealistic. We were stretching ourselves too thin, trying to meet impossible deadlines. This new approach allows us to focus on the partnerships that are already working, build a stronger foundation in Europe, and then expand to Asia when the time is right. It's the only way we can deliver something sustainable."

Raghav's eyes narrowed, but he didn't interrupt. "We know you want results," Priya added, her voice steady. "And we can deliver them. But they have to be real results, not rushed promises that will fall apart in the long run."

For a long moment, Raghav said nothing. The silence in the room was thick, and Nikhil could feel his heart pounding in his chest. This was the moment of truth.

Finally, Raghav leaned back in his chair, his expression softening slightly. "You've got guts," he said, his tone less harsh than usual. "I'll give you that. Fine. I'll give you a little more time. But don't waste it."

Nikhil exhaled, feeling a wave of relief wash over him. They had done it. They had bought themselves the time they needed to make the project work.

"We won't waste it," Nikhil said firmly.

Raghav nodded once, signaling the end of the meeting. "See that you don't."

As they left the building, Priya let out a long breath, a smile spreading across her face. "We did it."

Nikhil smiled too, though the weight of what lay ahead still pressed down on him. They had bought themselves time, but now they had to deliver.

"We're not done yet," Nikhil said, glancing at Priya. "But we've got a shot now."

Priya nodded, her expression determined. "And this time, we're doing it our way."

CHAPTER 53

THE FINAL TEST

The morning sunlight gleamed off the towering glass walls of Raghav's office building, casting long shadows over Nikhil and Priya as they approached. Today wasn't like the others—this meeting wasn't just another progress check. It was everything.

Nikhil felt the weight of it pressing on his chest, making every breath just a little bit harder. He could feel Priya's presence beside him, steady but focused. She looked just as calm as she always did, but Nikhil knew better. They were both nervous. The stakes had never been higher, and there was no more room for error.

As they rode the elevator up to the top floor, the quiet hum of the machinery was the only sound between them. The tension in the small space was suffocating. Nikhil's heart thudded heavily in his chest, and every possible scenario of how this meeting could go wrong ran through his head. What if Raghav refused to listen? What if he saw their pivot as a step back, not forward?

Priya broke the silence as the elevator doors slid open. "No matter what happens in there, we've done the right thing," she said, her voice firm but quiet. Nikhil nodded, his throat tight. She was right. They couldn't go back now. The pivot was their best option—the only option if they wanted to build something meaningful and sustainable. But convincing Raghav of that was another story.

They stepped out of the elevator and into the polished, minimalist reception area. The familiar sleek decor of Raghav's office greeted them—expansive glass windows overlooking the city, the air thick with the scent of leather and expensive wood polish. Everything about this place screamed power.

Raghav's assistant motioned them in, and Nikhil's pulse quickened as they walked into the large conference room. Raghav was already seated at the far end of the long table, his back straight and his fingers drumming rhythmically against the polished surface. His expression was unreadable, as it always was, but there was an intensity in his eyes that made Nikhil's stomach twist.

He motioned for them to sit without a word, and Nikhil and Priya took their seats across from him.

"So," Raghav began, his voice sharp and to the point. "You've changed the plan."

Nikhil exchanged a glance with Priya before leaning forward slightly. "Yes. After reviewing the scope of the project and the demands we were facing, we realized we were spreading ourselves too thin. Trying to expand into too many markets too quickly was putting the entire project at risk."

Raghav's fingers stopped drumming. He stared at Nikhil with a piercing gaze. "You're pulling back. You're asking me to be patient when I've made it very clear that I want results."

Nikhil swallowed, but his voice stayed steady. "We're not pulling back. We're refocusing. We've streamlined the plan to prioritize Europe first, where we already have traction. Once we've solidified our presence there, we can expand into Asia and other markets. This way, we ensure that the project has a stable foundation and doesn't collapse under its own weight."

There was a pause. Raghav's gaze shifted to Priya. "And you agree with this?"

Priya nodded confidently. "I do. The current pace is unsustainable. We're confident that by focusing our efforts and resources, we can deliver something real. Rushed expansion would lead to unstable partnerships and undermine the credibility of what we're building."

Raghav leaned back in his chair, crossing his arms over his chest. The silence that followed was suffocating. Nikhil felt the seconds stretch out like hours.

"You're asking me to trust you," Raghav finally said, his voice low but laced with tension. "You're asking me to put off the results I want to see. Why should I? Why should I believe that this new approach will succeed when you've already missed several deadlines?"

Nikhil felt his stomach tighten, but he didn't flinch. This was the moment. "Because we're playing the long game. We know the pressure is on to deliver fast, but if we focus solely on speed, we risk building something fragile. If you give us a little more time and allow us to build strategically, you'll see returns that last. This pivot is the only way to ensure that."

Raghav's eyes narrowed. He was silent for a long time, and Nikhil could feel the tension in the room thickening with every passing second. His mind raced, trying to predict Raghav's next move, but his expression gave nothing away.

Finally, Raghav leaned forward, his fingers pressed together in front of him. "You've got guts, I'll give you that. Most people would be scrambling to meet my demands, not telling me I'm asking for too much."

Priya didn't blink. "We believe in what we're building. That's why we're taking this risk."

Raghav studied them both, and for the first time, Nikhil thought he saw a flicker of something other than skepticism in his eyes. Was it approval? It was impossible to tell.

"I don't like being told to wait," Raghav said slowly, his voice measured. "But I also don't like wasting money. If you think this is the right move, then fine. I'll give you more time. But—" he held up a finger—"if you don't deliver, if you come back to me with excuses or delays again, this entire thing is over. No second chances."

Nikhil let out a breath he hadn't realized he'd been holding. Relief washed over him, but it was tinged with the weight of the ultimatum. They had more time, but the stakes were higher than ever.

"We understand," Nikhil said, his voice steady despite the surge of emotions inside him. "We won't waste this opportunity."

Raghav nodded once, signaling that the conversation was over. "Good. Now go make it happen."

The ride down in the elevator felt different this time. They had done it—they had convinced Raghav to give them more time, to trust them to follow through with their pivot. But as the reality of the meeting settled in, Nikhil knew that this was only the beginning. They had bought themselves time, but now they had to prove that their strategy was the right one.

"We did it," Priya said quietly, a small smile tugging at her lips. "He actually listened."

Nikhil smiled too, though it was a tired, cautious smile. "Yeah, but we're not out of the woods yet. He gave us time, but he made it clear—no more second chances."

Priya nodded, her expression turning more serious. "I know. But this time, we're doing it on our terms. And that's worth something."

Nikhil glanced at her, appreciating the calm confidence in her voice. She was right. They had taken control of the project, and while the pressure was still immense, it felt different now. They were no longer scrambling to meet someone else's demands—they were executing a plan they believed in.

The elevator doors slid open, and the noise of the bustling lobby filled the air. Nikhil took a deep breath, feeling a mix of relief and determination. They had more time. Now it was up to them to make sure they didn't waste it.

"We've got this," Nikhil said as they stepped out into the sunlight. "Let's show him what we can really do."

CHAPTER 54

SMALL WINS

The week that followed the meeting with Raghav felt like a whirlwind, but for once, it wasn't driven by panic. It was driven by purpose. They had a plan now, and more importantly, they had time—not much, but enough to make their pivot work if they stayed focused.

The team sensed the shift too. Sanya, who had been with them through the most chaotic days, noticed it immediately when Nikhil and Priya walked into the office the morning after the meeting. She raised an eyebrow as Nikhil dropped his bag onto the desk, a small but tired smile on his face.

"So?" she asked, crossing her arms. "How did it go with Raghav?"

Nikhil glanced at Priya, who gave him a nod. He exhaled slowly and smiled, though the weight of the responsibility still sat heavily on his shoulders.

"He gave us more time," Nikhil said, leaning against his desk. "But it's not without conditions. He made it clear—this is our last chance. No more mistakes."

Sanya looked between them, her expression serious. "And you think we can pull this off?"

"We have to," Priya said simply, her voice steady. "But this time, we're doing it on our terms. We're focusing on what we can deliver, not chasing impossible targets."

Sanya nodded, her usual calm demeanor returning. "Good. That's the only way this is going to work."

The next few days were all about execution. The team was re-energized, with everyone focused on building a solid foundation in Europe. They spent hours on calls with their partners, refining the details of their partnerships and ensuring that the groundwork was solid before they made any promises to Raghav.

For the first time in weeks, Nikhil felt a sense of control. They weren't rushing from one task to the next, scrambling to meet deadlines they knew were impossible. Instead, they were moving deliberately, focusing on the core of the project and building it step by step.

But that didn't mean the pressure was gone. Raghav's ultimatum still loomed large in the background. Every time Nikhil looked at the timeline on his screen, he could feel the weight of the ticking clock. They had more time, but it was still limited, and if they didn't deliver by the new deadline, it would all be over.

Still, there were moments of hope—small wins that reassured Nikhil that they were on the right path. One morning, as Nikhil was reviewing the latest market analysis for Europe, Sanya walked into his office, a rare smile on her face.

"We got a response from one of the key partners in Germany," she said, handing him a printed email. "They're in."

Nikhil looked down at the email, the words blurring slightly as the relief washed over him. They had been waiting on this partnership for weeks, and finally, they had confirmation.

"This is big," Nikhil said, running a hand through his hair. "This is really big."

Sanya nodded, her expression matching his excitement. "I know. It's a huge step. Once we get the contract finalized, we can leverage this to secure the other partnerships we've been working on."

Nikhil felt a wave of energy surge through him. This was it—the first real proof that their pivot was working. It wasn't a massive win, not yet, but it was something. And right now, that was enough.

Later that afternoon, Nikhil called Priya into his office. She walked in, holding a stack of papers, her expression as tired as his. But when she saw the smile on his face, she raised an eyebrow.

"What's up?" she asked, setting the papers down on his desk. Nikhil handed her the email from the German partner. "We've got them."

Priya scanned the email quickly, her eyes widening as she read. It was exactly the confirmation they had been waiting for.

"This is huge," Priya said, her voice filled with cautious excitement. "If we can lock this down, we're on track to meet the first phase of the plan."

Nikhil leaned back in his chair, the tension in his chest loosening just a bit. "I know. It's not everything, but it's a start. And right now, I'll take it."

Priya smiled, though there was still a seriousness in her eyes. "It's definitely a win, but we've still got a lot to do. We can't lose focus."

"I know," Nikhil said, his tone softening. "But it's nice to have a win for a change."

Priya nodded, her smile fading slightly. "It is. But we've got to keep pushing."

The following days continued in the same vein. They secured another partnership in the UK and made significant progress on contracts with two other European partners. The small wins were starting to add up, and the energy in the office was noticeably different.

Even Sanya, who was usually the most reserved, seemed more upbeat. The team worked late into the night, but it no longer felt like a slog. There was momentum now—a feeling that they were finally building something real.

One evening, as Nikhil sat at his desk, reviewing the latest contract drafts, Priya walked into his office, two cups of coffee in hand. She set one down in front of him and sat across from him, her face serious but calm.

"We're getting there," she said quietly, sipping her coffee.

Nikhil looked up from his papers, his own coffee forgotten for the moment. "Yeah, we are."

"But it's still not enough," Priya continued, her voice thoughtful. "Raghav's not going to be satisfied with just a few contracts. We need something bigger to show him."

Nikhil sighed, leaning back in his chair. She was right. The progress they had made was good, but it wasn't enough to fully satisfy Raghav. He had made it clear that he wanted results, and they weren't quite there yet.

"I know," Nikhil said, his voice quiet. "We need a breakthrough. Something that will make him see that this pivot was the right move."

Priya nodded, her expression serious. "And we're running out of time."

The next day, Nikhil received a message that made his heart skip a beat. It was from one of the biggest potential partners in Europe—the one they had been courting for months. He quickly opened the email, his pulse quickening as he read.

It was brief, but it was the news they had been waiting for.

"They want a meeting," Nikhil said aloud, his voice filled with a mix of excitement and anxiety.

Priya, who had been reviewing a contract at her desk, looked up sharply. "Who?"

Nikhil turned the screen toward her. "The big one.

They're interested."

Priya's eyes widened as she read the email. "This could be it."

"I know," Nikhil said, his mind already racing. This was the breakthrough they needed. If they could secure this partnership, it would be the proof Raghav needed to see that their pivot was working.

"Set up the meeting," Priya said, her voice steady but urgent. "This could change everything."

CHAPTER 55

THE FINAL PUSH

The day of the meeting with the major European partner came faster than Nikhil expected. The air in the office felt charged, almost electric, as the team worked tirelessly to prepare for what could be their biggest moment yet. This was the opportunity they had been building toward for months.

Nikhil and Priya had spent the last few days preparing every detail of their pitch. They knew this meeting wasn't just about securing a partner—it was about proving that their pivot had been the right move. This was the final push, the moment that would either validate everything they had worked for or bring it all crashing down.

"We've got everything lined up," Sanya said as she handed Nikhil a final draft of the pitch deck. "I've gone through it twice. Everything's tight."

Nikhil scanned the document, his mind racing with every possible question or scenario that could come up during the meeting. "Good. I don't want any surprises."

Priya, seated across the table, gave a slight nod. "This has to be perfect. Raghav's expecting results, and this partnership is the closest thing we have to a game-changer." Nikhil looked up at her, sensing the tension beneath her calm exterior. They were all feeling it—the weight of the moment. He knew that even though they had secured smaller partnerships, this was the one that would make or break their standing with Raghav.

The meeting was scheduled for the afternoon, giving them just enough time to review everything one last time before heading to the video conference. As they gathered in the conference room, the atmosphere was tense but focused. This was it.

Priya glanced at the clock, her fingers drumming lightly on the table. "They'll be on in five minutes."

Nikhil's eyes darted between the pitch deck on the screen and the notes in front of him. His nerves were buzzing, but he couldn't let it show. He had to project confidence. This wasn't just about him—this was about the entire team, about proving that the pivot they had made was the right decision.

"Just remember, we've done the work," Priya said softly, sensing his tension. "We're ready."

Nikhil nodded, his hands steadying on the table.

They were ready.

The call connected, and the screen filled with the faces of their potential partners from Germany, France, and Switzerland—the key players in the European market they had been targeting. Nikhil forced a smile, feeling the familiar thrum of adrenaline as the introductions were made.

"We're pleased to finally connect," said Markus, the lead representative from the German company. His tone was polite, but there was a distinct air of seriousness in his words. "We've been following your progress closely."

Nikhil nodded, feeling the weight of each word. "We're excited to be here. We believe that what we're building has the potential to create something transformative, not just in Europe but globally."

Markus glanced at his colleagues on the call before leaning forward. "We've seen your projections, and we're impressed with the recent focus on the European market. That was a smart move. But we have some concerns about the timeline."

Nikhil felt his heart skip a beat. Of course, they would bring up the timeline. It had been the one aspect that had plagued them since the beginning. But he was prepared.

"We've made significant progress over the last few months, and we've adjusted our timeline to focus on building strong partnerships first, before expanding too quickly," Nikhil said, his voice calm but firm. "We believe this approach gives us the best chance at long-term success, and it allows us to move faster once the foundation is solid."

There was a brief pause as Markus and the others considered his words. The silence felt like it stretched on forever, but Nikhil held his ground, keeping his expression steady.

Finally, Markus nodded. "That's a fair point. Rushing expansion could lead to instability. But what we need to know is—how committed are you to making this work in the long term?"

Nikhil felt a surge of determination. This was the moment. He glanced at Priya, who gave him a slight nod, urging him forward.

"We're fully committed," Nikhil said, his voice strong and clear. "This isn't just about short-term results for us. We're building something sustainable, something that will last. We've already secured key partnerships in Europe, and we're in it for the long haul. We're asking for your partnership not just for a quick deal, but to be part of something that will redefine how we operate across markets."

The silence that followed was heavy with anticipation. Nikhil's heart pounded in his chest, but he refused to let it show. He had given it everything—now it was up to them.

Markus glanced at his colleagues again, exchanging silent looks before turning back to the camera.

"Well," Markus said slowly, "we've been impressed with your recent progress. Your strategy shows a level of foresight we haven't seen in many of your competitors. We're prepared to move forward."

Nikhil felt the air rush out of his lungs in a quiet, controlled exhale. They had done it.

Priya, sitting beside him, allowed herself a brief, satisfied smile before returning her attention to the screen. "We'll get the paperwork ready. This is the start of something great."

Markus nodded. "We believe it is. Let's make it happen."

The moment the call ended, the conference room erupted into quiet celebration. It wasn't loud, it wasn't over the top—but the feeling of relief and accomplishment was palpable. They had secured the partnership that would take their project to the next level.

Sanya walked in, a huge grin on her face. "I'm guessing that went well?"

Priya stood up, stretching her arms. "Better than we could've hoped. They're in."

Nikhil leaned back in his chair, a slow, tired smile spreading across his face. "This changes everything."

That evening, the office was quiet as the team wound down from the intensity of the day. Nikhil sat at his desk, staring at the contracts that had come in, his mind buzzing with everything that had happened. The breakthrough had finally come.

Priya knocked lightly on his door before stepping in. "You did great today."

Nikhil looked up, the exhaustion evident in his eyes, but he smiled. "We did great. I couldn't have done this without you."

Priya sat down across from him, her expression serious again. "We've crossed a big milestone, but you know what this means, right?"

Nikhil nodded slowly. "Yeah. It means we've got to prove it now. This partnership is the first step, but

Raghav's going to want to see more."

Priya sighed, rubbing her temples. "He's never going to be satisfied, is he?"

"No," Nikhil admitted. "But we're not doing this for him anymore. We're doing it for us, for the team, for the vision we believe in."

Priya smiled softly, her expression lightening. "That's true. And now we have something real to show for it."

As they sat in the quiet office, the weight of the day's success settled in. They weren't done yet—there was still more work to do—but for the first time in a long time, it felt like they were on solid ground.

"We've got this," Nikhil said, his voice full of quiet confidence.

Priya nodded. "Yeah, we do."

CHAPTER 56

SEEING THE LIGHT

The days after the major partnership agreement flew by in a blur of activity. Nikhil and Priya knew that their work was far from over—this was only the beginning of the real challenge. They had secured the deal, but now they had to deliver, and Raghav's deadline still loomed in the background, unyielding.

But something was different now. The constant pressure that had once felt suffocating was still there, but it didn't seem as overwhelming. The small wins were adding up, and with the momentum of the big partnership behind them, Nikhil could feel a shift in his outlook. For the first time in months, it felt like they weren't just chasing deadlines; they were building something real.

The team was more focused than ever, and as they began to execute the next phase of the plan, Nikhil found himself falling into a rhythm. Meetings, contract reviews, project updates—it was still a lot to juggle, but the panic that had once gripped him was gone. There was a quiet confidence now, a sense that they were finally in control.

One afternoon, as Nikhil reviewed the final integration plans for the new European partnerships, Priya knocked on the door of his office, a calm but thoughtful look on her face.

"Got a minute?" she asked, stepping inside.

Nikhil nodded, setting his papers aside. "What's up?"

Priya sat down across from him, her fingers tapping lightly against the edge of the desk. "I've been thinking about something," she began, her voice thoughtful. "About where we are now compared to where we started."

Nikhil raised an eyebrow. "You mean how we went from chasing deadlines to actually building something sustainable?"

Priya smiled faintly. "Exactly. It feels different now, doesn't it? Like we're not just scrambling to survive. We're actually creating something meaningful."

Nikhil leaned back in his chair, crossing his arms over his chest. "Yeah, I've been feeling the same thing. I guess... I guess it's because we've stopped letting Raghav dictate everything. We've taken control of our own vision."

Priya nodded slowly. "That's what I was thinking too. It's like, for the first time, we're not just doing this to please someone else. We're doing it because we believe in it."

Nikhil smiled, the truth of her words settling over him. They had come a long way. The stress, the sleepless nights, the constant fear of failure—it had all been for something. They had fought through the chaos, and now, they were starting to see the light at the end of the tunnel.

"We've made it through the worst of it," Nikhil said quietly, his voice filled with quiet confidence. "But we're not done yet. We still have to deliver."

Priya nodded, her smile fading slightly as the weight of their ongoing work returned. "I know. But it's different now, Nikhil. We're in control. We're not just reacting to everything that's thrown at us—we're steering this ship."

Nikhil looked at her, appreciating the calm confidence in her voice. She was right. They weren't just surviving anymore—they were building, step by step, and the foundation they had laid was solid. But there was still more to do.

That evening, after the team had left and the office had quieted down, Nikhil found himself sitting at his desk, reflecting on how far they had come. The last few months had been a rollercoaster of emotions—highs and lows, successes and failures, doubts and breakthroughs.

He remembered the early days of the project when he and Priya had been full of energy and optimism, chasing big dreams with a sense of invincibility. But then reality had set in—Raghav's demands, the impossible deadlines, the constant pressure to deliver faster, better, more.

There had been moments when Nikhil wasn't sure if they were going to make it. Moments when the weight of it all felt too much, and he had wondered if they should just walk away. But they hadn't. They had pushed through, they had adapted, and they had found their way.

Nikhil looked around the quiet office, the papers and contracts spread out across his desk. This was their project now. Not Raghav's, not anyone else's. The vision they were building was their own, and they were finally seeing the fruits of their labor.

Priya was right—it did feel different. The fear that had once driven him had been replaced by something else. A quiet determination, a sense of purpose that wasn't tied to someone else's expectations. They had proven to themselves that they could do this, and now they were steering the ship.

As Nikhil sat there, the buzzing of his phone broke the silence. He glanced down at the screen and saw an email from Raghav. His heart skipped a beat—even though things were going well, Raghav's name still had a way of triggering that old sense of anxiety.

He opened the email quickly, scanning the message.

"I've seen the updates. Looks like you're finally delivering. Keep this up, and we might actually have something here. Let's review the next phase next week."

Nikhil let out a breath he hadn't realized he was holding. It wasn't glowing praise, but from Raghav, it was as close to approval as he was likely to get. The hard part wasn't over yet, but the email felt like a small victory—a sign that, even in Raghav's eyes, they were on the right track.

Priya walked back into the office, holding a cup of coffee. She saw the look on Nikhil's face and raised an eyebrow. "Good news?"

Nikhil held up his phone. "Raghav just sent me an email. He's... pleased with our progress. Well, as pleased as Raghav ever gets."

Priya smiled, sitting down across from him. "That's something, at least."

Nikhil leaned back in his chair, the tension in his shoulders easing just a bit. "Yeah. We're not done yet, but we're getting there."

Priya took a sip of her coffee, her eyes thoughtful. "You know, when we first started, I thought success meant getting Raghav's approval. But now, I'm realizing that it's about so much more than that. It's about building something we can be proud of, something that lasts."

Nikhil nodded slowly, her words echoing his own thoughts. Success wasn't about Raghav anymore. It wasn't about hitting arbitrary targets or meeting someone else's expectations. It was about the work they we're doing, the team they had built, and the vision they were bringing to life.

"We're on our way," Nikhil said quietly, his voice filled with quiet determination. "We're building something real."

The next week passed in a flurry of activity as they prepared for the next phase of the project. The European partnerships were progressing smoothly, and the momentum they had built was carrying them forward. The challenges were still there—the pressure to deliver, the deadlines, the constant juggling of priorities—but something had shifted.

Nikhil and Priya had stopped chasing perfection and had started focusing on what mattered most: building a foundation that could stand the test of time.

The day of the review with Raghav came, and this time, Nikhil didn't feel the same crushing anxiety that had plagued him before. He felt prepared. Confident.

When they entered the conference room for the video call, Raghav's expression was, as always, unreadable. But Nikhil wasn't focused on reading Raghav's mood anymore—he was focused on delivering what they had built.

"We've made significant progress," Nikhil said, pulling up the presentation on the screen. "Our European partnerships are solid, and we're already seeing early returns. We've laid the groundwork for expansion into Asia, but we're not rushing it. We're focused on sustainability and long-term growth."

Raghav listened, his gaze never leaving the screen. As Nikhil continued the presentation, walking him through the numbers, the partnerships, and the strategy for the next phase, he could feel the calm confidence in his voice. This was their plan. Their vision.

When he finished, there was a moment of silence.

Then, Raghav nodded once.

"Looks good," Raghav said simply. "Keep this up, and you'll have something worth showing to investors. We'll check in again in a month."

Nikhil felt a wave of relief wash over him. It wasn't high praise, but it was enough. They were on the right track.

As they left the conference room, Priya turned to Nikhil, a satisfied smile on her face. "I think we've finally got this."

Nikhil smiled back, feeling a sense of accomplishment settle over him. "Yeah. I think we do."

CHAPTER 57

THE SHIFT IN FOCUS

The days following Raghav's review were a whirlwind of activity. The pace of work had accelerated, but this time, it was fueled by progress rather than panic. The European partnerships were beginning to bear fruit, and the initial numbers were promising. They had finally turned a corner.

But with that progress came new challenges. Nikhil and Priya were no longer fighting to survive—they were preparing to scale. The next phase of their plan was expansion into Asia, but they knew they had to be careful. Rushing into new markets too quickly was what had nearly sunk them before. Now, with the foundation laid, they had to approach this expansion with the same discipline and focus that had gotten them this far.

"We're going to need more resources," Priya said one morning as they reviewed their expansion strategy. "If we're serious about moving into Asia, we can't do it with the current team. We're stretched too thin as it is."

Nikhil nodded, scanning the data in front of him. "You're right. We've been lucky that Sanya and the rest of the team have been able to handle Europe so well, but Asia's going to be a whole different ballgame. We need people on the ground, local expertise."

Priya looked thoughtful for a moment. "I think it's time to start thinking about bringing in a senior partner.

Someone who can take on some of the load and help manage the expansion."

Nikhil raised an eyebrow. "A senior partner? You think we're ready for that?"

"I do," Priya said, her voice steady. "We've built something real, but if we're going to grow, we need more leadership. We can't do it all ourselves anymore."

Nikhil leaned back in his chair, considering her words. She was right, of course. They had been running this project with a skeleton crew, pulling more than their share of late nights and long hours. But if they wanted to take the next step, they needed to expand—not just in markets, but in leadership.

"Okay," Nikhil said, nodding slowly. "Let's start looking. We'll need someone with experience, someone who understands the markets we're targeting."

The next few weeks were a flurry of meetings and interviews. Finding the right partner wasn't going to be easy. They needed someone who could not only help manage the growing business but who shared their vision and understood the delicate balance between growth and sustainability.

Sanya, ever reliable, had taken on much of the European work, freeing up Nikhil and Priya to focus on the search for a new senior partner. They met with candidates from across the industry, but none of them seemed quite right. Some were too focused on rapid expansion, eager to replicate the same mistakes they had worked so hard to avoid. Others lacked the strategic insight they needed for the Asian market.

"This is harder than I thought it would be," Nikhil admitted one evening after another long day of interviews. He leaned against the edge of his desk, rubbing his temples. "I thought there would be more people who understood what we're trying to do here."

Priya, seated across from him, sighed. "We're looking for something very specific. Most people are focused on the bottom line—they want growth, fast. But we're playing a different game."

"Yeah," Nikhil agreed, his voice heavy with frustration. "And if we don't find the right person soon, we're going to be in trouble. We can't handle the expansion on our own."

Priya nodded. "We'll find someone. It's just going to take time."

A week later, they finally found the person they had been searching for.

Her name was Amira Patel, and from the moment she walked into the office, Nikhil and Priya knew she was different. Amira had an impressive background—she had worked for several major corporations, managing expansions in Asia and Europe. But what set her apart wasn't just her experience. It was her understanding of the delicate balance between growth and sustainability.

"I've seen companies grow too fast and fall apart because they didn't have the right foundation," Amira said during her interview. "And I've seen companies that were too cautious and missed their window of opportunity. The trick is finding the right pace—knowing when to push and when to hold back."

Nikhil exchanged a glance with Priya, who gave him a small nod. This was the partner they had been looking for.

"We're not looking to just grow for the sake of growth," Nikhil said, leaning forward. "We want to build something that lasts, something that's sustainable over the long term."

Amira smiled. "That's why I'm here. I believe in that too."

With Amira on board, the next phase of the project began in earnest. The shift in focus was immediate. Amira brought a level of expertise and strategic insight that Nikhil and Priya hadn't realized they were missing. She quickly integrated into the team, taking over much of the heavy lifting on the expansion into Asia.

"We're going to approach this carefully," Amira said during one of their first strategy meetings. "We'll start by solidifying partnerships in key markets—India, Singapore, and Japan. These are the places where we already have some traction. Once we've built a strong foundation, we can expand further."

Nikhil and Priya watched as Amira laid out the plan in meticulous detail, her confidence and clarity shining through. For the first time in months, Nikhil felt a weight lift off his shoulders. They weren't alone in this anymore. They had a partner who could share the load, someone who understood the complexity of what they were building.

"I think we've got something real here," Priya said later that evening, as they sat together reviewing the day's work. "With Amira on board, we can handle this."

Nikhil nodded, feeling the same sense of relief. "Yeah. She's exactly what we needed."

The weeks that followed were some of the most productive Nikhil had experienced since the project began. With Amira handling much of the expansion into Asia, he and Priya were able to focus on deepening their European partnerships and refining their long- term strategy. The pieces were finally starting to fall into place.

One afternoon, as Nikhil reviewed a contract for a new partnership in Japan, his phone buzzed with a message from Raghav. He opened it, his heart pounding slightly out of habit, but this time, the anxiety wasn't as sharp.

"Heard about the new partner. Good move. Let's discuss next steps next week."

Nikhil let out a breath, a small smile forming on his lips. Even Raghav was acknowledging the progress they had made. They weren't scrambling anymore—they were executing.

Priya walked into his office, a stack of papers in hand. "I'm assuming by that look on your face that you got good news?"

Nikhil held up his phone. "Raghav's finally recognizing that we're moving in the right direction. He wants to talk next week."

Priya grinned. "About time."

Nikhil laughed, feeling a lightness that he hadn't felt in a long time. They had come so far from those early, frantic days, and now, with the right team and the right strategy, they were ready for the next phase.

As he looked around the office, filled with the quiet hum of focused work, he realized something. This was no longer just a project—they were building something bigger than themselves. Something that could last.

"We've got this," Nikhil said quietly, more to himself than to Priya. "We're really doing this."

Priya smiled, sensing the shift in his tone. "Yeah, we are."

CHAPTER 58

THE ROAD AHEAD

The shift in momentum continued in the weeks that followed. With Amira at the helm of their expansion into Asia, Nikhil and Priya had more space to breathe. They were no longer chasing deadlines or scrambling to meet impossible expectations. Instead, they were executing a carefully planned strategy, and the results were beginning to show.

The office had a new energy to it—one that Nikhil hadn't seen in a long time. The team was focused, energized by the small wins they were stacking up day by day. There was a sense of optimism that hadn't been there before. For the first time in months, they weren't just surviving—they were thriving.

One afternoon, Nikhil found himself sitting at his desk, reviewing the latest reports from Amira. The numbers were better than he had expected. Their partnerships in India and Singapore were progressing smoothly, and the early indicators from Japan were promising. It was the kind of progress they had dreamed of when they first started this project.

As Nikhil read through the reports, Priya walked into his office, a look of quiet satisfaction on her face. "We're on track," she said, sitting down across from him. "Amira's plan is working."

Nikhil nodded, still scanning the numbers. "I know. It's almost hard to believe how far we've come. A few months ago, I wasn't sure if we'd even make it to this point."

Priya smiled, leaning back in her chair. "Well, we did. And now we're stronger for it."

Nikhil set the reports down and looked at her, a thoughtful expression crossing his face. The journey they had been on together had changed them—not just as business partners, but as individuals. They had learned the hard way that success wasn't just about hitting targets or pleasing investors. It was about resilience, about adapting to challenges and staying true to their vision, even when everything seemed to be falling apart.

"What's next?" Priya asked, her tone curious.

Nikhil leaned back, crossing his arms as he considered the question. "We keep pushing forward. We solidify our position in Asia, and then... maybe it's time to start thinking about what comes after."

Priya raised an eyebrow. "What comes after?"

Nikhil smiled, the idea forming in his mind as he spoke. "We've built something real here. But this project isn't just about scaling for the sake of it. We've built a foundation—now it's time to think about how we can use it to do more. Maybe it's time to start looking at how we can give back."

Priya's eyes lit up. "You're talking about social impact, aren't you?"

Nikhil nodded slowly, his mind racing with possibilities. The idea had been simmering for a while, but now that they were on solid ground, it felt like the right time to explore it. They had focused so much on building a successful business, but what if they could also make a difference in the world? What if they could use the platform they had created to impact the lives of others in a meaningful way?

"I think we're in a position where we can start thinking about it," Nikhil said, his voice thoughtful. "We've been so focused on growth, on building something sustainable. But now that we've got that, maybe it's time to start thinking about how we can give back."

Priya leaned forward, her excitement palpable. "I love it. We've always talked about creating something more than just a business. This could be the next phase."

Nikhil nodded, the excitement building inside him as they brainstormed ideas. The vision for their project was expanding once again, but this time, it wasn't just about profits or market share—it was about purpose. Over the next few weeks, Nikhil and Priya began working on a new initiative within their company. They called it Project Uplift, a program designed to invest in communities in the markets they were expanding into. The idea was simple: as they grew their business, they would also grow opportunities for those who needed it most.

"We're going to start with education," Priya explained one morning as they outlined the details of the program. "There's a huge need for skills training in some of the markets we're working in, especially in rural areas. If we can create a program that trains young people in tech and business, we can give them the tools to build their own futures."

Nikhil nodded, his mind racing with possibilities. "We can partner with local organizations, create scholarship programs, offer internships... The potential is huge."

Amira, who had joined them for the discussion, smiled. "This is exactly the kind of initiative that will set us apart from the competition. It's not just about doing good—it's about creating a lasting impact. People want to work with companies that have a purpose."

As Project Uplift began to take shape, Nikhil felt a renewed sense of purpose. The pressure of running a business was still there, but now, it was balanced by something bigger—something that went beyond profits. They were building more than just a company. They were building a legacy.

One afternoon, as Nikhil sat in his office reviewing the latest draft of the Project Uplift proposal, his phone buzzed with an incoming call. He glanced at the screen—it was Raghav.

Nikhil took a deep breath before answering, still cautious whenever Raghav's name appeared.

"Hey, Raghav," Nikhil said, keeping his tone neutral.

"I've been hearing some good things," Raghav said, his voice as sharp as ever, though there was a hint of something else—approval? "The European numbers are strong, and the Asian partnerships are on track. Looks like you're finally delivering."

Nikhil smiled, though he kept it to himself. It wasn't about proving anything to Raghav anymore—they were doing this for themselves now. But still, hearing Raghav acknowledge their progress was satisfying.

"Thanks," Nikhil said simply. "We've got a solid team, and things are moving in the right direction."

Raghav paused, and for a moment, Nikhil wondered what was coming next.

"I also heard about this new project you're working on—Project Uplift?" Raghav's tone was unreadable, but Nikhil could sense the curiosity.

"Yeah," Nikhil said cautiously. "It's something we're passionate about. We want to create opportunities for the communities we're working in."

There was a long silence on the other end of the line before Raghav spoke again.

"Interesting move," he said slowly. "Could be a good story for investors—show them you're not just focused on profits. Keep me in the loop."

Nikhil couldn't help but smile. Raghav, ever the businessman, had found a way to spin their purpose into a selling point. But for once, it didn't bother him. They were doing this for themselves and for the people they wanted to help. If Raghav wanted to market it, that was fine. As long as they stayed true to their vision.

"We will," Nikhil said, keeping his tone even. "Talk soon."

As he hung up the phone, Priya walked in, raising an eyebrow at the look on his face.

"Raghav?" she asked.

Nikhil nodded, setting his phone down. "He's heard about Project Uplift. He thinks it'll play well with investors."

Priya grinned. "Of course he does. But that doesn't matter, right? We're doing this for us."

Nikhil smiled, leaning back in his chair. "Exactly."

CHAPTER 59

BALANCING THE SCALE

Project Uplift was gaining traction faster than Nikhil and Priya had expected. Word of their initiative had spread through their partners in Europe and Asia, and the response was overwhelmingly positive. People wanted to be part of something bigger, something that wasn't just about profit margins or market share. It was about creating opportunities, and it was clear that Project Uplift resonated deeply with many of their stakeholders.

But with that enthusiasm came new challenges. The balance between running their core business and managing Project Uplift wasn't easy. Nikhil found himself constantly toggling between meetings with investors, reviewing expansion plans, and overseeing the development of Uplift's training programs. The work was fulfilling, but it was also exhausting.

One evening, as Nikhil sat at his desk, his computer screen filled with emails and reports, Priya knocked on his door. She walked in, holding a cup of coffee, her expression serious.

"You look like you haven't slept in days," she said, handing him the coffee.

Nikhil smiled wearily, taking the cup. "You're not wrong. There's just so much to do. I feel like every time we make progress on the business, I'm pulled back into something with Project Uplift. And vice versa."

Priya sat down across from him, crossing her arms. "I've been thinking the same thing. Uplift has taken off faster than we anticipated, and now it feels like we're running two separate companies."

Nikhil nodded, rubbing his temples. "I know. And as much as I love what we're doing with Uplift, it's starting to take a toll. We need to find a way to balance both, or we're going to burn out."

Priya was quiet for a moment, her eyes thoughtful. "Maybe it's time we bring someone in to manage Uplift full-time. Someone who can focus solely on the social impact side while we handle the business."

Nikhil looked at her, considering the idea. She was right—Uplift had grown too big for them to manage on their own. They needed someone who could dedicate themselves fully to the initiative, someone with experience in running social programs and making an impact on the ground.

"It makes sense," Nikhil said slowly. "We're stretched too thin as it is. If we're going to make Uplift sustainable, we need someone who can take the lead."

Priya smiled, her expression softening. "I'll start reaching out to my contacts. I know a few people who could be a good fit."

A week later, they had found the perfect person for the job.

Her name was Anjali Nair, and from the moment she walked into the office, Nikhil and Priya knew she was exactly what they needed. Anjali had a background in non-profit management, working with organizations across India and Southeast Asia to develop education and skills training programs for underprivileged communities. But more than that, she had a passion for social impact that matched Nikhil and Priya's vision for Project Uplift.

"I've spent the last ten years working with communities that have been left behind by rapid economic growth," Anjali said during their first meeting. "There's so much potential in these young people, but they lack the skills and opportunities to thrive. What you're doing with Project Uplift—it's exactly the kind of initiative that can make a real difference."

Nikhil and Priya exchanged a glance, both of them feeling the same sense of certainty. Anjali was the one.

"We want Uplift to be more than just a side project," Nikhil said, leaning forward. "We want it to grow alongside the business, to be a core part of our vision. But we need someone who can focus on its full- time, someone who can take it to the next level." Anjali smiled, her eyes filled with enthusiasm. "I'd love to take on that challenge."

With Anjali on board, the weight that had been pressing down on Nikhil and Priya began to lift. Anjali took over the day-to-day management of Project Uplift, overseeing the development of the training programs and building partnerships with local organizations in India, Singapore, and beyond. Her expertise and passion quickly became evident, and Uplift began to grow in ways that Nikhil and Priya hadn't imagined.

"She's a powerhouse," Priya said one afternoon as they reviewed the latest updates from Anjali. "I feel like we're finally getting the right people in place."

Nikhil nodded, his expression one of quiet satisfaction. "Yeah. For the first time, it feels like we're not just holding everything together by sheer willpower. We've got a team that can make this work."

The balance between running the business and managing Uplift was no longer a constant struggle. Anjali's leadership allowed Nikhil and Priya to refocus on their core business, knowing that Uplift was in capable hands.

But as Uplift continued to grow, so did the attention it attracted. Investors, partners, and even competitors began to take notice of what Nikhil and Priya were doing. Project Uplift was more than just a social initiative—it was becoming a key differentiator for their business. People wanted to work with a company that wasn't just focused on profits, but also on making a real impact in the world.

One afternoon, as Nikhil sat in a meeting with Raghav, discussing the latest numbers from their Asian partnerships, Raghav leaned back in his chair, his eyes sharp.

"I've been hearing a lot about Uplift," Raghav said, his tone casual but loaded with meaning. "It's getting a lot of attention. Investors are starting to take notice."

Nikhil glanced at Priya, who was sitting beside him. They had expected this—Uplift had always been more than just a side project, and now it was starting to shape the way people viewed their entire business.

"Yeah, it's been growing faster than we anticipated," Nikhil said, keeping his tone measured. "But that's a good thing. It shows that we're not just another company chasing profits—we're building something with real impact."

Raghav nodded slowly, his gaze thoughtful. "It's smart. People want to invest in companies with a purpose. You've found a way to tie that purpose to the business. Keep it up, and you'll have a story investors can't ignore."

Nikhil smiled faintly, sensing the approval beneath Raghav's words. It wasn't about Raghav's approval anymore, but hearing him acknowledge their success still felt good.

"We're just getting started," Priya said confidently, her eyes meeting Raghav's. "There's a lot more we can do with Uplift."

As they left the meeting with Raghav, Priya turned to Nikhil, a grin spreading across her face. "That went better than I expected."

Nikhil chuckled, running a hand through his hair. "Yeah, it did. It's nice to see Raghav actually acknowledging the work we've put into Uplift."

Priya nodded, her expression turning more serious. "But we can't lose sight of why we're doing this. Uplift is important, but it's not just a tool to impress investors. It's about making a difference."

Nikhil looked at her, appreciating the clarity in her words. She was right. They had started Uplift because they wanted to create something meaningful, something that could change lives. The attention it was getting from investors was a bonus, but it wasn't the reason they were doing it.

"We won't lose sight of that," Nikhil said firmly. "This is about more than just business. We're building something bigger."

CHAPTER 60
THE BIGGER PICTURE

The success of Project Uplift was undeniable. What had once been a side initiative had grown into something much larger than Nikhil or Priya had anticipated. Uplift was no longer just a social impact project—it was becoming the heart of their company's identity. It wasn't just about driving profits; it was about changing lives. Clients, partners, and employees were drawn to the idea that they were part of something meaningful, something that could leave a lasting impact.

But with growth came new challenges. Nikhil could feel the weight of it all pressing down on him. Every day seemed like a sprint to keep up with the demands of both the business and Uplift. There were new markets to enter, new deals to secure, and constantly shifting priorities that kept piling up on his plate.

It was a Monday afternoon, and Nikhil had spent the entire day buried in reports. Expansion plans for their Asian partnerships were coming in, and while the numbers were strong, the pressure to deliver was constant. Every success only led to more responsibilities.

He leaned back in his chair, staring at the ceiling for a moment. The hum of the office around him barely registered as his mind raced through the endless to-do lists, deadlines, and investor meetings on the horizon. He was exhausted, but he couldn't afford to slow down.

The door to his office opened, and Priya walked in, her expression a mix of concern and focus. "You've been in here all day," she said, setting a cup of coffee down in front of him. "You look like you haven't slept in a week."

Nikhil smiled weakly, taking the coffee but not drinking it. "Feels like it, honestly. There's just... too much. Every time I think we're catching up, something else comes up."

Priya sat down across from him, her eyes scanning the piles of reports and proposals on his desk. "That's the price of success, right? The more we grow, the more there is to manage."

Nikhil sighed, running a hand through his hair. "It's just... overwhelming. The business is doing well, Uplift is taking off, but it's all moving so fast. I can't keep up with everything, and it's starting to feel like I'm barely holding it all together."

Priya leaned forward, her tone gentle but firm. "Maybe it's time we take a step back."

Nikhil blinked, looking at her as though the thought had never occurred to him. "A step back? What do you mean?"

Priya paused, choosing her words carefully. "We've been running at full speed for months now, trying to juggle everything. The business, Uplift, the expansion plans... it's all piling up. But we can't keep going like this. You can't keep going like this. You're going to burn out."

Nikhil shook his head, feeling the familiar surge of resistance rising in him. "I can't slow down, Priya. We're on the verge of something big. The partnerships in Asia, Uplift's expansion—it's all happening now. If I slow down, we could lose momentum."

"I get that," Priya said, her voice calm but insistent. "But at what cost? You're exhausted, Nikhil. You're doing everything yourself, and it's unsustainable. We've already brought in Amira to help with the expansion, and Anjali is running Uplift. You don't need to be in the weeds of every single detail."

Nikhil looked at her, the frustration clear in his eyes. "I know, but it's hard to let go. I need to be sure everything's on track."

Priya leaned back, crossing her arms as she studied him. "You don't have to do it all alone. That's why we built this team. We've got people we trust—Amira, Anjali, Sanya—they can handle the day-to-day. You need to focus on the bigger picture."

Nikhil sat back, staring at the piles of work on his desk, the weight of her words settling in. He knew she was right. He had been so caught up in the day-to-day operations, in managing every detail, that he hadn't stopped to think about what it was costing him—and the company.

"I don't know how to do that," Nikhil admitted quietly. "I've always been the one driving things forward. If I step back, what if something falls apart?"

Priya smiled softly. "That's the thing—you've already built something that can stand on its own. You've built a team that believes in this as much as you do. If you don't step back, you'll never be able to see the bigger picture."

The conversation stuck with Nikhil over the next few days. He couldn't shake the feeling that Priya was right—he was too deep in the details, too focused on keeping everything moving to realize how much progress they had actually made. The team was stronger than ever, the partnerships were solidifying, and Project Uplift had taken on a life of its own. Yet, he still felt like he was holding everything together by sheer force of will.

One afternoon, Nikhil found himself sitting in on a meeting with Anjali and some of their Uplift partners. The discussion was centered on expanding their educational programs into rural parts of India, providing skills training to communities that had been left behind by rapid industrial growth. It was exactly the kind of impact they had hoped Uplift would make, and Anjali was leading the charge with precision and passion. As Nikhil listened to Anjali speak, he realized something—he didn't need to be in this meeting. Anjali had it covered. She knew the project better than he did, and she was driving it forward without needing his input. It was a strange feeling—both freeing and unsettling.

After the meeting, Priya found Nikhil sitting in his office, staring out the window.

"You okay?" she asked, sitting down beside him.

Nikhil nodded slowly. "Yeah. I just... I think you're right. I've been holding on to things that I don't need to hold on to. Anjali's running Uplift better than I ever could. Amira's managing the expansion. I've been so focused on the work that I haven't stopped to see how much we've actually accomplished."

Priya smiled, leaning back in her chair. "It's hard to let go, I know. But this isn't just your project anymore. It's ours. It's the team's. You've built something that can stand without you micromanaging every part of it."

Nikhil looked at her, the weight of the last few months finally starting to lift. She was right. He had been so focused on doing everything himself that he hadn't realized how far they had come as a company, as a team. They had built something strong, something that could thrive without him pushing every lever.

"You're right," Nikhil said, his voice steady. "It's time to step back. Time to trust the team we've built."

Priya nodded, her smile widening. "Exactly. Focus on the bigger picture, Nikhil. That's where you're needed now."

The decision to step back wasn't easy, but over the next few weeks, Nikhil began to make a conscious effort to shift his focus. He delegated more, trusting Amira to manage the expansion into Asia and Anjali to drive Uplift forward. He spent more time thinking about the long-term strategy of the company, about where they were headed and how they could continue to grow while staying true to their vision.

It wasn't an overnight change, but slowly, Nikhil began to see the benefits of letting go. The team flourished under the increased autonomy, and their results spoke for themselves. The partnerships in Asia were stronger than ever, and Uplift was expanding into new markets, providing education and skills training to thousands of people.

One evening, as Nikhil sat in his office reviewing the latest reports from Anjali, he felt a sense of peace that had been missing for a long time. The company was thriving, and for the first time in months, he didn't feel like he was barely keeping his head above water.

Priya walked in, a smile on her face. "I see you're not buried under a mountain of reports tonight."

Nikhil laughed, setting the papers down. "No, not tonight. I'm actually starting to feel like I can breathe again."

Priya sat down across from him, her expression soft. "It suits you. The team's doing great, Nikhil. You've built something amazing."

Nikhil nodded, a smile tugging at his lips. "We've built something amazing. And it's only going to get better."

CHAPTER 61

A NEW HORIZON

Nikhil stood by the window of his office, watching the last traces of sunlight dip below the city skyline. He often found himself in this spot, gazing out at the sprawling city that had come to represent so much of his journey. This view had seen him through countless moments of doubt, struggle, and triumph—and today, for the first time in what felt like years, he felt a deep sense of peace.

It wasn't just about the success of his business anymore, or the growth of Project Uplift, though both had exceeded his wildest expectations. It was about the path he had taken to get here—the lessons learned, the battles fought, and the relationships built along the way.

Priya walked in, her footsteps soft on the hardwood floor. She joined him at the window, gazing out at the same cityscape. "You're thinking again," she said, smiling gently.

Nikhil chuckled. "Always. But this time, it's different."

Priya turned to him, raising an eyebrow. "Different how?"

Nikhil took a deep breath, still staring out at the city. "For the first time, it feels like we've made it. Not just in the business sense—but in a way that really matters."

Priya smiled, leaning against the window frame. "Yeah. I know what you mean. We've built something real, something that's going to last."

Nikhil nodded, his thoughts drifting back over the years. "There were so many moments when I thought we wouldn't make it. So many nights when it felt like everything was slipping away."

Priya's voice was soft, filled with understanding. "But we didn't give up. We pushed through. And look at where we are now."

Nikhil smiled, feeling the truth of her words sink in. They had come so far, and now they stood at the precipice of something even bigger. But the best part? He didn't feel the same overwhelming pressure he had felt when they first started. This time, he felt in control.

"We've only just begun," Nikhil said, turning to look at Priya. "There's so much more we can do. Uplift has already changed lives, but now we can take it to the next level. We can go beyond just education and skills training. We can help shape the future for so many more people."

Priya's eyes sparkled with excitement. "You're right. We've barely scratched the surface of what's possible." Nikhil nodded, his mind racing with ideas. The company had become more than just a business—it was a platform for change. They had the resources, the people, and the drive to make a real difference. And now that they had built a solid foundation, it was time to think bigger.

"I want to focus on sustainability," Nikhil said, his voice filled with purpose. "Not just in business, but in how we operate globally. Clean energy, healthcare access, entrepreneurship—there's so much more we can do to make sure our impact is lasting."

Priya smiled, her expression proud. "I'm with you. We've built something incredible, and it's time to use it to create real change."

Over the next several months, Nikhil and Priya dedicated themselves to expanding Project Uplift. They brought on new partners with expertise in sustainable development, healthcare, and clean energy. Uplift was no longer just an initiative—it had become a movement, reaching communities across continents and changing lives in ways they had once only dreamed of.

One afternoon, Nikhil sat in his office reviewing a proposal from a group of young entrepreneurs in rural India. They had started a company focused on solar energy solutions for small villages, and they were seeking Uplift's help to scale their business. As Nikhil read through the proposal, he felt a wave of emotion wash over him. This was why they had started

Uplift—to give people the tools and opportunities to build their own futures.

Priya walked in, holding a cup of tea. "You've got that look on your face again," she said with a grin.

Nikhil glanced up, smiling. "What look?"

"The look that says you've found something that makes all the hard work worth it."

Nikhil laughed softly, handing her the proposal. "Take a look at this."

Priya skimmed the pages, her eyes widening as she read. "This is incredible. They're using what they learned in Uplift to start their own company. This is exactly what we wanted—people creating their own opportunities."

Nikhil nodded, his heart full. "Yeah. This is what it's all about."

As the months turned into years, Project Uplift continued to grow, touching more lives than Nikhil had ever imagined. The company was thriving, but more importantly, they had created something that went beyond profit and success. They had built a legacy of impact.

One evening, as Nikhil sat alone in his office, the quiet hum of the city below him, he received a message from Raghav.

He opened it, expecting the usual business update.

But instead, the message was short and to the point:

"Well done. You've proven it's possible to build something that matters. Keep going."

Nikhil smiled to himself. It wasn't about Raghav's approval anymore, but reading those words felt like closing a chapter in his life—a chapter where he had been driven by the need to prove himself, to achieve success at all costs. Now, it was different. Now, success wasn't measured by numbers on a balance sheet—it was measured by the lives they had changed.

Priya entered the room, noticing the smile on his face. "Raghav?"

Nikhil nodded. "Yeah. He finally gets it."

Priya sat down beside him, her expression thoughtful. "Took him long enough."

They both laughed, the tension that had once surrounded Raghav's name now a distant memory. They had come so far, and while the road ahead was still filled with challenges, it didn't feel as daunting as it once had. They had built something stronger than they ever imagined, something that would continue to grow long after they were gone.

Nikhil leaned back in his chair, gazing out at the city that had witnessed every step of their journey. "We did it," he said quietly, his voice filled with quiet pride.

Priya smiled, resting her hand on his. "Yeah. We did."

The Journey Continues

As Nikhil looked back over the years, he could see how far he had come—from the quiet boy from a small town, unsure of his place in the world, to the entrepreneur who had built a company driven by purpose, resilience, and innovation. But the true success of his journey wasn't the business itself—it was the lives they had touched, the communities they had empowered, and the opportunities they had created.

Success, he realized, wasn't about the destination. It was about the impact you made along the way.

The lessons he had learned weren't just about business—they were about growth, perseverance, and learning to trust in something bigger than yourself. They were about building relationships, lifting others up, and using the tools you've gained to create lasting change.

As Nikhil stood at the cusp of the next phase of his life, he knew that the journey would never truly end. There would always be new challenges to face, new dreams to chase, and new ways to make a difference. But for the first time, he felt ready. Ready to embrace the future, whatever it held.

Because success, in the end, wasn't about how much you achieved. It was about how you inspired others, how you lifted them up, and how you left the world a little better than you found it.

Final Reflection

To everyone reading this, I hope you find your own journey—your own path to success and purpose. The road will never be easy. There will be challenges, setbacks, and moments of doubt where you'll wonder if it's worth it. But I can tell you from experience—it is.

Success isn't a destination. It's a journey. And the most important part of that journey is the impact you make along the way—the people you inspire, the lives you touch, and the legacy you leave behind.

So keep going. Keep dreaming. Keep pushing forward, even when the world feels like it's against you. Because in the end, success isn't measured by how much you've achieved—but by how much you've helped others achieve their own dreams.

This is your journey. Own it. And remember—anything is possible.

Epilogue

A Legacy of Purpose

Years later, Nikhil would look back on his journey with a deep sense of pride and fulfillment. Project Uplift had expanded across continents, reaching countless communities and inspiring future generations of entrepreneurs, innovators, and change-makers.

The business had grown, but more importantly, it had become a beacon of hope and opportunity. The lives they had touched, the futures they had helped shape—this was the real legacy.

And as Nikhil watched the young entrepreneurs who had once been part of Uplift now leading their own companies, creating their own impact, he knew that this was the greatest success of all.

They had built something that would outlast them—a legacy of purpose, resilience, and hope.

Conclusion

Nikhil's journey from the small town of Ernakulam to the heights of entrepreneurial success is a story of perseverance, resilience, and the unwavering belief that greatness can be achieved, no matter where one starts. His journey serves as a reminder that success is not measured solely by financial gains or accolades but by the impact one makes on others and the legacy one leaves behind.

Through failures, setbacks, and moments of doubt, Nikhil never wavered in his belief in his vision. His story is a testament to the power of resilience, adaptability, and continuous learning. As Nikhil looks ahead to the future, he knows that the journey is far from over. New challenges and opportunities lie ahead, and he is ready to face them with the same determination and courage that has carried him this far.

For those who dream big and are willing to work tirelessly to achieve those dreams, Nikhil's story serves as an inspiration. It reminds us all that with hard work, perseverance, and a belief in oneself, anything is possible